Taiwanese Literature as World Literature

Literatures as World Literature

Can the literature of a specific country, author, or genre be used to approach the elusive concept of "world literature"? **Literatures as World Literature** takes a novel approach to world literature by analyzing specific constellations—according to language, nation, form, or theme—of literary texts and authors in their own world-literary dimensions.

World literature is obviously so vast that any view of it cannot help but be partial; the question then becomes how to reduce the complex task of understanding and describing world literature. Most treatments of world literature so far either have been theoretical and thus abstract, or else have made broad use of exemplary texts from a variety of languages and epochs. The majority of critical work, the filling in of what has been traced, lies ahead of us. **Literatures as World Literature** fills in the devilish details by allowing scholars to move outward from their own areas of specialization, fostering scholarly writing that approaches more closely the polyphonic, multiperspectival nature of world literature.

Series Editor:
Thomas O. Beebee

Editorial Board:
Eduardo Coutinho, Federal University of Rio de Janeiro, Brazil
Hsinya Huang, National Sun-yat Sen University, Taiwan
Meg Samuelson, University of Adelaide, Australia
Ken Seigneurie, Simon Fraser University, Canada
Galin Tihanov, Queen Mary University of London, UK
Mads Rosendahl Thomsen, Aarhus University, Denmark

Volumes in the Series
German Literature as World Literature, edited by Thomas O. Beebee
Roberto Bolaño as World Literature, edited by Nicholas Birns and Juan E. De Castro
Crime Fiction as World Literature, edited by David Damrosch, Theo D'haen and Louise Nilsson
Danish Literature as World Literature, edited by Dan Ringgaard and Mads Rosendahl Thomsen
From Paris to Tlön: Surrealism as World Literature, by Delia Ungureanu

American Literature as World Literature, edited by Jeffrey R. Di Leo
Romanian Literature as World Literature, edited by Mircea Martin, Christian Moraru, and Andrei Terian
Brazilian Literature as World Literature, edited by Eduardo F. Coutinho
Dutch and Flemish Literature as World Literature, edited by Theo D'haen
Afropolitan Literature as World Literature, edited by James Hodapp
Francophone Literature as World Literature, edited by Christian Moraru, Nicole Simek, and Bertrand Westphal
Bulgarian Literature as World Literature, edited by Mihaela P. Harper and Dimitar Kambourov
Philosophy as World Literature, edited by Jeffrey R. Di Leo
Turkish Literature as World Literature, edited by Burcu Alkan and Çimen Günay-Erkol
Elena Ferrante as World Literature, by Stiliana Milkova
Multilingual Literature as World Literature, edited by Jane Hiddleston and Wen-chin Ouyang
Persian Literature as World Literature, edited by Mostafa Abedinifard, Omid Azadibougar, and Amirhossein Vafa
Mexican Literature as World Literature, edited by Ignacio M. Sánchez Prado
Beyond English: World Literature and India, by Bhavya Tiwari
Graphic Novels and Comics as World Literature, edited by James Hodapp
African Literatures as World Literature, edited by Alexander Fyfe and Madhu Krishnan
Feminism as World Literature, edited by Robin Truth Goodman
Polish Literature as World Literature, edited by Piotr Florczyk and K. A. Wisniewski
Taiwanese Literature as World Literature, edited by Pei-yin Lin and Wen-chi Li
Pacific Literatures as World Literature, edited Hsinya Huang and Chia-hua Yvonne Lin (forthcoming)
Central American Literature as World Literature, edited by Sophie Esch (forthcoming)
Kazuo Ishiguro as World Literature, by Chris Holmes (forthcoming)
Hungarian Literature as World Literature, edited by Péter Hajdu and Zoltán Z. Varga (forthcoming)

Taiwanese Literature as World Literature

Edited by
Pei-yin Lin and Wen-chi Li

BLOOMSBURY ACADEMIC
NEW YORK • LONDON • OXFORD • NEW DELHI • SYDNEY

BLOOMSBURY ACADEMIC
Bloomsbury Publishing Inc
1385 Broadway, New York, NY 10018, USA
50 Bedford Square, London, WC1B 3DP, UK
29 Earlsfort Terrace, Dublin 2, Ireland

BLOOMSBURY, BLOOMSBURY ACADEMIC and the Diana logo
are trademarks of Bloomsbury Publishing Plc

First published in the United States of America 2023
This paperback edition published 2024

Volume Editor's Part of the Work © Pei-yin Lin and Wen-chi Li, 2023
Each chapter © Contributors, 2023

For legal purposes the Acknowledgments on p. 208 constitute
an extension of this copyright page.

Cover design by Simon Levy

All rights reserved. No part of this publication may be reproduced or transmitted in any form or by any means, electronic or mechanical, including photocopying, recording, or any information storage or retrieval system, without prior permission in writing from the publishers.

Bloomsbury Publishing Inc does not have any control over, or responsibility for, any third-party websites referred to or in this book. All internet addresses given in this book were correct at the time of going to press. The author and publisher regret any inconvenience caused if addresses have changed or sites have ceased to exist, but can accept no responsibility for any such changes.

Library of Congress Cataloging-in-Publication Data
Names: Lin, Pei-yin, editor. | Li, Wen-chi (Sinologist), editor.
Title: Taiwanese literature as world literature / edited by Pei-yin Lin and Wen-chi Li.
Description: New York : Bloomsbury Academic, 2023. | Series: Literatures as world literature | Includes bibliographical references and index. |
Summary: "Explores the richness of 20th-century Taiwanese literature as multilingual and diverse-styled world literature, accentuating how it intersects with world literary trends and how it is perceived globally through translation"– Provided by publisher.
Identifiers: LCCN 2022027071 (print) | LCCN 2022027072 (ebook) | ISBN 9781501381348 (hardback) | ISBN 9781501381386 (paperback) | ISBN 9781501381355 (epub) | ISBN 9781501381362 (pdf) | ISBN 9781501381379 (ebook other)
Subjects: LCSH: Chinese literature–Taiwan–History and criticism. | Chinese literature–Appreciation. | LCGFT: Literary criticism. | Essays.
Classification: LCC PL3031.T3 T3568 2023 (print) | LCC PL3031.T3 (ebook) | DDC 895.109/951249–dc23/eng/20220805
LC record available at https://lccn.loc.gov/2022027071
LC ebook record available at https://lccn.loc.gov/2022027072

ISBN:	HB:	978-1-5013-8134-8
	PB:	978-1-5013-8138-6
	ePDF:	978-1-5013-8136-2
	eBook:	978-1-5013-8135-5

Series: Literatures as World Literature

Typeset by Integra Software Services Pvt. Ltd.

To find out more about our authors and books visit www.bloomsbury.com
and sign up for our newsletters.

Contents

List of Figures ix
Editorial Notes x
Foreword *Karen Thornber* xi

Introduction: Framing Taiwanese Literature as World Literature
   Pei-yin Lin and Wen-chi Li 1

Part I Bridging Taiwan and the World: Frameworks and Tactics

1 Taiwanese Literature in Two Transnational Contexts: Sinophone Literature and World Literature *Kuei-fen Chiu* 19
2 Worlding Taiwan: Taiwanese Literature's Contingent Constructions *Carlos Rojas* 35
3 Worlding Modalities of Taiwanese Literature: Family Saga, Autobiographical Narrative, and Bildungsroman *Pei-yin Lin* 51

Part II Bringing the World Home: Transcultural Practice in Taiwanese Literature

4 Reading Taiwan through Japanese and French Literatures: The Surrealism of *Le Moulin* Poetry Society *Yi-chen Liu (translated by Blake Brownrigg)* 69
5 Responsible Primitivism: Wu Ming-yi's *The Man with the Compound Eyes* as Indigenous-Themed Environmental World Literature *Darryl Sterk* 81
6 The Foreign at Home: World Literature, Viral Postmodernism, and *Notes of a Desolate Man* *Nicholas A. Kaldis* 97

Part III Bringing Taiwan to the World: Taiwanese Literature in Translation

7 Anthologizing Taiwan: Taiwanese Literature toward the Anglophone World *John Balcom* 113
8 Settling in the World Republic of Letters: Taiwanese Literature in French *Gwennaël Gaffric* 129
9 Voices from Alternative Literary Fields: Translating Taiwanese Literature into Italian *Federica Passi* 143

10 From Taiwan's Literature to Taiwanese Literature: A Paradigm Shift in
    Japanese Translation *Ying-che Huang (translated by Sherlon Chi-yin Ip)*   157
11 Made in Taiwan: Reading Chiu Miao-chin's Lesbian Tales as World
    Literature *Wen-chi Li*   171
12 Translation Matters: The Case of *The Butcher's Wife* in English
    Sheng-chi Hsu   189

Notes on Contributors   205
Acknowledgments   208
Index   209

Figures

11.1 Ratings of *Notes* on Goodreads, September 3, 2021 — 185
11.2 Ratings of *Last Words* on Goodreads, September 3, 2021 — 185

Editorial Notes

This book takes non-Chinese collections as primary sources for any footnotes referring to the targeted literary contents. For the sake of readability, English translation precedes other non-English translation and the original texts. Square brackets are used to provide missing words, mark phonetic notation, correct errors, and assimilate quoted texts into surrounding texts. Although the default for proper names, places, and dynasties is the pinyin system, Taiwanese personal names are particularly spelled out in the Wade-Giles without apostrophes and umlauts. Certain personal names, such as Kuo-ch'ing Tu, Chu T'ien-wen, Ng Kim Chew, Wang Chen-ho, and Lōa Hô, show as they are known in the English-speaking world. Asian names, including Japanese ones, consist of a family name followed by a given name in order. Exceptions are the book contributors, internationally renowned scholars such as Shu-mei Shih and David Der-wei Wang, and certain Japanese authors such as Haruki Murakami and Ryūnosuke Akutagawa.

Foreword

Karen Thornber

The field of world literature has broadened considerably in recent years. Since the mid-2000s, increasing numbers of scholars trained in Asian literatures written in Asian languages have been publishing in the field of world literature, revealing its lacunae, and often advocating explicitly for transformational change. In addition to the exceptional scholarship created and cited in Pei-yin Lin and Wen-chi Li's *Taiwanese Literature as World Literature*, books, articles, chapters, journals, and book series by Wiebke Denecke (MIT), Satoru Hashimoto (Johns Hopkins), Francesca Orsini (SOAS), Ronit Ricci (Hebrew University of Jerusalem), Haun Saussy (University of Chicago), and Karen Thornber (Harvard), among other scholars with primary research expertise in Asia, have contributed significantly to diversifying the field of world literature.[1]

The barriers facing such specialists are high. Discourse on world literature remains dominated by academics without training in Asian literatures. It is far more common for these individuals to teach and publish about "the world," including Asia, than it is for those with training in Asian literatures to do so—even though Asia is home to 60 percent of the global population and has thousands of years of literary history, and scholars of Asia generally have far more knowledge of non-Asian literatures than the reverse. The world literature publications of individuals well-versed in Asian literatures often are consigned to or even dismissed as "area studies," even though the "areas" with which they are most familiar often are more diverse than the "areas" covered by scholars whose expertise lies outside Asia. Moreover, these world literature publications frequently are overlooked by scholars of world literature of all backgrounds, including, paradoxically, other scholars of Asian literatures who write on world literature.[2] In other words, even as we call for more rigorous inclusion of a broader range of Asian literatures within the field of world literature, we all too frequently continue to prioritize Western languages, literatures, and cultures. Similarly, we continue to turn to earlier generations of world literature scholarship (e.g., Cassanova, Damrosch, Moretti) as our

---

[1] Thornber, for instance, has published three large single-authored monographs that engage with Asian literatures, including Taiwanese literature, as world literatures, in addition to nearly twenty articles/chapters with "world literature" in the title. Denecke likewise has an extensive publishing and editing record in the field of world literature, particularly as pertains to premodern literatures and cultures.

[2] The same dynamic takes place in other burgeoning fields of the humanities, including the environmental, medical, and health humanities. Conventional lineages of these fields are given far more attention than newer scholarship that integrates these fields with the study of Asia. The term "conventional lineages" is from Robin Truth Goodman's description of her *Feminism as World Literature* (2022).

guideposts and foundations rather than engaging more deeply with world literature scholarship on the very narratives, cultures, literatures, and languages that we are advocating be included more responsibly in the field of world literature.

By calling attention to this phenomenon here in the opening pages of *Taiwanese Literature as World Literature*, my hope is that readers of this book interested in Taiwanese literature and/or Asian and world literature will commit to engaging in their own teaching, research, and broader studies with the innovative voices articulated in this volume, as well as those mentioned above and similar voices, rather than returning primarily to conventional Euro-dominated lineages and dynamics of world literature. Benefiting from the important insights and appreciating the challenges facing the contributors to this volume, readers can more successfully decenter Western languages, literatures, and cultures in discussions of world literatures.

Taiwanese Literature as World Literature makes vital contributions to scholarship on Asian literatures and world literature. This volume rightly problematizes current trends in world literature, including the field's tendency to focus primarily on how "first world" works are

> disseminated and read beyond Anglo-European zones. Individual works of the Global South such as African, South American, and Asian canons are consequently assessed without a comprehensive understanding of the history of local literature. Their circulation in the Global North is limited to the readers' eyes that at any point can flatten, homogenize, disrupt, and even discriminate.
> (Introduction, 5–6)

The editors of *Taiwanese Literature as World Literature* also speak eloquently of the very real impacts of the "imbalanced cultural capital between the West and non-West," including the politics of recognition, whereby "Western works are considered almost universal and widely applicable worldwide because they are thought to tackle intellectual issues," in sharp contrast with those from other parts of the world (Introduction, 6). Divided into three sections—Bridging Taiwan and the World, Bringing the World Home, and Bringing Taiwan to the World—*Taiwanese Literature as World Literature* argues powerfully and convincingly for conceptualizing Taiwanese literature as world literature (rather than solely as Sinophone literature), and it skillfully analyzes "the import of world literature to Taiwan and the export of Taiwanese literature to the world" (Introduction, 13). The book's twelve chapters, by scholars from a range of backgrounds, are expertly researched and written.

At the same time, this volume embodies many of the challenges facing scholars of world literature who have expertise in Asian literatures. Even as it pushes back against conventional conceptions of world literature, *Taiwanese Literature as World Literature* ultimately places Western languages, literatures, and cultures very near if not at the center of world literature. For instance, the editors astutely evoke the importance of the relational comparison and oceanic epistemology advocated by Édouard Glissant, Shu-mei Shih, and Epeli Hau'ofa. The editors also are correct in affirming in the introduction that "Taiwanese literature, in a quasi-national literary sense, was born as a result of writers' transcultural practices" (9). In addition to the examples provided, it is important to recognize the myriad transcultural practices vis-à-vis other Asian literatures. Without question, Tokyo was the most common place "for colonial Taiwanese intellectuals to access global knowledge," and Japanese-language translations facilitated access to European literature and thought in the early twentieth century (Introduction, 10). However, we also need to understand colonial Taiwanese intellectuals as actively transculturating hundreds of volumes of Japanese literature and engaging with literature by preeminent Korean writers and writers from mainland China.[3]

To give another example, four of the five chapters of Part Three—Bringing Taiwan to the World: Taiwanese Literature in Translation—focus on Western translations of Taiwanese literature (i.e., English, French, and Italian translations), with an additional chapter on Japanese translations. In the introduction, the editors mention that because of space limitations, they were not able to include as many case studies as they had hoped, including Dutch and Czech translations as well as those in "Asian languages" (Introduction, 14), which we can identify more specifically. Particularly important going forward will be studies of Korean translations and Vietnamese translations of Taiwanese literature. Similarly, German and Spanish are given as languages in which there are an "insufficient number of translations" to warrant exploration (Introduction, 14). The same could be said for Bengali, Hindi, Indonesian, and many Asian languages.

Taiwanese literature always has been part of world literature, despite its rarely having been adequately recognized as such. Thoroughly researched, gracefully written, and unfailingly insightful and instructive about the vibrant corpus of creative writing, translation, and transculturation emanating from and through Taiwan over the past century, the individual chapters of Pei-yin Lin and Wen-chi Li's *Taiwanese Literature as World Literature* contribute significantly both to scholarship on Taiwan and to scholarship on world literature. No reader can fail to gain a deep appreciation for the literary works and dynamics skillfully analyzed here, as well as for the need to continue to work assiduously to decenter Western literatures from the field of world literature and to continue to open the discipline to new and diverse voices.

---

[3] Transculturation in early twentieth-century East Asia is discussed in detail in Karen Laura Thornber, *Empire of Texts in Motion: Chinese, Korean, and Taiwanese Transculturations of Japanese Literature* (2009). Yi-chen Liu's chapter in this volume on "Reading Taiwan through Japanese and French Literatures: The Surrealism of *Le Moulin* Poetry Society" gives a case study of this dynamic.

Introduction: Framing Taiwanese Literature as World Literature

Pei-yin Lin and Wen-chi Li

Beyond Sinophone, Japanophone, and "Free China" Literatures

As an island with multi-ethnic and palimpsestic colonial history, Taiwan has been a confluent site where different languages and cultures intersect and coexist. During the fifty years of Japanese colonial rule, particularly after the adoption of the assimilation policy in 1919, Taiwan was regarded as a cultural and linguistic extension of the Japanese Empire. Increased Japanese proficiency enabled a great number of Taiwanese intellectuals to access world literature through Japanese translation. As Japan prepared for its military expansion southward, colonial control intensified and writers were mobilized to produce works in support of imperialization. Under such circumstances, articulations of Taiwan's literary autonomy were challenging. Taiwanese writers often had to navigate with caution through colonial censorship to continue publishing. Following Japan's surrender, the Chinese Nationalist Party (Kuomintang, hereafter the KMT) assumed control over Taiwan. To enhance the legitimacy of its rule over the island, the KMT implemented various strategies of "de-Japanization" and "re-Sinicization," aiming to remove the Japanese colonial impacts and reinstate Taiwan as a repository of Chinese culture. Consequently, Taiwanese literature was conceptualized within the KMT's grand Chinese narrative. The subjectivity of Taiwanese literature was once again suppressed by the ruling party. Further, the linguistic barrier marginalized Taiwanese authors who were by this time well-versed in Japanese.[1]

Through the KMT-imposed Chinese lens, Taiwan's postwar literary establishment during the 1950s and 1960s was dominated by émigré authors' anticommunist or nostalgic writing. In the Cold War context, literary works from Taiwan were exported abroad, beginning in the 1970s as examples of literature from "Free China." Stories by diasporic modernist authors were preferred by book editors such as Pang-yuan Chi and C. T. Hsia in this early phase of "literary diplomacy." Although native

---

[1] The use of Japanese language was allowed for about one year after the KMT's takeover. In the second half of 1946, many Japanese books containing pro-Japan messages were censored and the use of Japanese in newspapers and magazines was banned in October 1946.

Taiwanese writers' works were selected in *Chinese Stories from Taiwan: 1960–1970*, the foreword written by C. T. Hsia considers them (Taiwan-oriented) regionalists.[2] The "provincialized" treatment of Taiwanese literature continued throughout the first few years of the 1980s, but identification with Taiwan continued to grow as Taiwanese literature played an important role in the island's democratization. Toward the end of the decade, particularly after the lifting of martial law in 1987, researchers and literary historians have widely recognized the subjectivity of Taiwanese literature.[3] Ideological constraints found often in the pre-1987 English anthologies of Taiwanese literature also became relaxed.[4] The publication of Yeh Shih-tao's (葉石濤) Taiwan-centric *A History of Taiwan Literature* (台灣文學史綱) serves a milestone of this transition.[5] Writers, too, endeavored to represent Taiwan's past, such as the previously suppressed February 28th Incident,[6] from various perspectives different from the KMT's master narrative. After 1990, the contribution of works from the colonial era, marginalized until the mid-1970s, was acknowledged. Translations into Mandarin, compilation, and canonization have together broadened Taiwanese literary history and enabled us to reflect on a new dimension of bilingualism. This Taiwan-centric literary reorientation has led to the revival of colonial Taiwanese literature, a process that culminated in the institutionalization of Taiwanese literature in 1997 as an independent academic discipline distinct from Chinese literature.

The 1990s witnessed not merely the collapse of KMT authoritarianism but also the rise of the Chinese Communist Party (hereafter the CCP). When Taiwan started to utilize its name as an act of self-recognition, Chinese scholars (and also pro-China literary critics from Taiwan) took measures to reemphasize Taiwan's inseparable link with China. While this third marginalization, after Japanese colonial control and the KMT's martial law rule, generated repercussions—especially after Chen Shui-bian's success in the 2000 Taiwanese presidential election[7]—it also ushered in innovative explanatory paradigms for the study of Taiwanese literature. The Sinophone paradigm, for which postcolonialism serves as one pillar in Shu-mei Shih's conceptualization, is one example.[8] By questioning China's hegemony, the Sinophone model lends weight to

---

[2] C. T. Hsia, "Foreword," in *Chinese Stories from Taiwan: 1960–1970*, ed. Joseph Lau and Timothy Ross (New York: Columbia University Press, 1976), xii.

[3] See Xiaobing Tang, "On the Concept of Taiwan Literature," *Modern China* 25, no. 4 (1999): 379–422, for more details.

[4] See Balcom's chapter in this volume for details.

[5] It was serialized in the magazine 文學界 [*Literary World*] in the early 1980s. In the book form, Yeh's Taiwan-centric perspective became more noticeable. Its English version, translated by Christopher Lupke, was published by Cambria Press in 2020.

[6] An anti-government uprising that happened on February 28, 1947. The KMT's troops arrived on March 8 and launched a violent crackdown on protestors. Public discussion of the event was banned, but the incident has exerted tremendous impact on the formation of Taiwanese identity.

[7] For example, a book entitled 「文學台獨」面面觀 [*Aspects of Taiwan Independence through Literature*] was published by two Chinese scholars Zhao Xiaqiu and Zeng Qingrui (Beijing: Jiuzhou, 2001).

[8] The term "Sinophone" becomes popular after the publication of Shu-mei Shih's *Visuality and Identity: Sinophone Articulations across the Pacific* (Berkeley: University of California Press, 2007). See *Sinophone Studies: A Critical Reader*, ed. Shu-mei Shih, Chien-hsin Tsai, and Brian Bernards (New York: Columbia University Press, 2013) for more details.

the discourse of Taiwanese cultural and literary nationalism. Employing a Sinophone perspective, the subjectivity of Taiwanese literature, as well as that of Chinese-language works from other Sinophone sites (such as Hong Kong) and communities (such as the Malaysian Chinese), is celebrated.

Sinophone works are purposefully distinguished from the obsolescent category of Chinese literature, a term assigned to literature written in the Chinese language that fails to escape China-centrism.[9] As a theoretical framework, it gained momentum in Taiwan around 2012 and 2013, with the publication of Issue 22 in *Modern Chinese Literature* (中國現代文學) and Issue 35 of *Sun Yat-sen Journal of Humanities* (中山人文學報) respectively.[10] Interestingly, the two oft-quoted critics Shu-mei Shih and David Der-wei Wang, while based in America, are initially Taiwan-trained. This explains why some critics see Sinophone framework as partially a "Taiwan-made" theory.[11] Because Sinophone studies engages with minority studies and calls attention to different forms of Chinese colonialism, it prompts Taiwanese Han scholars to reflect on the "settler colonialism" imposed on Taiwan's Indigenous peoples. The applicability of this framework for Taiwan therefore is twofold: to accentuate Taiwan's literary autonomy and facilitate the analysis of Taiwanese literature vis-à-vis other Sinitic-language communities instead of China alone, and to redress the imbalanced Han-indigene relations. The unequal power relationship between Taiwan's Han and Indigenous population is addressed in two edited volumes—*Knowledge Taiwan* (知識台灣), in which Shu-mei Shih made an acute analogy between the marginalization of Taiwan's Indigenous people and that of Taiwan studies in global knowledge establishment,[12] and *Indigenous Knowledge in Taiwan and Beyond*.[13]

Shih's continued effort of positioning Taiwan studies in a global context is laudable, and Sinophone framework does serve as one possible way of bridging Taiwan with other Sinitic-language literatures produced elsewhere. Yet, like most theories, the Sinophone framework has constraints. Its focus on Sinitic works cannot account for the rich Japanese-language works produced in Taiwan under Japanese rule. Moreover,

---

[9] In Shu-mei Shih's 2004 definition, "Sinophone" literature means "literature written in Chinese by Chinese-speaking writers in various parts of the world outside China," as distinguished from "Chinese literature"—literature from China. See Shih, "Global Literature and the Technologies of Recognition," *PMLA* 119, no. 1 (2004): 16–30. But in *Visuality and Identity*, she adds minority writing in Chinese from China to the scope of "Sinophone" (See fn.8, 31).

[10] Four other special issues are worth noting—the *Chung Wai Literary Monthly* 44, no. 1 (2015), *Sun Yat-sen Journal of Humanities* (2016) on "Sinophone Articulations and *Mahua* Literature," *Taiwan Journal of Southeast Asian Studies* (2016), and 中國現代文學 [*Modern Chinese Literature*] 32 (2017). For the introduction of Sinophone studies to Taiwan, see Huang Mao-shan, "跨時空糾葛：華語語系研究在台灣小史" [Entanglements across Time and Space: A Brief History of Sinophone Studies in Taiwan], *Taiwan Lit* 1, no. 2 (Fall 2020).

[11] Zhan Min-xu, "華語語系研究的種族化轉向：談史書美、蔡建鑫、貝納德合編的 *Sinophone Studies: A Critical Reader*" [The Ethnic Turn of Sinophone Studies: *Sinophone Studies: A Critical Reader*, ed. Shu-mei Shih, Chien-hsing Tsai, and Brian Bernards], 台灣文學研究 [*Taiwan Literature Studies*] 4 (2013): 265–71.

[12] See 知識台灣 [*Knowledge Taiwan*], ed. Shu-mei Shih et al. (Taipei: Rye Field, 2016), 78.

[13] See *Indigenous Knowledge in Taiwan and Beyond*, ed. Shu-mei Shih and Lin-chin Tsai (Singapore: Springer Singapore, 2021).

the anti-Sinocentric schema does not sufficiently scrutinize the implicit relationship with the KMT's regime.[14] During the White Terror, certain writers such as Yu Kuang-chug (余光中), Ya Hsien (瘂弦), and Lo Fu (洛夫) in Taiwan developed ambivalent cooperation with the Sinocentric Republic of China (hereafter, ROC). In the process of becoming established writers, they acquired their cultural capital in various ways: by cultivating relationships with politicians and other influential people, winning grants and prizes, having their work included in textbooks and anthologies, playing the role of cultural ambassador for their homeland, getting sponsorship for translation and international marketing, and gaining global recognition tied to their national identity. Rather than revolting against Sinocentric ideology, they benefitted from the KMT's patronage and shrewdly employed strategies such as ambivalence and mimicry to acclaim their distinct Chinese identity that did not conform to the official discourse on Chineseness. The anti-Sinocentric schema also cannot comprehend why Yang Mu (楊牧) insists that Taiwanese writers are "legitimate heirs" to Chinese cultural tradition and that their writings are "authentic embodiments" of the Chinese cultural heritage.[15] Although these issues can be investigated through Sinophone studies, a more nuanced clarification of its applicability to Taiwanese literature is needed.

Likewise, the "Japanophone" framework favored by comparatists has its pros and cons. It enables valuable transcolonial comparisons (such as colonial Taiwan versus colonial Korea) and facilitates transculturation within the Japanese Empire. It, however, reinforces the already unequal prestige between writers of Japan proper and those from its former colonies. While some writers continued to compose in Japanese after 1945, the Japanophone framework is less relevant to postwar Taiwan, not to mention that it precludes Chinese writing, in both classical and vernacular styles, produced during Taiwan's Japanese colonial era. Bert Scruggs and Pei-yin Lin have both addressed the multilingual nature of colonial Taiwanese literature; Lin in particular calls for the examination of Taiwanese literature as world literature.[16] Still, a more thorough treatment of this topic, covering both colonial and postcolonial Taiwan, has yet to be offered. In sum, while the Sinophone and Japanophone frameworks "rescue" Taiwanese literature from the KMT's mis-conceptualization of it as Chinese literature from "Free China," and from China's emphasis on a monolithic and homogenized Chinese literature based on a common language and race, neither can comprehensively elucidate the situatedness of Taiwan in a different sense.

---

[14] We do not mean to reduce the Sinophone framework to merely a theory that challenges China-centrism, especially it can serve as a conjecture intersecting with other fields such as queer studies. However, the anti-hegemonic characteristic remains an important aspect of it.
[15] See Kuei-fen Chiu's chapter in this volume.
[16] Bert Scruggs, *Translingual Narration: Colonial and Postcolonial Taiwanese Fiction and Film* (Honolulu: University of Hawai'i Press, 2015); Pei-yin Lin, *Colonial Taiwan: Negotiating Identities and Modernity through Literature* (Boston and Leiden: Brill, 2017), 12–13.

Toward a Relational Comparison within the Framework of World Literature

To carve out the richness of Taiwanese literature, a fresh analytical framework is necessary. In light of its particularities, which are always liminal and ceaselessly negotiating with the collective experiences of national identity and cultural values, we propose to conceptualize Taiwanese literature as world literature. This approach allows for an exploration of the intricate dynamics, similar to an ongoing *fort/da* game, in which literary works constantly shuttle back and forth from Taiwan to multiple foreign cultures and then return to local discourses. It is only through this framing that the multilingual nature of Taiwanese literature and its writers' worldly visions can be holistically appreciated and thoughtfully appraised.

"World literature," a term for which Goethe is usually given credit as the first proponent, has generated various discussions in the West since the second half of the twentieth century, and particularly since the late 1990s. Casanova's sociological studies of the "world republic of letters," Moretti's call for a "distant reading" and attention to variations in the genre, and Damrosch's shying away from the literary canon to the circulation of texts are oft-quoted examples.[17] One may also add Apter's criticism of Franco Moretti's world literature system and Thomsen's analysis of the international circulation of literary "constellations" that share similar formal and thematic properties.[18] These discussions have left noticeable impacts on the discipline of comparative literature, encouraged us to step out of the usual aesthetics confined by "great tradition" as Leavis notes,[19] and expanded our understanding of a literary canon beyond Shakespeare and Flaubert to include Mahfouz and Cao Xueqin. Nevertheless, these narratives cannot escape their European and North American backgrounds. Examples proposed by scholars or readers, such as *The Guardian*'s "The 100 Greatest Novels of All Time,"[20] are often colored by the Euro-American centrism in which Western works emerge, receive canonization, circulate within Europe and North America, and subsequently are distributed to the rest of the world.

Extant scholarship on world literature focuses primarily on how Global North works are disseminated and read beyond Anglo-European zones. Individual works of the Global South such as African, South American, and Asian canons are consequently

---

[17] Pascale Casanova, *The World Republic of Letters*, trans. M. B. DeBevoise (Cambridge, MA: Harvard University Press, 2004); Franco Moretti, "Conjectures on World Literature," *New Left Review* 1 (2000): 54–68; David Damrosch, *What Is World Literature?* (Princeton: Princeton University Press, 2003).

[18] Emily Apter, *Against World Literature: On the Politics of Untranslatability* (London: Verso, 2013); Mads Rosendahl Thomsen, *Mapping World Literature: International Canonization and Transnational Literatures* (New York: Continuum, 2008).

[19] F. R. Leavis, *The Great Tradition: George Eliot, Henry James, Joseph Conrad* (London: Chatto & Windus, 1948). For the discussion on the relationship between canonicity and world literature, see Longxi Zhang, "Canon and World Literature," *Journal of World Literature* 1, no. 1 (2016): 119–27.

[20] Robert McCrum, "The 100 Greatest Non-Fiction Books," last modified October 12, 2003, https://www.theguardian.com/books/2003/oct/12/features.fiction.

assessed without a comprehensive understanding of the history of local literature. Their circulation in the Global North is limited to the readers' eyes that at any point can flatten, homogenize, disrupt, and even discriminate. Take the translation of Taiwanese literature as an example: feminism and queer issues attract more attention than anticolonial resistance, a dominant theme of modern Taiwanese literature.[21] This is likely because modern readers are keener to learn about issues that are most immediately relevant to them, as opposed to those that reference a specific historical context.

This matter of taste has contributed to a literary industry that constantly seeks the exciting and unexpected but does not necessarily attend to each literary tradition. Once favored, non-Western writers and their works are treated as privileged to be included for the purpose of showcasing variety within the (actually monotonic) literary world. The superiority of Western literature, the absence of non-Western literatures, or—in a nutshell—the asymmetry between the West and the "rest of the world" has been problematized by numerous scholars. For instance, Ngũgĩ wa Thiong'o identifies how local syllabi cover English-language literature in a neocolonial sense, Chakrabarty critiques Eurocentric knowledge production about "Indian" history, and Shu-mei Shih and Françoise Lionnet raise concerns about Western disciplines and methodologies espousing "universal" values to subjugate the rest of the world.[22] Without redressing the power discrepancy, world literature either results in studies of one-way (West to non-West) transculturation or is merely a false utopian premise.

As the concept "world" in world literature is de facto grounded in Western practice, discussion of the topic in reference to Chinese-language literature tends to concentrate on its connection to the "world," mainly Western readers. Chinese writers zealously draw on transnational and transcultural substances, resulting in a trap—the idea that modern China is a country of passive acceptance rather than active influence. Chakrabarty's words about India are equally relevant to China: "Third-world historians feel a need to refer to works in European history; historians of Europe do not feel any need to reciprocate."[23] The nearly zero obligation of the West gives rise to a subsequent question—the politics of recognition. Western works are considered almost universal and widely applicable worldwide because they are thought to tackle intellectual issues, whereas the latter are required to characterize these issues according to "geopolitical realism" and to stabilize the content by way of a "nation, ethnic, and cultural location."[24] Mo Yan's winning the Nobel Prize for using "older Chinese literature and popular

---

[21] From Pei-yin Lin's informal conversation in 2019 with Su Shuo-bin, director of Tainan-based National Museum of Taiwan Literature, a main organization promoting Taiwanese literature's translation projects, Su remarked that foreign readers are more interested in gender-related issues than anticolonial ones.

[22] Ngũgĩ wa Thiong'o, *Writers in Politics: Essays* (London: Heinemann, 1981); Dipesh Chakrabarty, "Postcoloniality and the Artifice of History: Who Speaks for 'Indian' Pasts?" in "Imperial Fantasies and Postcolonial Histories," special issue, *Representations* 37 (1992): 1–26; *Creolization of Theory*, ed. Shu-mei Shih and Françoise Lionnet (London: Duke University Press, 2011).

[23] Dipesh Chakrabarty, *Provincializing Europe: Postcolonial Thought and Historical Difference* (Princeton: Princeton University Press, 2000), 28.

[24] Rey Chow, "On Chineseness as a Theoretical Problem," in *Sinophone Studies: A Critical Reader* (New York: Columbia University Press, 2013), 43–56.

oral traditions as a starting point, combining these with contemporary *social* issues" (emphasis added), is an illustrative case.[25] Peter Handke, the 2019 Nobel laureate in literature, in contrast, is applauded more generically for his "linguistic ingenuity."[26] In 2020, the prize was given to the American poet Louise Glück for her "unmistakable poetic voice that with austere beauty makes individual existence *universal*" (emphasis added).[27] These different comments give rise to the following questions: Do Asian writers have to be local or socially realistic to win world recognition? Are they less competent than their Western counterparts in composing universally themed or linguistically creative works?

Mo Yan's case prompts us to pay heed to the difference between Asian local particularities and Western universality when it comes to world recognition. The imbalanced cultural capital between the West and non-West leads to the predicament of how to reach world readership as authors of "minor" languages.[28] Anxious about the limited visibility of Chinese literature in the West, Wang Ning urges Chinese writers to increase their proficiency in foreign languages so as to catch up with the West,[29] whereas Yingjin Zhang, more mindful of cultural unevenness, invites readers to recognize "other maps and other modes" in order to sustain the openness of world literature—a term predicated largely on Western values.[30]

Both the issues of asymmetric transculturation and global recognition (or circulation) are common concerns of Taiwanese literature and have been addressed by scholars. Lisa Wong concentrates on the transcultural poetics of Yang Mu, whereas Serena Chou and David Wang both employ the term "worlding" to discuss, respectively, Wu Ming-yi's (吳明益) eco-criticism and the complex and constantly developing state of Taiwanese literature.[31] In a similar vein, the edited volume *Positioning Taiwan in a Global Context* regards Taiwanese literature as a continuous and dynamic worlding process of becoming with a "practical-actional dimension," as Pheng Cheah puts it.[32] Shu-mei Shih calls for Taiwan to take its place on the map of global postcolonial studies,[33] and Hsinya Huang uses Taiwan to explore transnational and trans-Pacific

---

[25] https://www.nobelprize.org/prizes/literature/2012/yan/facts/.
[26] https://www.nobelprize.org/prizes/literature/2019/handke/facts/.
[27] https://www.nobelprize.org/prizes/literature/2020/gluck/facts/.
[28] "Minor" here refers to its symbolic capital instead of the population of its speakers.
[29] Wang Ning, "Chinese Literature as World Literature," *Canadian Review of Comparative Literature* 43, no. 3 (2016): 387.
[30] Yingjin Zhang, "Mapping Chinese Literature as World Literature," *CLCWeb: Comparative Literature and Culture* 17, no. 1 (2015): 9.
[31] Lisa Lai-ming Wong, *Rays of the Searching Sun: The Transcultural Poetics of Yang Mu* (New York: Peter Lang, 2009); Shiuhhuah Serena Chou, "Wu's *The Man with the Compound Eyes* and the Worlding of Environmental Literature," *CLCWeb: Comparative Literature and Culture* 16, no. 4 (2014): 1–9; David Wang's European Association of Taiwan Studies annual conference's keynote lecture "Worlding Taiwan: Translation, Transgression, Transmigration" delivered in March 2017.
[32] Bi-yu Chang and Pei-yin Lin, eds., *Positioning Taiwan in a Global Context: Being and Becoming* (London: Routledge, 2019); Peng Cheah, *What Is a World? On Postcolonial Literature as World Literature* (Durham: Duke University Press, 2016).
[33] Shu-mei Shih, "Globalization and the (In)significance of Taiwan," *Postcolonial Studies* 6, no. 2 (2003): 143–53.

Indigenous cultural flows.³⁴ The latest additions investigating the transnational context of Taiwanese literature are the Chinese edited volume *The Structure of Feeling Resonating with the World: Papers on Taiwan Literature* and Szu-wen Kung's translation-focused study of the asymmetrical cultural relationships between Taiwan and the English-speaking world.³⁵ As to how exactly Taiwanese literature can reach an international audience, Kuei-fen Chiu in her recent articles has initiated four practical strategies for "peripheral" literature, like Taiwanese literature, to go global and consider the online circulation.³⁶ Nevertheless, those Taiwan-friendly tactics still cannot escape from the shadow of Western eyes or Chinese hegemony. Western readers find it difficult to actively distinguish Taiwan from China and tend to prefer translating and circulating Chinese works for effortless commercialization and packaging. Labels such as "translation from Chinese language (Taiwan)" or "translation from Taiwan" in bookstores are not merely unappealing. Instead, they to a considerable degree constrict the international space of Taiwanese literature. If Taiwan is not important, then why should foreign readers peruse Taiwanese literature?

This question can only be tackled when the map of world literature and world studies is replaced by theories of knowledge exchange that seek to annul subjugation and discrimination. Epeli Hauʻofa's concept of "a sea of islands," Édouard Glissant's poetics of relation, and Shu-mei Shih's relational comparison—from the islands of Tonga and Fiji, Martinique, and Taiwan, respectively—mark three attempts at redress. Altogether, they demonstrate how an oceanic view continuously challenges the rigid epistemology within Western institutions, capitalism, and hegemony.³⁷ From a European view, the Pacific islands are small, isolated, and poor in terms of resources and economic growth. Noting this belittlement, Hauʻofa proposes the perspective of "a sea of islands" to substitute the old, continental idea of "islands in a far sea."³⁸ The difference between the two perceptions is reflected in how the sea is perceived. The ocean is not a barricade but an expressway to reach other islands; an individual can be a seafarer and travel along the oceanic highway to break the island-state boundaries

---

34 Hsinya Huang, "Indigenous Taiwan as Location of Native American and Indigenous Studies," *CLCWeb: Comparative Literature and Culture* 16, no. 4 (2014), http://docs.lib.purdue.edu/clcweb/vol16/iss4/2.

35 Huang Mei-er, ed., 世界中的台灣文學 [*The Structure of Feeling Resonating with the World: Papers on Taiwan Literature*] (Taipei: National Taiwan University Press, 2020); Szu-wen Kung, *Translation of Contemporary Taiwan Literature in a Cross-Cultural Context: A Translation Studies Perspective* (New York: Routledge, 2021).

36 Kuei-fen Chiu, "Worlding World Literature from the Literary Periphery: Four Taiwanese Models," *Modern Chinese Literature and Culture* 31, no. 1 (2018): 13–41; Kuei-fen Chiu, "World Literature in an Age of Digital Technologies: Digital Archive, Wikipedia, and Goodreads.com," in *The Making of Chinese-Sinophone Literatures as World Literature*, ed. Kuei-fen Chiu and Yingjin Zhang (Hong Kong: Hong Kong University Press, 2022).

37 Epeli Hauʻofa, *We Are the Ocean: Selected Works* (Honolulu: University of Hawaiʻi Press, 2008); Édouard Glissant, *Poetics of Relation*, trans. Betsy Wing (Ann Arbor: The University of Michigan Press, 2010); Shu-mei Shih, "World Studies and Relational Comparison," *PMLA* 130, no. 2 (2015): 430–38.

38 Hauʻofa, "Our Sea of Islands," in *We Are the Ocean*, 31.

imposed by European colonizers. Glissant holds an analogous opinion when he states, "our boat is open, and we sail them for everyone."³⁹

The voyage embodies nomadism, errantry, and a detour, which establishes relations beyond economic exploits and cultural pressures, giving birth to a hybrid identity. Inspired by Glissant's poetics of relation, Shih sees all continents as nothing but bigger islands that are connected to other islands by the ocean.⁴⁰ Recognizing that literatures emit their literary arcs to interrelate and reciprocate each other, she argues, "world literature must be understood as a field of relations that expend horizontally across space and are transmitted vertically across time."⁴¹ These ideas do not merely abolish the continental dichotomies of the colonizer and the colonized, the oppressor and the oppressed, and influence and acceptance but also embrace an open oceanic spirit. They aptly capture the distinct global and oceanic features of Taiwanese literature, as many individual works are informed by social and literary trends that are not restricted to a single country. This further endorses the necessity of framing Taiwanese literature as world literature.

Taiwanese Literature in Relation to the World: Transculturation and Translation

Taiwanese literature, in a quasi-national literary sense, was born as a result of writers' transcultural practices. During the early phase of Japanese colonial rule, before Japanese became prevalent, most works by Taiwanese authors were written in a mixture of classical and vernacular Chinese. The first few stories have rather exotic foreign settings. For instance, Hsieh Hsueh-yu's (謝雪漁) "An Unusual Romance during the War" (陣中奇緣, 1905) is set against the backdrop of the French Revolution, whereas Wei Ching-te's (魏清德) "Tooth Marks" (齒痕, 1918) is an adaptation of Maurice Leblanc's "The Teeth of the Tiger." When vernacular Chinese gained greater momentum beginning in the mid-1920s, the early work "Scales of Injustice" (一桿「稱仔」, 1926) by Lōa Hô (賴和) is inspired by French writer Anatole France's *L'Affaire Crainquebille*. Rather than taking this case as evidence of the prestige of French literature per se, Lai's transnational humanitarian concerns for those of the lower social stratum warrant attention.

Entering the 1930s, a Japanese-language generation emerged among Taiwan's literary establishment. They, like Japanese-language Korean authors, sought recognition from Tokyo's central literary arena, because they witnessed the shift from Paris to Tokyo for Japanese-language writers from the colonies. Throughout

---

³⁹ Glissant, "The Open Boat," in *Poetics of Relation*, 9.
⁴⁰ Shu-mei Shih, "關係的比較學" [Comparison as Relation], 中山人文學報 [*Sun Yat-sen Journal of Humanities*], no. 39 (2015): 7.
⁴¹ Shih, "World Studies and Relational Comparison," 431.

the colonial era, Taiwanese writers continued to gain inspiration from global literary trends through the mediums of Japanese and Chinese. Lung Ying-tsung (龍瑛宗), one of the most productive colonial Taiwanese writers, when recollecting his literary career in the 1980s, commented on his fortune of being able to buy several affordable *enbun* sets, such as the *Complete Collection of World Literature* published by Shinchōsha in the 1930s. He specifically admitted that books from writers including Heinrich Heine, Nikolai Gogol, Ivan Turgenev, Émile Zola, and Honoré de Balzac have become the "blood and meat" of his writing.[42] Other remarkable cases include the multilingual Liu Na-ou (劉吶鷗),[43] the globally minded Yang Kuei (楊逵), the surrealist advocate Yang Chih-chang (楊熾昌), and the French-literature aficionado Yeh Shih-tao.

While Tokyo appeared to be the option for colonial Taiwanese intellectuals to access global knowledge, Liu decided to head to Shanghai—a city about which he harbored mixed feelings, after studying in Tokyo—to seek a more conducive environment for his literary career. In a cosmopolitan city like Shanghai, Liu would not worry about his colonized background, and he managed to blend in well. Yang Kuei, a humanitarian socialist, strove to write from the global perspective of the worker[44] and is hailed as a world-class writer.[45] Yang Chih-chang's student career in Tokyo (1932–34) overlapped with the heyday of surrealism in Japan. Through Japanese translation, he was in sync with the latest European surrealist trends at that time. Upon returning to Taiwan, he and his Le Moulin Poetry Society peers strove to transcend political reality with their avant-garde surrealist poetics. Its world-embracing aesthetics, albeit short-lived, complement the otherwise realism-dominant Taiwanese literary establishment, making a peculiar case for colonial Taiwanese literature that eschews the conundrum of identity politics. As for Yeh, his two 1943 works were inspired by Alphonse Daudet and André Gide, whereas Rimbaud's verse poem "The Drunken Boat" was his antidote to the suffocating 1950s.[46] Rather than a passive imitator, Yeh selectively learned from Daudet's "The Old Folks" and Gide's *Strait Is the Gate*. The results are substantially different from the two French texts.

In postwar Taiwan, modernism—which emerged in the mid-1950s against the context of the KMT's promotion of anticommunist literature—became the mainstream style in the 1960s. It began initially in the genre of poetry, with Chi Hsien's (紀弦) bold and controversial claim that Taiwan's postwar modern poetry was a practice of "horizontal transplantation"—meaning learning from the West—instead of "vertical

---

[42] Lung Ying-tzung, "讀書遍歷記" [My Reading Experience], 民眾日報 [*The Commons Daily*], January 28, 1981.

[43] Liu's 1927 diary shows that his reading includes Chinese, Japanese, French, and English books. Liu's ex-colleague at the Central Film Company considers him as "a man of the world" rather than Chinese or Japanese. Quoted from Peng Hsiao-yen, "浪蕩天涯：劉吶鷗1972年日記" [The Flâneur of the World: Liu Na-ou's 1927 Diary], 中國文哲研究集刊 [*Bulletin of the Institute of Chinese Literature and Philosophy*] 12 (1998): 35.

[44] Yang Kuei, "藝術是大眾的" [Arts Are for the Masses], 台灣文藝 [*Taiwan Literature and Arts*] 2, no. 2 (1935): 11.

[45] Hayama Yoshiki, "世界的作家たれ" [Be World-Class Writers], 台灣新文學 [*Taiwan New Literature*] 2, no. 2 (1937): 59.

[46] Yeh was imprisoned by the KMT government under the charge of "harboring communist agents" from 1951 to 1954. See his "A Painful Confession," in *The Columbia Sourcebook of Literary Taiwan*, ed. Sung-sheng Yvonne Chang, Michelle Yeh, and Ming-ju Fan (New York: Columbia University Press, 2014), 362–68.

inheritance"—meaning adhering to the Chinese classical lyrical tradition—being one of the best-known examples. While this declaration has elicited criticism, such as a rootless exercise and an inferior imitation of the West, especially among realist critics, it remained a sensible practice for writers to experiment with new styles and themes as well as navigate the KMT's authoritarian rule. It is more accurate to consider those modernist practitioners who appropriated Western techniques to respond to Taiwan's sociocultural particularities, such as challenging the conservative middle-class value systems in *Family Catastrophe* (家變, 1973) by Wang Wen-hsing (王文興) and portraying the spiritual paralysis of mainlander émigrés in *Taipei People* (台北人, 1971) by Pai Hsien-yung (白先勇). Nevertheless, several modernist works became the target of criticism in the 1970s due to critics' calls for more socially engaged literature to respond to Taiwan's diplomatic setbacks and engage in the push for social reform.[47]

The 1980s saw an even more rapidly urbanizing and open society. Following the visits of Fredric Jameson and Ihab Hassan in 1986 and Lo Ching's (羅青) translation of postmodern theories, such as those of Jean-François Lyotard and Steven Henry Madoff, Taiwanese writers quickly employed postmodern techniques in their works to challenge long-accepted views and "absolute" truth. Debates took place among Taiwanese scholars as to whether the country had entered late capitalism, as in the case of its Western model, to classify Taiwan as a postmodern society. In 1987, Taiwan's nearly four-decade-long martial law (1949–87) was lifted. This symbolic collapse of KMT hegemony engendered great collective postcolonial efforts to "rediscover" Taiwan from a non-KMT angle. Depending on political stance, how one should understand the post-1945 KMT rule of Taiwan remains contentious. The 1995 debate in the journal *Chung-Wai Literary Monthly* and that between the pro-Taiwan literary historian Chen Fang-ming (陳芳明) and the China-yearning writer Chen Ying-chen (陳映真) in the journal *Unitas* in the late 1990s serve as two salient examples.

In 1999, Chen Fang-ming claimed that the postcolonial framework is more suitable to explain the social condition of post-1980s Taiwan because postmodern theory overlooks Taiwanese people's subjectivity under Japanese colonialism and KMT authoritarianism.[48] He also criticized the simplified and out-of-context appropriation of postmodernism from the United States and France by postmodernists in Taiwan. Ping-hui Liao, however, was more sympathetic toward Taiwan's embrace of postmodernism.[49] He regards postmodernism in Taiwan as an act of cultural unconsciousness to respond to Taiwan's double marginalized state of being under the shadow of China, and its isolation on the international political stage. For him, the postmodern wave in Taiwanese academia in the late 1980s was closely connected with Taiwan's colonial past. To highlight the complexity of Taiwan's social and cultural contexts, he proposes understanding its postmodern conditions as alternative

---

[47] Taiwan lost its United Nations seat in 1971. Japan and America switched diplomatic recognition from Taipei to Beijing in 1972 and late 1978 respectively.
[48] Chen Fang-ming, "台灣新文學史的建構與分期" [The Construction and Periodization of Taiwan's New Literary History], 聯合文學 [*Unitas*] 178 (1999): 162–73.
[49] Ping-hui Liao, "台灣：後現代或後殖民？" [Taiwan: Postmodern or Postcolonial?], in 書寫台灣 [*Writing Taiwan*], ed. Chou Ying-hsiung and Joyce Chi-hui Liu (Taipei: Rye Field, 2000), 85–99.

modernity. Taiwan's sociocultural trajectory demonstrates an intricate coexistence of the two -isms. As the Han Taiwanese establish their "postcolonial" identity, they concurrently encounter the aftereffect of the KMT and Japanese authorities and the need to redress their relations with émigrés, Indigenous peoples, and migrants from Southeast Asia. As the claim for a singular identity becomes almost impossible in an era marked by globalization, articulations of Taiwanese-ness ought to remain plural and recognize its inherent hybridity, just as cultural identity is situational and never static.

In addition to transculturation, Taiwanese literature develops its arcs to the world via translation. The United States played a role in promoting anticommunist literature in Taiwan via the USIS (United States Information Service) and in translating literary works from Taiwan, which commenced in the 1950s. The first few years focused on English-to-Chinese translation, with an aim to help establish an imagined anticommunist community among overseas Chinese. To offset the communist state's ambitious Chinese-to-English translation plan, English translation received more attention toward the end of the decade. The first Chinese work from Taiwan, translated into English by the renowned writer Eileen Chang in 1959, is Chen Chi-ying's (陳紀瀅) *Fool in the Reeds* (荻村傳), often considered an anticommunist novel. Although it was facilitated by the USIS in Hong Kong, the USIS in Taiwan launched a book translation program between 1952 and 1962.[50]

From 1963 to 1972, *Today's China*, edited by Lung Ying-tsung, joined the effort by introducing works from Taiwan in Japanese translation. The journal is not merely propaganda that aims to expand investment in Japanese; it also implicitly conveys a feeling of ambivalence and revolt within the KMT discourse. When émigré writers grew to enjoy the privileges of discourse and occupy pivotal literary positions, translations by native writers born under Japanese rule somehow became a literary field fairly free of restrictions and censorship. The journals also include writings on colonial memories, the Taiwanese experience in Vietnam, and Chinese culture. They compare some writings to European or Japanese works to render a multicultural impression.[51]

The arcs of translation were mostly institutionalized by government authorities, translators, and scholars. In 1973, Pang-yuan Chi, while working in the National Institute for Compilation and Translation, edited *An Anthology of Contemporary Chinese Literature*. From 1990 to 2011, the Council for Cultural Affairs (CCA, 文建會) sponsored 149 English translations, 66 Japanese translations, and 18 works in French. When the CCA was upgraded to the ministerial level in 2012—under the name Ministry of Culture—the National Museum of Taiwanese Literature (hereafter NMTL)

---

[50] For details, see Wang Mei-hsiang, "冷戰時代的台灣文學外譯：美國新聞處譯書計畫的運作 (1952–1962)" [Translating Taiwan Literature into Foreign Languages in the Cold War Era: The Operation of USIS Book Translation Program (1952–1962)], 台灣文學研究學報 [*Journal of Taiwan Literary Studies*] 19 (2014): 223–54.

[51] Wang Hui-chen, "六零年代台灣文學的日譯活動：今日之中國的文學翻譯與文化政治" [Taiwanese Literature in Japanese Translation in the 1960s: *Today's China*'s Literary Translation and Cultural Politics], 台灣文學研究學報 [*Journal of Taiwan Literary Studies*] 23 (2016): 255–90.

established the Center for Taiwanese Literature in Translation. Patronage was extended by the museum for three years. In 2015, the Ministry of Culture reappropriated the system of sponsorship, giving it the new name "Books from Taiwan."

Two university-based publication channels warrant special mention, although the readership of their publications is smaller than works published by mainstream presses. These are the journal *Taiwan Literature: English Translation Series*, which is operated under the charge of Kuo-ch'ing Tu at the University of California, Santa Barbara since 1996, and the Columbia University series "Modern Chinese Literature from Taiwan," edited by David Der-wei Wang from 2000 onward. The former explores a wider range, including poetry, dialects, and works under Japanese rule, whereas the latter focuses on canonical novels. Tu has, in fact, been promoting the notion of "world literatures in Chinese" (世華文學), which refers to the multilingual writing of Chinese people worldwide.[52] The latest addition is the "Taiwan Literature" series in Cambria Press, a joint effort with the NMTL and National Taiwan Normal University. In recent decades, Taiwanese literature in translation has encountered a variety of sources of patronage, readership, institutional attention, and aesthetic tastes. Authors have participated in global issues, such as climate change and ethnic and gender equality, to different degrees. While Taiwanese works continue to develop literary relations to the world at large, there remains a long way to go before we witness a more balanced cultural exchange.

Chapter Outline

Cautious about Western theories, this volume shares the idea of relational comparison and oceanic epistemology put forward by Glissant, Shih, and Hauʻofa, offering an approach that situates Taiwanese literature with respect to the world and that reframes world literature by reducing the effects of American-European centrism. To flesh out in depth the issues in which we are particularly interested—the framing, transculturation, and translation of Taiwanese literature—the book is divided into three interconnected parts. Each represents one important dimension of approaching Taiwanese literature as world literature.

Starting with methodology, the first part explores frameworks and tactics to conceptualize Taiwanese literature as world literature. The second and third parts investigate respectively the import of world literature to Taiwan and the export of Taiwanese literature to the world. Taken together, the twelve chapters respond to the three interrelated questions of Taiwanese literature in a global sense: To what extent can Taiwanese literature be viewed as world literature? What kinds of world inspirations have led to the creation of Taiwanese literature? What is the political background behind the translation of Taiwanese literary works into foreign languages? Due to

---

[52] Kuo-ch'ing Tu, 台灣文學與世華文學 [*Taiwanese Literature and World Literatures in Chinese*] (Taipei: National Taiwan University Press, 2015).

spatial limitations, we are unable to include as many case studies as we had hoped. The increases in Dutch translations as well as translations in Czech and other Asian languages promoted by the government are therefore unaccounted for here. Studies related to German and Spanish translation are not explored, mainly because of the insufficient number of translations.

Part One contains three chapters. Kuei-fen Chiu uses the example of Taiwanese literature to challenge the theoretical framework of Sinophone literature and embrace transculturalism within world literature. Through carefully selected case studies, she compares the advantages and limits of both the Sinophone and world literature models. Carlos Rojas discusses the different contingent constructions of Taiwanese literature as the "worlding" tactics of the literary works themselves. Focusing on Wu Ming-yi, he maintains that political and institutional constraints may foster writers' creativity at the outset. Concerned with the literary modes in a global context of production, circulation, and reception, Pei-yin Lin investigates three forms—family saga, autobiographical narrative, and bildungsroman—that she characterizes as classifying Taiwanese literature as "worldly." Her selected texts tackle the "back" circulation, "non-Western" circulation, and even "non-circulation" of works with a transnational vision, which are usually overlooked in world literature studies.

Part Two presents three case studies of transculturation in Taiwanese literature. Yi-chen Liu reevaluates the circulation of knowledge and the localization of *Le Moulin* Poetry Society. She posits that their Japanese inspirations and emphasis on intellectualism made them quite different from French surrealism, at least Breton's automatism. They were not as politically radical as their Western counterparts because their literary rebellion was against the left-leaning Taiwanese literary establishment in the mid-1930s instead of colonialism. Continuing the glocal circulation of Taiwanese literature, Darryl Sterk revisits Wu Ming-yi's environmentally informed works, which have been hailed for their symbiosis of local concern and global vision. He takes Wu's eco-cosmopolitanism as his departure point, delving critically into the relationship between Wu's eco-writing and his portrayal of Indigenous people. Nicholas A. Kaldis explores how Chu T'ien-wen's (朱天文) gay novel *Notes of a Desolate Man* (荒人手記, 1994) conflates postmodernity and homosexuality, with the former aligning with Western techniques and the latter reflecting a unique Taiwanese reaction to global literary trends.

The final part examines Taiwanese literature in various translations. We start with the English translation primarily because it is the main foreign language in which Taiwanese literature has been circulated globally. Resonating with Lefevere's observation that the selection of texts is subject to the mainstream aesthetics and ideologies of the specific historical context in which the translation is produced,[53] John Balcom investigates several anthologies ranging from the 1970s to 2021 and maintains that the cultural variety has finally been emphasized in recent anthologies. Gwennaël

---

[53] André Lefevere, "Anthologizing Africa," in *Translation, Rewriting, and the Manipulation of Literary Fame* (London: Routledge, 1992).

Gaffric, analyzing selected French series of Taiwanese literature, argues that Taiwan's image has changed from an area reserved for Chinese culture to a multicultural and multilingual society. Federica Passi illustrates how two minor literatures—Taiwan and Italy—can equally exchange their cultural capitals. She also demonstrates how Taiwan can provide an alternative voice for Western readers to understand the complexity of the Chinese-speaking world, transgress the hegemony of China, and embrace other Sinophone regions like Taiwan, Hong Kong, and Malaysia. Ying-che Huang scrutinizes the shifting conceptualization of Taiwanese literature among Japanese scholars and translators from "Taiwan's literature," which entails an absence of national identity, to an entity with its autonomy facilitated by governmental patronage since the 1990s.

After investigating the politics and implications of translating Taiwanese literature into four different languages, we focus on two celebrated authors—Chiu Miao-chin (邱妙津) and Li Ang (李昂), both mentioned in Huang's chapter—to delve into the effectiveness and complications of cultural equivalence in translation. Wen-chi Li implements a field research method to provide an understanding of Western readership concerning non-Western literature—Chiu Miao-chin's lesbian works specifically. Admitting that the strategy of distant reading adopted by English-speaking people risks reducing Taiwan's distinctiveness, Li nevertheless confirms the possibility of their appreciation and opportunities for their discovery of new Taiwanese queer texts. Sheng-chi Hsu highlights two translations of Li Ang's *The Butcher's Wife* (殺夫, 1983), demonstrating how different translators might manipulate the rendering of sexuality in feminist work. The chapters in this part altogether offer valuable insights into the current state of introducing Taiwanese literature through translation to a global audience.

Part One

Bridging Taiwan and the World: Frameworks and Tactics

1

Taiwanese Literature in Two Transnational Contexts: Sinophone Literature and World Literature

Kuei-fen Chiu

Taiwanese Literature in Transnational Contexts

This chapter examines two transnational frameworks for the study of Taiwanese literature: Sinophone literature and world literature.[1] Both emerged around the turn of the twenty-first century in response to increasing transnational cultural flows. These two concepts gained currency in Western academic communities almost concomitantly.[2] Although world literature began to be taught at the undergraduate level in the United States in the mid-twentieth century, it began to emerge as a vibrant research domain only after the publication of several seminal theoretical pieces by prominent scholars of Western literature, such as Pascale Casanova, Franco Moretti, and David Damrosch, between 1999 and 2004. Its major proponents and participants are mostly scholars of Western literature and comparative literature. While world literature was drawing attention from the international community of Western literature, the concept of the Sinophone also began to make its impact on the US academic community of Chinese literary studies. Shu-mei Shih first articulated the Sinophone as a theoretical concept and research method in her ground-breaking *Visuality and Identity: Sinophone*

---

[1] This chapter expands on points I made in several previously published journal articles and the introductory chapter in an edited volume, including "Cosmopolitanism and Indigenism: The Use of Cultural Authenticity in an Age of Flows," *New Literary History* 44, no. 1 (2013): 159–78; "'Worlding' World Literature from the Literary Periphery: Four Taiwanese Models," *Modern Chinese Literature and Culture* 30, no. 1 (2018): 13–41; "「世界華文文學」、「華語語系文學」、「世界文學」：以楊牧探測三種研究台灣文學的跨文學框架" [World Literature in Chinese, Sinophone Literature, and World Literature: Yang Mu and Three Theoretical Frameworks for Taiwan Literary Studies], 台灣文學學報 [*Bulletin of Taiwanese Literature*], no. 35 (2019): 127–57; the introduction to *The Making of Chinese-Sinophone Literatures as World Literature*, co-authored with Yingjin Zhang (Hong Kong: Hong Kong University Press, 2022), 1–21. I would like to thank the Ministry of Science and Technology in Taiwan for its continuous support of my research.

[2] Kuei-fen Chiu, "World Literature in an Age of Digital Technologies: Digital Archive, Wikipedia, and Goodreads.com," in *The Making of Chinese-Sinophone Literatures as World Literature*, ed. Kuei-fen Chiu and Yingjin Zhang (Hong Kong: Hong Kong University Press, 2022), 217–36.

Articulations across the Pacific in 2007. In the words of Brian Bernards, "Shu-mei Shih gave the term 'Sinophone' its first critical theorization—and inaugurated the new field of Sinophone studies" with her tripartite framework of continental colonialism, settler colonialism, and overseas migration.[3] An examination of *Sinophone Studies: A Critical Reader* (2013) shows that the main participants in the discussion are scholars with expertise in Chinese-related studies. The vitality of world literature studies and Sinophone studies is testified by the recent establishment of institutions and book series—for example, the Institute for World Literature at Harvard University and the *Journal of World Literature* for the promotion of the study of world literature, the Society of Sinophone Studies, University of California Press Sinophone Studies Series, and Cambria Sinophone World Series for the development of Sinophone studies.

The Sinophone approach situates Taiwanese literature in relation to Chinese literature as well as literatures in Sinitic languages produced in different countries. It tends to focus on the problematics of Chinese and Chineseness and underscores the importance of place-based imagination. The world literature approach, on the other hand, situates Taiwanese literature in relation to works beyond the Sinosphere. How Taiwanese literary texts move across borders is often the focus of attention. In Sinophone studies, China is seen as the literary center whose exercise of cultural hegemony is subject to critique. In world literature studies, China and Chinese literature are seen to inhabit the margins of the world literary space. Western literatures written in dominant languages such as English, French, and German constitute the literary center of world literature, whereas Chinese literature takes up the position of small literature. Using the Sinophone as a critical method would highlight the notion of resistance toward the Chinese literary center. Situating Taiwanese literature within world literature studies usually pays more attention to how Taiwanese texts negotiate with the literary center dominated by Western mechanisms of recognition and less to the relationship between Taiwanese literature and Chinese literature. Sinophone studies often show a great interest in how Sinophone literatures may work to dismantle the hierarchical relationship between mainland Chinese literature and Sinophone literatures. For world literature studies, a crucial question is how small literature writers work within, rather than against, the hierarchical structure of world literature to claim recognition in the realm of world literature.[4]

Therefore, studying Taiwanese literature as Sinophone literature and studying Taiwanese literature as world literature often address quite different sets of issues. In its current practice, the issue of identity, very often in terms of content and the use of Chinese as a literary language, is cast in the limelight. Taiwanese Indigenous literature is a case in point. Taiwanese Indigenous writers often tell stories about how Indigenous communities have been oppressed by the Han settlers and how the adoption of the

---

[3] Brian Bernards, "Sinophone Literature," in *The Columbia Companion to Modern Chinese Literature*, ed. Kirk Denton (New York: Columbia University Press, 2016), 76.
[4] Pascale Casanova, *The World Republic of Letters*, trans. M. B. DeBevoise (Cambridge, MA: Harvard University Press, 2004), 176; Johan Heilbron, "Obtaining World Fame from the Periphery," *Dutch Cross: Journal of Low Countries Studies* 44, no. 2 (2020): 137–39.

Chinese language enacts symbolic violence.⁵ The study of Taiwanese literature as world literature—compared to the Sinophone approach—is more interested in the travel of Taiwanese literature beyond Chinese-speaking communities. Take the Man Booker International Prize nominee Wu Ming-yi (吳明益) as an example. Studies of Wu have framed the writer within the context of environmental world literature and magical realism or focused on the problems of cross-cultural transaction in translating his works. They are more interested in how Wu's works engage in dialogues with traveling world literature or literary trends.

These two transnational approaches suggest new ways of studying Taiwanese literature and introduce new research topics. In traditional literary studies in and outside Taiwan, Taiwanese literature as a subject of research and teaching used to be placed under Chinese literature as national literature. This literary hierarchy was challenged by the postcolonial approach to Taiwanese literature that emerged in Taiwan in the 1990s as the issue of Taiwan's sovereignty was put on the table.⁶ The postcolonial approach promoted by Taiwanese scholars conceptualizes Taiwanese literature as national literature. Like the postcolonial approach, the Sinophone approach challenges the hierarchy in Chinese literary studies that subsumes the study of Taiwanese literature under the umbrella of Chinese literature. It tries to clear up space for Taiwanese literature and other Sinitic-language literatures, such as Hong Kong and Malaysian Chinese literature, to be studied as literatures on par with Chinese mainland literature, not just the supplements to Chinese literature. The Sinophone approach replaces the national literature paradigm with a transnational paradigm. It places Taiwanese literature within a context beyond the boundaries of national literature. World literature as a theoretical framework shares with Sinophone theory the transnational approach to Taiwanese literature. While the Sinophone approach connects Taiwanese literature to other literatures in Sinitic languages, the world literature approach connects Taiwanese literature with literature at large in the global literary market. In the following, I discuss further "Taiwanese literature as Sinophone literature" and "Taiwanese literature as world literature" in terms of domain, definition, central issues, and favored texts.

The Domain of Sinophone Taiwanese Literature

All valid studies begin with an adequate definition of the subject under investigation. The fundamental question for Sinophone studies is therefore the demarcation of the domain. Shu-mei Shih defines the domain of the Sinophone as follows: "I coin the notion of the Sinophone to designate Sinitic-language cultures and communities

---

⁵ Brian Bernards and Chien-hsin Tsai, "Part III: Sites and Articulations," in *Sinophone Studies: A Critical Reader*, ed. Shu-mei Shih, Chien-hsin Tsai, and Brian Bernards (New York: Columbia University Press, 2012), 188; Hsinya Huang, "Sinophone Indigenous Literature of Taiwan: History and Tradition," in *Sinophone Studies*, 250.
⁶ Chen Fang-ming, 台灣新文學史 [*A New History of Modern Taiwanese Literature*] (Taipei: Linking, 2011).

outside China as well as those ethnic communities within China, where Sinitic languages are either forcefully imposed or willingly adopted."[7] By this definition, Sinophone literature refers to literary works produced by writers of these Sinitic-language communities. The "Sites and Articulations" section in the influential edited volume *Sinophone Studies: A Critical Reader* gives us an idea of the domain of Sinophone literature. It includes Hong Kong literature, Taiwanese literature, Tibetan literature, and literary works by ethnic Chinese writers across different countries. Therefore, the 2012 Nobel Laureate Gao Xingjian, who now lives in France as a French citizen, Malaysian Chinese writers such as Kim Chew Ng, and Chinese American writers are considered Sinophone writers.

However, if the Sinophone is, as Shu-mei Shih points out, "often the site where the most powerful articulations against China-centrism are heard,"[8] does the concept of Sinophone literature designate all literatures produced by Sinitic-language writers or only those works endorsing the Sinophone critique of China-centrism? In other words, is the "Sinophone" of Sinophone literature a linguistic referent or a critical stance? Brian Bernard's discussion of Sinophone literature suggests the former: "'Sinophone literature' is an updated translation of 華文文學, a term that until recently had been defined as 'literature in Chinese' or 'overseas Chinese literature' (海外華文文學)."[9] This view of Sinophone literature as an updated version of literature in Chinese may not be shared by Shih, for she considers "literature in Chinese" as upholding "Chinese" as the hegemonic sign.[10] Nevertheless, her discussion of Sinophone literature reveals that she also takes the Sinophone of Sinophone literature as a linguistic referent rather than a critical stance against China-centrism. Thus, she acknowledges that China-centrism may be found in some Sinophone literary works. They demonstrate a strand of Sinophone literature that, in her view, "is the nostalgic kind that forever looks back at China as its cultural motherland or the source of value."[11] We may say that Sinophone literature refers to literature written in Sinitic languages regardless of the writers' identity or ideological positions.

It is important to note that the meaning of the term "Sinophone" in Sinophone literature is different from "Sinophone" as a critical concept and a research method. In Shih's words, "The Sinophone as a concept, then, allows for the emergence of a critical position that does not succumb to nationalist and imperialist pressures and allows for a multiply-mediated and multiply-angulated critique. In this way, Sinophone can be considered a method."[12] Using the Sinophone as a critical method to study works written by Taiwanese writers means adopting the critical position proposed by Shih. This critical stance may not be shared by writers who are classified as Sinophone

---

[7] Shu-mei Shih, "Against Diaspora: The Sinophone as Places of Cultural Production," in *Sinophone Studies*, 30.
[8] Shih, "Against Diaspora," 33.
[9] Bernards, "Sinophone Literature," 73.
[10] Shih, "Against Diaspora," 34.
[11] Shih, "Against Diaspora," 33.
[12] Shih, "Against Diaspora," 39.

writers. In other words, the ethnic or ideological identification of the writers is not a criterion for the inclusion in or exclusion from Sinophone Taiwanese literature. It is the language that decides eligibility. Thus, Sinophone Taiwanese literature would exclude Japanese-language literature by Taiwanese writers in colonial Taiwan. Works in a Sinitic language by Taiwan's Indigenous writers would be considered as part of Sinophone Taiwanese literature, whereas those written with the Romanization of their Indigenous languages would not.

The Domain of Taiwanese Literature as World Literature

In contrast to the concept of Sinophone Taiwanese literature which encompasses most Taiwanese literary texts, "Taiwanese literature as world literature" designates only a very small part of Taiwanese literature if we adopt David Damrosch's influential notion of world literature as literary works that are actively "present in a literary system beyond that of its original culture."[13] In his view, "world literature" is neither the total of all literatures in the world, but "a mode of circulation and of reading."[14] Only works that can "take on a new life as they move into the world at large" can be considered as world literature.[15] By this definition, the term "Taiwanese literature as world literature" is restricted to a very small group of translated Taiwanese literary works that resonate with an international readership. "Taiwanese literature as world literature" does not include all Taiwanese literary works or all Taiwanese literature in translation. As I have argued elsewhere, spatial movement alone does not turn a literary work into a work of "world literature."[16] Translation does not guarantee readership; Taiwanese literature in translation becomes world literature only when it enjoys an active life in other literary systems. This is why world literature is conceptualized by Damrosch as "a mode of circulation," in addition to "a mode of reading." To configure the literary life of a writer in world literature, I have proposed a scheme of international recognition indicators (IRI). Multiple factors are considered to define a Taiwanese writer as a world literature writer, including the number of translations, international awards, presence in international anthologies or websites, book reviews in languages other than Chinese, special issue or reports in languages other than Chinese, adaptations by non-Chinese communities, research publications in languages other than Chinese, and invited writers-in-residence from foreign countries.[17] In a recent essay, I added digital platforms such as English Wikipedia, websites devoted to a specific writer, and Goodreads.com to this IRI list which takes into account the increasingly significant role of media technologies in shaping world literature on the internet.[18] These

[13] David Damrosch, *What Is World Literature?* (Princeton: Princeton University Press, 2003), 4.
[14] Damrosch, *What Is World Literature*, 4–5.
[15] Damrosch, *What Is World Literature*, 24.
[16] Chiu, "'Worlding' World Literature from the Literary Periphery," 14.
[17] Chiu, "'Worlding' World Literature from the Literary Periphery," 16.
[18] Chiu, "World Literature in an Age of Digital Technologies," 13–41.

international recognition indicators can be regarded as part of the mechanisms of what Pascale Casanova calls "littérisation" in the internet age.[19] By this term, Casanova means a metamorphosis that transforms a writer from an unrecognized writer of small literature to a writer of world literature recognized by the authorities in the literary center. Understood this way, the domain of "Taiwanese literature as world literature" is the domain of traveling Taiwanese literary texts, mostly in translation. Thus, Taiwanese literature as world literature is part of Sinophone Taiwanese literature, but only a small portion of Sinophone Taiwanese literature belongs to the category of Taiwanese literature as world literature.

Issues and Topics for Sinophone Studies

Because of the difference in their agendas, the main issues and topics for these two fields of research are noticeably different. Shu-mei Shih provides an answer to the question "What does Sinophone studies do?" as follows. First, it problematizes the essentialist notions of "Chineseness" and the "Chinese." In addition, it decouples home-ness and origin and links home-ness with the place of residence to rethink the relationship between roots and routes. Finally, it articulates a critical position toward both the country of origin and the country of settlement.[20]

The collection *Sinophone Studies: A Critical Reader* consists of three parts. Part I is devoted to "issues and controversies." Chien-hsin Tsai's introduction to the first part of the reader, titled "issues and controversies," makes the following remarks: "Sinophone studies underscores issues and controversies surrounding multiple identities, ethnicities, languages, and cultures in contrast to the singular and all-consuming 'obsession with China.'"[21] Bernards makes a similar point when he states in the short essay "Sinophone Literature" included in *The Columbia Companion to Modern Chinese Literature*, "The primary purpose of the Sinophone designation—as alternative or counterpoint to 'Chinese'—is to highlight commonly conflated distinctions between ethnicity, language, and nation in literary categorization."[22]

An examination of the structure of *Sinophone Studies: A Critical Reader* gives us an idea of the main issues and topics for the study of Sinophone literature. Part I, titled "Issues and Controversies," includes six essays. Almost all of them address the issue of "Chineseness." These six articles that map the issues and controversies in Sinophone literature studies are followed by another four essays in Part II titled "Discrepant Perspectives." In his introduction to this section, Brian Bernards remarks that the articles try to "locate and offer theoretical paradigms for understanding different kinds of Chineseness outside mainland China, from Taiwan and Hong Kong to Southeast

---

[19] Casanova, *The World Republic of Letters*, 136.
[20] Shih, "Against Diaspora," 38–39.
[21] Chien-hsin Tsai, "Part I: Issues and Controversies," in *Sinophone Studies*, 17.
[22] Bernards, "Sinophone Literature," 72.

Asia and the United States."²³ He identifies four paradigms: the Chinese diaspora, cultural China, the Wandering Chinese exile, and the structure of dual domination.²⁴ Clearly, the problematics of Chinese identity take the center stage.

For scholars of Sinophone studies, two corpora of Taiwanese literary works incite particular interest because they help demonstrate two major paradigms of Sinophone Taiwanese literature: The Sinophone Malaysian literature in Taiwan often serves to illustrate the transnational paradigm, whereas Taiwan's Indigenous literature exemplifies the Indigenous paradigm. Tee Kim Tong argues that "In many cases, Sinophone literature is not one-place based, for it often travels or diffuses to other Sinophone spheres."²⁵ Taking Sinophone Malaysian literature in Taiwan as an exemplary case, he draws attention to the transnationalism of Sinophone literature and the intersystemic relationships within Sinophone literatures.²⁶ Works by Malaysian Chinese writers are often associated with minority writing within the contexts of Taiwanese literature and Malaysian literature, respectively. As I discussed elsewhere, "the raison d'etre of Chinese Malaysians depends very much on the preservation of the prefix of the term, a project that is feasible only when the Chinese language functions properly in a congenial environment to carry on Chinese cultural tradition."²⁷

However, this ethnic stance seems out of joint in both Malaysian and Taiwanese fields of cultural production, where the Chinese identity has become a problem. Sinophone Malaysian writers in Taiwan like Ng Kim Chew (黃錦樹) regard the rise and development of Taiwanese literature after the lifting of martial law with a suspicious eye.²⁸ They believe that the Taiwanese nativist writers' and literary historians' emphasis on place-based imagination and critique of the Chinese identity would trigger a form of political and cultural oppression very much like what they experienced in Malaysia. The nativist turn to notions such as "roots," "place," and "home" runs counter to the diasporic position of many Sinophone Malaysian writers.²⁹ They argue that to be a Sinophone Malaysian writer in Taiwan is to live without home, in a perpetual condition of being always en route.³⁰

Thus, while Tee echoes Shih's emphasis on Sinophone literature as transnational and comparative, he challenges two points in her theorization of the Sinophone. Tee defines Sinophone Malaysian literature as "deterritorialized" rather than celebrating "place-based imagination" because of its ambiguous position in relation to Malaysian literature and Taiwanese literature.³¹ He also questions Shih's conceptualization of

---

²³ Brian Bernards, "Discrepant Perspectives," in *Sinophone Studies: A Critical Reader*, 126.
²⁴ Bernards, "Discrepant Perspectives," 126.
²⁵ Tee Kim Tong, "(Re)mapping Sinophone Literature," in *Global Chinese Literature: Critical Essays*, ed. Jing Tsu and David Der-wei Wang (Leiden: Brill, 2010), 86.
²⁶ Tee, "(Re)mapping Sinophone Literature," 87.
²⁷ Kuei-fen Chiu, "Empire of the Chinese Sign: The Question of Chinese Diasporic Imagination in Transnational Literary Production," *The Journal of Asian Studies* 67, no. 2 (2008): 606.
²⁸ Chiu, "Empire of the Chinese Sign," 608–9.
²⁹ Chiu, "Empire of the Chinese Sign," 609.
³⁰ Chiu, "Empire of the Chinese Sign," 608.
³¹ Tee, "(Re)mapping Sinophone Literature," 85.

Sinophone literature in terms of resistance because "Sinophone Malaysian literature does not resist the position of Malaysian national literature" but is expelled from the definition of Malaysian national literature.[32] The term "Sinophone Malaysian literature in Taiwan" is, therefore, more appropriate than "Taiwan-based Sinophone Malaysian literature" or "Taiwanese-Malaysian Sinophone literature" because of its deterritorialization stance and carefully maintained a distance from "Taiwanese literature" as a specific category of literary products. This helps us understand why Tee, echoing Ng Kim Chew's point, defines the features of Sinophone Malaysian literature in Taiwan as questioning the "problematics of literary, cultural, and political identities in Taiwan and Malaysia."[33] The prominent role of Sinophone Malaysian literature in Taiwan, as compared to the works by other Taiwanese writers, is testified by the number of studies that center on identity politics in the works of Li Yung-ping (李永平), Chang Kuei-hsing (張貴興), and Ng Kim Chew.

In contrast to this paradigm of transnational Sinophone Malaysian literature in Taiwan, Taiwan's Indigenous literature underscores the importance of place-based imagination and the symbolic violence of the Chinese language. Brian Bernards sums up succinctly the different attitudes of these two strands of Sinophone literature toward Chineseness and Chinese languages: whereas Chinese is adopted by Malaysian Chinese writers to reclaim their ethnocultural identity, its use as a literary language implies a loss of ethnocultural identity for Taiwanese Indigenous writers.[34] As has been noted by many critics, Taiwan's Indigenous writers often use Indigenous words in romanization to interrupt the smooth flow of the Chinese language and to signify the inerasable traces of Indigenous otherness in Taiwanese Indigenous literature in Chinese.[35] "Homecoming," often embodied in topographical writing with a strong emphasis on "roots," has been a recurrent motif in Taiwanese Indigenous literature since the 1980s.[36] Using Syaman Rapongan (夏曼·藍波安) as an illustrative example, Hsinya Huang shows how the return to the tribal home empowers the Indigenous body.[37] She argues that "environmentality" is one of the most popular themes in Taiwan's Indigenous literature. She uses this term to describe the situation when the body at home finds ways to connect itself to ancestral immediacy and intimacy.[38] This

---

[32] Tee, "(Re)mapping Sinophone Literature," 85.
[33] Tee, "(Re)mapping Sinophone Literature," 88.
[34] Bernards, "Sinophone Literature," 75.
[35] Sun Da-chuan, "原住民文化歷史與心靈世界的摩寫：試論原住民文學的可能" [Representation of Indigenous Culture, History, and Spiritual World: Exploration of the Possibilities of Indigenous Culture], in 台灣原住民族漢語文學評論選集(上) [*Anthology of Taiwan Indigenous Literature: Critical Essays I*], ed. Sun Da-chuan (Taipei: Ink Books, 2003), 17–51; John Balcom, translator's introduction to *Indigenous Writers of Taiwan: An Anthology of Stories, Essays, and Poems*, ed. John Balcom and Yingtsih Balcom (Columbia: Columbia University Press, 2005), xi–xxiv; Kuei-fen Chiu, "The Production of Indigeneity: Contemporary Indigenous Literature in Taiwan and Cross-cultural Inheritance," *The China Quarterly* 200 (2009): 1071–87.
[36] Chiu, "The Production of Indigeneity," 1071–87; Hsinya Huang, "Sinophone Indigenous Literature of Taiwan: History and Tradition," in *Sinophone Studies: A Critical Reader*, 249–50.
[37] Huang, "Sinophone Indigenous Literature of Taiwan," 249.
[38] Huang, "Sinophone Indigenous Literature of Taiwan," 249.

is in sharp contrast to the deterritorializing homelessness of Sinophone Malaysian literature in Taiwan.

Issues and Topics for World Literature Studies

The issues and topics for the world literature approach, as illustrated by the works of Pascale Casanova, Franco Moretti, and David Damrosch, appear to be those addressing the mode of reading world literature as a specific kind of literary production and the mode of its circulation. It is not far-fetched to say that the core issue in Casanova's *The World Republic of Letters* lies in "littérisation" as writers compete for international recognition. Drawing upon Pierre Bourdieu's theory, she conceptualizes world literature as a space of literary rivalry, where writers of small literature struggle to claim the recognition of the literary center. For Moretti, world literature is "one and unequal."[39] The fundamental question for the study of world literature is how to deal with the "great unread."[40] He introduces the innovative method of "distant reading" which sketches how the world literary system works rather than the interpretation of selected texts.[41] Moretti's "distant reading" focuses on units smaller or larger than the text—for example, devices, themes, tropes, genres, or systems.[42] His innovative approach illustrates par excellence how world literature is a mode of reading and a mode of circulation—as David Damrosch proposes in his influential *What Is World Literature?* As a mode of reading, distant reading configures the circulation of world literature in terms of "waves" of diffusion.[43] In David Damrosch's discussion, the notion of "double refraction" lies at the heart of his theorization. World literature is conceptualized as a site of cultural exchange between host culture and source culture: "world literature is thus always as much about the host culture's values and needs as it is about a work's source culture."[44] As I discussed elsewhere, Damrosch's statement "Bei Dao in English *isn't* Bei Dao in Chinese"[45] urges for a mode of reading that shifts from the search for the internal logic of the work to an engagement with the complex dynamics of cultural exchange and contestation that transforms a text on its travel.[46]

Thus, while the reading of a Taiwanese work from the Sinophone perspective tends to focus on the problematics of Chineseness and stress the hybrid dimension of the Taiwanese text as a sign of resistance, a contextualization of Taiwanese literature within the framework of world literature would pay more attention to how and why

---

[39] Franco Moretti, *Distant Reading* (New York: Verso, 2013), 46.
[40] Moretti, *Distant Reading*, 87.
[41] Moretti, *Distant Reading*, 109.
[42] Moretti, *Distant Reading*, 47–49.
[43] Damrosch, *What Is World Literature*, 60.
[44] Damrosch, *What Is World Literature*, 283.
[45] Damrosch, *What Is World Literature*, 22.
[46] Kuei-fen Chiu and Yingjin Zhang, introduction to *The Making of Chinese-Sinophone Literatures as World Literature*, 1–21.

a restricted number of Taiwanese literary works manage to travel. Sinophone studies tend to highlight how Taiwanese literature is differentiated from Chinese literature. The world literature approach would investigate how Taiwanese literary works negotiate with an international readership. The issue of "worlding" is cast in the limelight. In Hayot's words, "Worlding is gestural; it is an attitude, by which one adjusts oneself, symmetrically, to one's inclusion in a whole that does not belong to one."[47] Taking Hayot's notion of "worlding" as essential to the constitution of world literature, I contend that the idea of "multiple world literatures," powered by a critique of West-centrism in the studies of world literature, does not address the question. The opposition of Chinese literature to world literature is a good case in point. The very concept of "Chinese literature," as Sinophone studies shows, is an exercise of cultural hegemony. Breaking down the unitary "world literature" into smaller "world literatures" based on the use of language does not solve the problems of literary hierarchies.

It is interesting to note that while Sinophone Malaysian literature and Indigenous literature take the center stage in Sinophone studies of Taiwanese literature, the world literature approach pays more attention to the works of dominant ethnic Han writers in Taiwan. From a historical perspective, Taiwanese writers' practice of a Sinitic literary language can be dated back to Taiwanese vernacular writing pioneered by Lōa Hô (賴和) in the 1930s. Unlike many Taiwanese writers under Japanese colonial rule, Lōa Hô insisted on the use of Chinese rather than Japanese. This choice of language was intended as a gesture against Japan-centrism imposed by the Japanese colonial government. He invented a Sinitic language that mixed Chinese with Taiwanese and Japanese vocabulary words. It can be regarded as the earliest example of Sinophone literary writing in Taiwan. This Sinitic language was revived in the 1970s with the rise of nativist literature. In the works of nativist writers like Wang Chen-ho (王禎和), Sung Tse-lai (宋澤萊), and Huang Chun-ming (黃春明), Sinitic language replaces standard Chinese as the dominant language. This literary practice has continued in the writing of renowned contemporary Taiwanese writers, such as Kan Yao-ming (甘耀明), whose language inflects Hakka cultural tradition, as well as millennial writers born in the 1980s. Interestingly, this rich corpus of Taiwanese literature, which plays a significant role in shaping the development of Taiwanese literature since the 1930s, has seldom been discussed in Sinophone studies, probably because the implicit agenda of Taiwanese literature to assert the sovereignty of Taiwan runs counter to the anti-nationalist orientation of Sinophone theory. As a result, works that have often been identified as masterpieces or part of the literary canon in Taiwanese literature seldom come under the purview of Sinophone studies.

In contrast to Sinophone studies' preference for works by Malaysian Chinese writers in Taiwan and Indigenous writers, writers of Han ethnicity play a more significant role in studies that address the relationship between Taiwanese literature and world literature. Take the present volume *Taiwanese Literature as World Literature* as an example. The Taiwanese writers discussed in the volume are mostly of Han ethnicity, including Yang

---

[47] Eric Hayot, "Commentary: On the 'Sainifeng賽呢風' as a Global Literary Practice," in *Global Chinese Literature*, 228.

Mu (楊牧), Li Ang (李昂), Chiu Miao-chin (邱妙津), Chu T'ien-wen (朱天文), and Wu Ming-yi among others. *The Making of Chinese-Sinophone Literatures as World Literature* has three chapters devoted to the discussion of Taiwanese literature.[48] They study the experimental poet Chen Li (陳黎), the award-winning picture book writer Chen Chih-yuan (陳致元), and the woman writer Li Ang.

The structures of these two edited volumes reveal how these Taiwanese writers are studied within the framework of world literature. *Taiwanese Literature as World Literature* is divided into three parts: the first part deals with the modalities and frameworks for the study of Taiwanese literature as world literature, the second part addresses the issues of transcultural practices, and the third is devoted to the translation of Taiwanese literature in various languages. In the book proposal that is shared with the contributors, the editors Pei-yin Lin and Wen-chi Li describe the book as follows: "This book focuses on three interrelated themes—the framing of Taiwanese literature, Taiwanese writers' experience of transculturation, and politics behind translating Taiwanese literature. It aims to stimulate new ways of conceptualizing Taiwanese literature, demonstrate remarkable cases of Taiwanese authors' co-option of world trends in their Taiwan-concerned writing, and explore its readership and circulation."[49] How the traveling world literature impacts Taiwanese writers' writing and how Taiwanese literature travels beyond the boundaries of Taiwan through translation are posed as the central issues. *The Making of Chinese-Sinophone Literatures as World Literature* consists of four parts. The first part focuses on conceptualization and methods. The second part discusses different translation circuits for literary importation and exportation. The third section brings attention to the issue of genre in world literature studies. Finally, the last two chapters examine the impact of transmedia and the internet on the shaping of world literature.

Three chapters in this book are devoted to the discussion of Taiwanese literature: Tong King Lee's chapter on Chen Li's concrete poetry addresses the issue of translatability, Andrea Wu's chapter on Chen Chih-yuan discusses the travel of Taiwanese children's picture books, and Kuei-fen Chiu's chapter on Li Ang explores the new mode of circulation on the internet and its impact on the shaping of world literature. All three articles share a common interest in the circulation of Taiwanese literature.

In addition to these two edited volumes, Michelle Yeh's "The Newman Prize for Chinese Literature Nomination Statement for Yang Mu" highlights the cosmopolitan outlook of Yang Mu, showing how he draws upon the literary resources from world literature, as well as Chinese classical literature, to craft his poetry.[50] Yeh underscores Yang Mu's achievement as a transcultural poet. Serena Chou's and Ben Holgate's studies of Wu Ming-yi, a nominee for the 2018 Man Booker International Prize, situate the

---

[48] Kuei-fen Chiu and Yingjin Zhang, eds., *The Making of Chinese-Sinophone Literatures as World Literature*.

[49] Pei-yin Lin and Wen-chi Li, the unpublished book proposal for *Taiwanese Literature as World Literature*.

[50] Michelle Yeh, "The Newman Prize for Chinese Literature Nomination Statement for Yang Mu," *Chinese Literature Today* 4, no. 1 (2013): 50.

writer within the global frameworks of environmental world literature.[51] They praise Wu for his eco-cosmopolitanism and investigate how Wu participates in world literary genres such as environmental world literature and magical realism.

While Taiwanese writers of Han ethnicity figure prominently in studies of Taiwanese literature from the vantage point of world literature, it does not mean that Malaysian Chinese literature and Indigenous literature are missing in the picture. Shu-mei Shih's "World Studies and Relational Comparison" proposes the method of "relational comparison" to highlight the importance of what she calls "world-historical perspectives" in the study of world literature.[52] Andrea Bachner focuses on Taiwanese Indigenous literature to reflect on the implications of the concept of the minor in response to Casanova's categorization of Chinese literature as small literature.[53] However, Shih and Bachner discuss Taiwanese literature in relation to world literature in a way different from most of the studies mentioned here. The definition of world literature as literature that travels does not assume an important position in their studies; nor is the issue of transcultural exchange between Taiwanese literature and world literature a focus of critical attention. An examination of the structures and Taiwanese writers studied in the aforementioned volumes tells us how situating Taiwanese literature within the context of world literature and within that of Sinophone literature impacts the choice of writers and the issues for discussion.

Yang Mu as a Sinophone Writer and World Literature Writer

Finally, I shall focus on the case of Yang Mu to investigate how these two transnational frameworks may help address important issues for the study of Taiwanese literature in a transnational context. Many critics have remarked on the cosmopolitanism of the Taiwanese poet Yang Mu.[54] His works are seen to be characterized by a remarkable blending of Chinese and Western literary resources. In the words of Michelle Yeh, "At the most obvious level, Yang Mu's biculturalism can be seen in his wide-ranging imagery, references, and motifs, which straddle China and the West. He draws not only on classical Chinese poetry and prose but also on Western literature and culture."[55] Transculturation is key to the interpretation of Yang's creative works. The following discussion will discuss how Yang's transculturation can be reinterpreted through a

[51] Shiuhhua Serena Chou, "Wu's *The Man with the Compound Eyes* and the Worlding of Environmental Literature," *CLCWeb: Comparative Literature and Culture* 16, no. 4 (2014): 1–9; Ben Holgate, "Planetary Perspective: Addressing Climate Change in Wu Ming-yi's *The Man with the Compound Eyes*," in *Climate and Crises: Magical Realism as Environmental Discourse* (New York: Routledge, 2019), 208–24.
[52] Shu-mei Shih, "World Studies and Relational Comparison," *PMLA* 130, no. 2 (2015): 431.
[53] Andrea Bachner, "Cultural Margins, Hybrid Scripts: Bigraphism and Translation in Taiwanese Indigenous Writing," *Journal of World Literature* 1, no. 2 (2016): 226–44.
[54] Michelle Yeh, introduction to *No Trace of the Gardener: Poems of Yang Mu*, by Yang Mu, ed. and trans. Lawrence R. Smith and Michelle Yeh (New Haven: Yale University Press, 1998), xxiv–xxv; Lisa Lai-ming Wong, *Rays of the Searching Sun: The Transcultural Poetics of Yang Mu* (New York: Peter Lang, 2009), 81; Kuei-fen Chiu, "Cosmopolitanism and Indigenism: The Use of Cultural Authenticity in an Age of Flows," *New Literary History* 44, no. 1 (2013): 161.
[55] Michelle Yeh, introduction to *No Trace of the Gardener*, xxiv.

Sinophone approach and a world literature approach, and how these two approaches open up new space for thinking about Taiwanese literature in a broader framework beyond that of national literature.

Yang Mu is a difficult case for Sinophone studies, for he insists on his identity as a Taiwanese writer while promoting ardently a poetics that makes Chinese literary tradition the ultimate referent of his creative works. Instead of challenging and critiquing the hegemonic position of Chinese literature and culture, he urges Taiwanese writers to acknowledge the debt to it and inherit it. In his Newman Prize acceptance speech, he makes the following remarks:

> At times our modern poetry displays a fondness for tumultuous images of the old and new Taiwan. Yet it isn't afraid to make traditional China its cultural referent. Acknowledging its enduring love and admiration, it uses traditional China as a foundation for literary creation, a foundation that has contributed its written language, imagery, and allusions, and thus presides over and guides the imagination.[56]

Michelle Yeh's nomination statement states clearly that Yang Mu holds "a reverence for the legacy of classical Chinese poetry."[57] Interpreting this peculiar feature of Yang Mu as a Taiwanese poet in terms of Derrida's notion of inheriting, I suggest that Yang Mu positions himself as an heir to Chinese cultural heritage, "declar[ing] [his] admiration, [his]debt, [his]gratitude—as well as the necessity to be *faithful* to the heritage for the purpose of reinterpreting it and endlessly reaffirming it."[58]

Thus, we find in Yang Mu an attitude toward Chinese language and literature quite different from that advocated by Sinophone critics. Instead of critiquing Chinese language and literature as symbolic violence or problematizing the very concept of Chinese, Yang Mu insists that Taiwanese writers are *legitimate heirs* to Chinese cultural tradition and their writings are *authentic* embodiments of the Chinese cultural heritage.[59] The Sinophone celebration of creolization and hybridity is missing. How should we understand Yang Mu's view of Chinese cultural tradition as a major, essential referent for Taiwanese literature from a Sinophone perspective?

I will elaborate on the main points of my previous studies to show how Yang Mu's insistence on appropriating Chinese classical literature contributes to a radical theorization of the Sinophone concept. It is important to note that Yang Mu's call for Taiwanese writers to take Chinese classical literature as a major resource took place at a time when de-Sinicization was gaining momentum in the post–martial law era in Taiwan.[60] For Yang Mu, the challenge for Taiwanese writers should not be met with

---

[56] Yang Mu, "Newman Prize for Chinese Literature: Yang Mu," YouTube video, 13:15, March 26, 2013, https://www.youtube.com/watch?v=vTmqOLocZAI.
[57] Yeh, "The Newman Prize for Chinese Literature Nomination Statement for Yang Mu," 50.
[58] Chiu, "Cosmopolitanism and Indigenism," 162.
[59] Chiu, "Cosmopolitanism and Indigenism," 162.
[60] Chiu, "Cosmopolitanism and Indigenism," 166.

a simple rejection of Chinese literature in the name of de-Sinicization. The task is to insist on Chinese literary tradition as an asset without falling prey to what can be called Sinocentric diasporism that essentializes Chineseness and rejects Taiwanese identity in favor of Chinese identity. In the Derridean sense, to inherit a cultural heritage of one's choice is to *critically* appropriate it by *radically* transforming it.[61] Writing in the most elegant Chinese language and often praised as a towering figure in modern Chinese poetry, Yang Mu demonstrates a mode of writing that redefines the relationship between Taiwanese writers and Chinese literary tradition. Inheriting means transformation and innovation, rather than subjection or mechanical reproduction.

Since Taiwan has maintained the use of traditional Chinese characters and the teaching of Chinese classical literature since the KMT retreated to the island after World War II, Taiwan has a special relationship to the tradition of Chinese classical literature. It stands in sharp contrast to Communist China that replaced traditional Chinese characters with simplified characters and sought to dismantle the tradition of Chinese classical literature. Yang Mu's elegant Chinese writing suggests that China, the place of origin of Chinese literary tradition, is not the only place for continuing Chinese literary tradition. He demonstrates through his creative works how Taiwanese literature can claim to be an heir to that tradition. Such an interpretation of Yang Mu radicalizes the implications of inheritance: China ceases to be seen as the center of Chinese literary tradition. Chinese literary tradition unfolds its afterlives in multiple places with multiple forms and multiple centers. This is a Sinophone deconstruction of China-centrism that does not negate the value and usefulness of Chinese literature.

Seen in this light, Yang Mu's cosmopolitanism is akin to the argument of Jorge Luis Borges in his discussion of the relationship of Argentine writers to Western culture: Argentine writers have a right to Western cultural tradition just like Irish writers have a right to English cultural tradition.[62] In Borges's view, it is easier for a non-Western writer to make innovations in Western culture than Western writers and a non-Briton to make innovations in English culture than native Britons. By the same logic, Taiwanese writers have a right to Chinese literary tradition because they can write within that tradition without feeling "bound to it by any special devotion," as Borges comments on the relationship of Jews to Western culture. [63]

Such a Sinophone interpretation tries to tease out the implications of Yang Mu's insistence on traditional China as a foundation for Taiwanese writers' literary creation, whereas the world literature approach would pay more attention to his relationship with world literature and the translation of his works in different languages. For example, L. Wong discusses Yang Mu's transcultural poetics in comparison with that practiced by Rainer Maria Rilke and Stephen Spender.[64] Yeh shows Yang Mu's indebtedness to

---

[61] Jacques Derrida and Elisabeth Roudinesco, *For What Tomorrow…: A Dialogue*, trans. Jeff Fort (Stanford: Stanford University Press, 2004), 4.

[62] Jorge Luis Borges, "The Argentine Writer and Tradition," in *World Literature in Theory*, ed. David Damrosch (West Sussex, England: John Wiley & Sons, Ltd, 2014), 391–7.

[63] Borges, "The Argentine Writer and Tradition," 397.

[64] Lisa Lai-ming Wong, "The Making of a Poem: Rainer Maria Rilke, Stephen Spender, and Yang Mu," *The Comparatist* 31 (2007): 130–47.

Western classics, such as *Sir Gawain and the Green Knight*, and the works of Romantic poets Coleridge and Shelley.[65] I also highlight Yang Mu's transcultural poetics in my previous studies.[66]

Yang Mu's indebtedness to Western and Chinese classics, often seen as a characteristic of his cosmopolitanism, can be understood as an attempt to cope with the problem of literary destitution that places a small literature writer in a disadvantaged position in international competition for recognition. A prominent trait of small literature is literary destitution. In Casanova's words, "literary capital is both what everyone seeks to acquire and what is universally recognized as the necessary and sufficient condition of taking part in literary competition."[67] Literariness is an important form of literary capital.[68] It is often associated with the age of literary tradition that a writer can access.[69] Since it was only in the late twentieth century that "Taiwanese literature" came to be recognized as literature with an independent literary history, it is difficult for Taiwanese writers to generate the literary capital they need by drawing exclusively upon Taiwanese literary resources. To overcome the problem of literary deprivation and boost the literariness in their works, many Taiwanese writers try to raise their literary capital by appropriating foreign patrimonies. Yang Mu's works are known for their dense intertextuality with world literature and Chinese classical literature, wherein a distinct form of literariness can be located. The identification of Yang Mu as a small literature writer in the world literary space offers an interpretation of Yang Mu's cosmopolitanism not simply in terms of the writer's aesthetic penchant but the positionality of a Taiwanese writer within a broader picture of literary rivalry in the world literary space.

Reframing Taiwanese Literature in the Twenty-First Century

This chapter examines two theoretical frameworks that open new space for studying Taiwan literature in international contexts. The Sinophone approach challenges the hierarchy of Chinese literary studies by advancing the Sinophone as an epistemological concept and research method. Taiwanese literature is no longer studied as a supplement to Chinese literature, as part of Chinese national literature, or as a branch of Chinese diaspora literature. It impacts the traditional hierarchy of Chinese literary studies. While the Sinophone approach scrutinizes critically the problematic of Chinese and Chineseness and celebrates the hybridity of Taiwanese literature, the world literature approach shows more interest in the relationship of Taiwanese literature to literatures

---

[65] Michelle Yeh, "Burning and Diffusing through Eternity: An Introduction to Yang Mu," in *Hawk of the Mind: Collected Poems*, by Yang Mu (New York: Columbia University Press, 2019), xviii–xxii.
[66] Chiu, "'Worlding' World Literature from the Literary Periphery," 13–41; Chiu, "World Literature in Chinese, Sinophone Literature, and World Literature," 127–57.
[67] Casanova, *The World Republic of Letters*, 17.
[68] Casanova, *The World Republic of Letters*, 17.
[69] Casanova, *The World Republic of Letters*, 18.

beyond the Sinosphere. The latter is interested in how Taiwanese literature gains an active life in non-Chinese literary systems. The focus is no longer on the internal logic of the Taiwanese literary texts but on how they engage in the competition for international recognition and how they manage to travel. Studying Taiwanese literature as Sinophone literature focuses on the literary text in its original language and form, whereas studying Taiwanese literature as world literature takes translated Taiwanese texts as the subject of investigation. Known for his poetics of transculturation, which includes Chinese classical literature as well as world literature as his literary referents, Yang Mu offers a good case for teasing out the respective contribution of these two approaches. He opens up new space for the study of Taiwanese literature as Sinophone literature and world literature.

2

Worlding Taiwan: Taiwanese Literature's Contingent Constructions

Carlos Rojas

In late 2019, a novel coronavirus began infecting residents of Wuhan, China, and while the precise source of the virus is not known, evidence suggests that the virus was most likely zoonotic in origin, having spilled over to humans from bats or some other nonhuman animals.[1] This new virus, dubbed SARS-CoV-2, was closely related to the one responsible for the 2003 SARS outbreak, SARS-CoV, although a crucial set of mutations helped make the new virus significantly more infectious in humans. Over the next several months, the virus quickly spread around the world, leaving enormous disruption in its wake. Scientists had long predicted the likelihood of precisely this sort of pandemic,[2] but the details of this crisis were shaped by a specific set of contingencies—including tiny mutations in the virus's genome, and whatever circumstances permitted the mutated virus to cross over to humans from its original animal hosts. In this respect, the pandemic can be viewed as a paradigmatic example of the so-called butterfly effect, wherein even tiny changes in the conditions of one state of a complex dynamic system can result in widely divergent conditions in later states.

One of the unexpected consequences of the pandemic is an intriguing literary project that was initiated in the spring of 2020. Before the pandemic started, comparative literature scholar David Damrosch had been commissioned by a major trade press to write a book on world literature, for which he eventually planned an around-the-world that would roughly mirror the trajectory of Phileas Fogg, the protagonist of Jules Verne's 1872 novel *Around the World in Eighty Days* (*Le tour du monde en quatre-vingts jours*). The original objective of this journey, Damrosch explains, would be to "recall, and often actually revisit, a group of particularly memorable locations and the books I associate with them, both to see how literature enters the world and to think about how the world bleeds into literature."[3] He had initially planned to make the trip

---

[1] "Origin of SARS-Cov-2," *World Health Organization*, last modified March 26, 2020, https://www.who.int/emergencies/diseases/novel-coronavirus-2019/origins-of-the-virus.
[2] For instance, a 2019 UN-sponsored report concluded that "there is a very real threat of a rapidly moving, highly lethal pandemic of a respiratory pathogen killing 50 to 80 million people and wiping out nearly 5% of the world's economy." See *A World at Risk: Annual Report on Global Preparedness for Health Emergencies* (Geneva: Global Preparedness Monitoring Board, 2019), 6.
[3] See the "Introduction to the Project" page of the website *Around the World in Eighty Books*, https://projects.iq.harvard.edu/80books/about.

during the summer of 2020, but after international travel was shut down as a result of the pandemic, he decided instead to pursue a virtual journey around the world. Each weekday for sixteen weeks, he published a blog entry on a different literary work that he found particularly significant. Damrosch shared the blog entries in real time, with the intent to later republish them as a stand-alone volume.[4]

Damrosch—who is the chair of Harvard's Department of Comparative Literature and founder of Harvard's Institute for World Literature—is a polyglot who works professionally in more than a dozen languages, ranging from Egyptian and Biblical Hebrew to Old Norse and Nahuatl. Despite himself being able to read numerous relatively obscure languages, Damrosch has nevertheless advanced a vision of world literature that focuses on works that can be accessed by large numbers of readers. For instance, in his 2003 book *What Is World Literature?* Damrosch famously defined world literature as a category that includes "all literary works that circulate beyond their culture of origin, either in translation or in their original language."[5] Consequently, for his 2020 *Around the World* project he selected only works that are readily available in English and have circulated widely. Although Damrosch did feature several regions that did not figure in Verne's original novel (in particular, while Fogg's fictional journey was limited to the northern hemisphere, Damrosch's virtual journey also included several sites in the Global South), there were nevertheless many regions that could not be included in the literary project, given inevitable constraints of time and space.

For instance, although Damrosch devotes one week to "Shanghai-Beijing" and another to "Tokyo-Kyoto," his project doesn't include any texts explicitly associated with Taiwan.[6] In fact, in Verne's novel, Phileas Fogg did not stop in Taiwan either—though it is true that in early November of 1872, while on his way from Hong Kong to Yokohama, Fogg did pass through the Taiwan Strait (or, as the novel puts it, "the Straits of Fo-kien, which separate the island of Formosa from the Chinese coast").[7] Just as Fogg was passing through the Taiwan Strait, however, his boat was unexpectedly knocked off course by a typhoon, forcing him to change course and head toward Shanghai.

It is not particularly surprising that Taiwan was not explicitly featured in Damrosch's 2020 literary journey, given that the country is not mentioned in his 2003 book on world literature either. In fact, even as Damrosch notes that, in the early 1990s, many world literature anthologies like the *Harper Collins World Reader* began attempting to "give something approaching proportionate representation to all the world's major literary

---

[4] The project was initially posted on the web as a daily blog, but Damrosch subsequently took down the blog entries to publish them as a book. Some portions of the project remain available online, and the book is scheduled to be published by Penguin in November of 2021: David Damrosch, *Around the World in Eighty Books* (New York: Penguin, 2021).
[5] David Damrosch, *What Is World Literature?* (Princeton: Princeton University Press, 2003), 4.
[6] During his "Shanghai-Beijing" week, Damrosch did devote one blog entry to Eileen Chang's *Love in a Fallen City, and Other Stories*. Although Chang composed these works while living in Shanghai in the 1940s, she later moved to Los Angeles, after which she spent two years in Taiwan in the 1960s. Like many of the works on Damrosch's *Around the World in Eighty Books* list, Chang's works were very influential in Taiwan, though few would consider her an actual Taiwanese author.
[7] Jules Verne, *Around the World in Eighty Days* (New York: Sterling, 2008), 106.

traditions" by including "greatly shortened selections from Western figures like Homer and Dante, making room for the inclusion of work not only from China, Japan, and India but also from Vietnam, Singapore, and Micronesia, among many other areas,"[8] his *discussion* of world literature in that same volume includes only passing references to works from "China, Japan, and India" (and makes no reference at all to works from "Vietnam, Singapore, and Micronesia," apart from the single sentence quoted here).[9] Generally speaking, *What Is World Literature?* gives more attention to discussing the *possibility* that non-Western literary works might enter the world literature canon than it does to analyzing actual non-Western literary works, and while the entire premise of Damrosch's subsequent *Around the World* project is to discuss works from "around the world," the nature of the project and the selection process means that many regions will inevitably not be represented.

Just as the protagonist of Verne's 1872 novel undertook his fictional journey to prove his contention that "the world has grown smaller,"[10] and Damrosch similarly frames his 2020 project as an attempt to reflect on a set of "worldly works, written by authors who are reflecting on the world around them and the wider world beyond their borders,"[11] in the following discussion I will examine some of the processes which constitute the category of world literature. Taking inspiration from the fictional storm that knocked Fogg off course when passing through the Taiwan Strait in Verne's original novel and the figurative storm of the pandemic that, nearly 150 years later, forced Damrosch to shift his own *Around the World* project to a virtual platform, I consider the role of similar contingencies in helping shape the formation of literary fields themselves. That is to say, while driven in part by macro-level trends, the constitution and development of a field like Taiwanese literature—including its shifting relationship to larger fields, such as Chinese and world literature, and to various subfields that are sometimes marked as marginal or "other" within the field of Taiwanese literature itself—is influenced by a vast array of contingencies with unpredictable consequences.

In addition to a set of broader reflections about the constitution of literary fields, I consider a recent novel that may be viewed as a figurative hinge between the fields of Taiwanese and world literature. First published in 2011, Wu Ming-yi's (吳明益) *The Man with the Compound Eyes* (hereafter *The Man*) was translated into English by Darryl Sterk in 2014[12]—making it, as Sterk notes, "the first Taiwanese novel to be published in English translation by a major trade publisher."[13] Rather than invoking Wu's novel simply to celebrate Taiwanese literature's symbolic entry into the field

---

[8] Damrosch, *What Is World Literature*, 128.
[9] The book's allusions to actual works of Chinese literature, for instance, are limited to a handful of references to Goethe's allusion, in his discussion of *Weltliteratur*, to having read an unnamed Chinese novel and Stephen Owen's more recent critique of the Chinese poet Bei Dao for producing a "secondhand American modernism." See Damrosch, *What Is World Literature*, 10–11 & 20.
[10] Verne, *Around the World in Eighty Days*, 13.
[11] See the "Introduction to the Project" page of the website *Around the World in Eighty Books*.
[12] Wu Ming-yi, 複眼人 [*Compound Eye Person*] (Taipei: Summer Festival, 2011), translated by Darryl Sterk as *The Man with the Compound Eyes* (London: Harvill Secker, 2013).
[13] Darryl Sterk, "The Apotheosis of Montage: The Videomosaic Gaze of *The Man with the Compound Eyes* as Postmodern Ecological Sublime," *Modern Chinese Literature and Culture* 28, no. 2 (Fall 2016): 184.

of world literature, however, I use the work to reflect on the processes by which the categories of Taiwanese and world literature are constituted in the first place. I suggest that the work's exploration of the serendipitous interactions between members of different communities offers a useful model for considering the interactions between different literary fields and subfields, while the novel's suggestion that loss and separation have the potential to be generative mirrors how a literary field's relative isolation may similarly be productive.

Storms and Realignments

Although Verne's *Around the World in Eighty Days* is a work of fiction, it was initially serialized in the French newspaper *The Times* (*Les Temps*) alongside news reports of contemporary events. Given that the dates of the novel's serialization (from November 6 to December 22 of 1872) coincided closely with the dates of Fogg's fictional journey (from October 2 to December 21 of the same year), readers could easily have been given the impression that they were following Fogg's journey in real time. This overlap of reality and fiction was occasionally reinforced by serendipitous points of convergence between these two representational plans. For instance, if any of Verne's original readers had been following weather developments in the Pacific region, they might have noticed that around the time the fictional Fogg encountered was blown off course by a typhoon while passing through the Taiwan Strait on November 8, an actual storm (a "baguio") was passing through the region, having already made landfall in the Philippines on November 5—and while it is not clear what November 5 storm's trajectory was after it passed the Philippines, it is certainly plausible that such a storm could have continued on a northward trajectory at a speed that would have put it in the general vicinity of the Taiwan Strait by November 8.[14]

These questions about the possibility of a real-life correlate to the fictional typhoon that makes a passing appearance in Verne's novel are, of course, merely hypothetical. However, a more historically significant storm did in fact strike Taiwan a year earlier, which led to the so-called Mudan Incident and contributed to a broader geopolitical realignment between Japan and China during the final decades of the nineteenth century. More specifically, in late November of 1871, four ships were heading from Okinawa to a pair of islands at the Southern end of the Ryukyu archipelago (which forms a long arc between Japan and Taiwan) when they encountered a typhoon and were blown off course. One of the ships was stranded on Taiwan's southeast coast, and the survivors were allegedly captured by members of the Indigenous Paiwan tribe

---

[14] For a brief description of the 1872 storm, see the online database "The Selga Chronology Part I: 1348–1900," compiled by R. García-Herrera, P. Ribera, E. Hernández, and L. Gimeno on the website *Paleocyclones UCM-UPO-UVIGO*. Given that tropical storms in the North Pacific Basin generally follow a northwestern trajectory and may travel between ten and twenty kilometers an hour, a storm could easily have passed the Philippines on August 5 and traveled a thousand kilometers northward to reach the Taiwan Strait three days later.

from the village of Mudan, and fifty-four of them were killed.[15] The incident resulted in a Japanese punitive strike in 1874, and memories of the massacre and of Japan's retaliatory strike have persisted up to the present. In the early twenty-first century, both Taiwan and Japan hosted a series of ceremonies and symposia commemorating the nineteenth-century encounter, which included formal apologies by both the Japanese and by descendants of the Paiwan aborigines.[16]

Apart from these recent attempts to commemorate those who perished during the Mudan Incident and its aftermath, the incident also had more immediate consequences. At the time of the shipwreck the Ryukyu Islands were part of the Ryukyu Kingdom, which had been established in the early fifteenth century and, although nominally independent, the kingdom had long been both a Chinese tributary state and a Japanese vassal state—meaning that, at the time of the 1871 shipwreck, it fell under the spheres of influence of both Japan and China. The shipwreck and the resulting conflict between two sets of peoples positioned at the outer margins of both the Chinese and Japanese empires (i.e., the Ryukyuans and the Aboriginal tribes from southern Taiwan) served as a flashpoint for the relationship between the two empires and the complicated nexus of communities and territories located along their interstices. For instance, in 1872, in the immediate aftermath of the shipwreck, Japan established the Ryukyu Domain, thereby officially making the Ryukyus part of the Japanese Empire. Moreover, when the Japanese launched the Taiwan Expedition in 1874 in retaliation for the Mudan Incident, part of the motivation appeared to retroactively underscore Japan's claims over the Ryukyus. Another function of the 1874 Taiwan Expedition, meanwhile, was to help lay the groundwork for Japan's ambitions to claim Taiwan itself, and therefore the military strike may be viewed as an important anticipation of Japan's invasion of Taiwan twenty years later. After China's defeat in the first Sino-Japanese War, the Qing court ceded Taiwan to Japan in 1894, and Japan launched a full-scale invasion of the island in 1895 to quell local resistance, which in turn established the foundation for the colonial regime that would persist for the next half century.

Although in hindsight it is easy to view Japan's victory over China and its subsequent colonization of Taiwan as overdetermined eventualities, a consideration of the 1871 typhoon underscores the role of seemingly minor contingencies in helping determine broader historical trajectories and corresponding literary and cultural formations. For instance, the category of Taiwanese literature is inextricably bound up with Japan's colonization of Taiwan in 1895, which was anticipated by the 1874 Taiwan Expedition, which was catalyzed by the 1871 Mudan Incident and the typhoon, and which in turn was influenced by a vast array of individual meteorological perturbations down

---

[15] Although it is usually claimed that it was Paiwanese from Mudan who killed the Japanese, Paul Barclay points out that it was instead residents of the small neighboring village of Kuskus who were responsible. See Paul D. Barclay, *Outcasts of Empire: Japan's Rule on Taiwan's "Savage Border,"* *1874-1945* (Berkeley: University of California Press, 2018), 52.

[16] Mizuno Norihito, "An Attempt of Reconciliation over History: The Case of the 1871 Ryukyu Shipwreck Incident," *International Journal of Social Science and Humanity* 5, no. 2 (February 2015): 157–61.

to the proverbial flap of a single butterfly wing. As a result, not only is the field of Taiwanese literature the product of a nearly infinite array of discrete contingencies, the category itself is determined not by a set of necessary and sufficient criteria (such as language, author's citizenship, publication site, etc.) but rather by a set of what Ludwig Wittgenstein calls family resemblances: a loose aggregate of factors that collectively shape our intuitive understanding of the category even if there is no single criterion that is essential to the category's identity.[17] As a result, some of the most useful insight into the nature of the category often comes from considering works that are not necessarily paradigmatic exemplars but rather positioned at the category's "fuzzy boundaries."[18]

For instance, the monthly periodical *Four-Way Voice* (四方報) was launched in 2011 to collect and publish original writings by Taiwan's Southeast Asian migrants, including both migrant workers and marriage migrants. Most of the works were published in migrants' original languages—with the periodical originally appearing in Vietnamese and Thai editions but later adding Indonesian, Cambodian, and Filipino editions. In 2014, the Taiwan Literature Award for Migrants was launched, similarly seeking to identify and recognize high-quality writing by Southeast Asian migrants in Taiwan.[19] Although most writers whose works were published in *Four-Way Voice* and were recognized by the prize were not Taiwanese citizens, did not write in Chinese, and did not even necessarily think of themselves as professional authors, Taiwanese literature scholar and inaugural migrant literature prize juror Chen Fang-ming (陳芳明) contends that "as long as [a] work expresses emotions or memories associated with this territory of Taiwan, it should count as Taiwanese literature."[20]

If, as suggested above, Wu Ming-yi's *The Man* represents a symbolically significant milestone in Taiwanese literature's entry into the field of world literature, projects like *Four-Way Voice* and the Taiwan Literature Award for Migrants mark an inverse moment where the position of the "world" within Taiwanese literature is emphatically affirmed. One of the interesting aspects of *The Man*, meanwhile, is that it is attentive to the sorts of transborder movements that drive the migrant literature projects discussed above, while at the same time remaining attentive to the ways by which the distinctive sociocultural space of Taiwan (and Taiwanese literature) is constituted.

---

[17] Carlos Rojas, "Introduction," in *Writing Taiwan: A New Literary History*, ed. David Der-wei Wang and Carlos Rojas (Durham: Duke University Press, 2007), 1–16.
[18] Carlos Rojas, "Reflections on Concepts, Categories, and Fuzzy Boundaries: An Interview with Carlos Rojas," interview by Ji Jin, *Chinese Literature Today* 7, no. 1 (2018): 131–42.
[19] Chang Cheng and Liao Yun-chang, "Song of Exile, Four-Way Voice: The Blood-and-Sweat Writings of Southeast Asian Migrants in Taiwan," in *The Oxford Handbook of Modern Chinese Literatures*, ed. Carlos Rojas and Andrea Bachner (New York: Oxford University Press, 2016).
[20] Chen Fang-ming, "我的文學歸鄉路" [My Literary Path Back to My Homeland], lecture given in 2011. See also Chang Cheng and Liao Yun-chang, "Song of Exile, Four-Way Voice."

The Man with the Compound Eyes

Wu Ming-yi's 2011 novel *The Man* was completed in the wake of the devastating 2009 typhoon Morakot that resulted in over 650 deaths, making it the deadliest typhoon to hit Taiwan in recorded history. The weather system was first identified as a tropical depression in the Philippine Sea and was named Kiko by the Philippines' meteorological agency on the morning of August 3 and was dubbed Morakot later that same day by the Japanese meteorological agency. Officially designated a typhoon on August 5, the storm made landfall in Hualien County on the east coast of Taiwan on August 7, passed over the northern part of the island, and then continued to the mainland.[21] Like many Pacific Basin storms, accordingly, Kiko/Morakot passed through the territories of several different nations and the jurisdictions of meteorological agencies run by the Philippines and Japan.

Perhaps taking inspiration from Morakot, Wu Ming-yi's *The Man* pivots around two sets of natural disasters that almost simultaneously impact Taiwan's eastern coast—though, unlike a typhoon, which is primarily an atmospheric disturbance, the natural disasters that drive the plot of *The Man* are instead the product of violent geological and oceanographic realignments. First, an earthquake strikes Taiwan's coast near where the novel's protagonist, Alice, lives alone in a seaside house in Hualien County that she used to share with her husband and son.[22] Bereft by the earlier loss of her husband and son (they both had disappeared under circumstances that are not clarified until near the end of the work), Alice had been contemplating suicide prior to the earthquake, and therefore she greets the post-quake tidal surge with grim anticipation. Unexpectedly, however, her will to live is renewed when she sees a shivering kitten float by on a piece of driftwood. Alice takes the kitten in and names it *Ohiyo*—meaning "good morning" in Japanese, in memory of how she once greeted her husband and son—and treats it as a partial surrogate for her missing loved ones.

Second, a shift in ocean currents causes a vast floating mass of debris in the middle of the Pacific to break up, whereupon one portion begins drifting westward toward Taiwan. Brought to shore by a tsunami, this "trash island" makes landfall during an extraordinary hailstorm in which "shooting hunks of hail pounded the seashore, glowing like mini-asteroids with a silver-blue light."[23] The resulting devastation draws a wide array of people to the coast, ranging from local Aborigines to European scientists—who come either to help clean up the trash or to study it. Also brought to this coastal region by the trash island is a young Aboriginal man by the name of

---

[21] Although the typhoon passed over the northern part of Taiwan, given the clockwise nature of the storm's winds, it was the southern portion of the island that was most directly affected by deadly flooding. See Steven Lang, "NASA's TRMM Satellite Sees Typhoon Morakot's Massive Flooding in Taiwan," *NASA*, August 12, 2009, https://www.nasa.gov/mission_pages/hurricanes/archives/2009/h2009_MorakotNews.html.

[22] The location of Alice's home is abbreviated as "H County" (H縣) in the novel (and for some reason is rendered as "Haven" in the work's English translation), but from the novel's description it is clear that this is meant to refer to Hualien.

[23] Wu, *The Man*, 129.

Atile'i from the (fictional) island of Wayo Wayo in the middle of the Pacific.[24] We are told that, in accordance with local ritual practice, when Atile'i turned fifteen, he built a small boat and then headed out to sea with only enough provisions to last him ten days. This ritual was designed to keep the human population of the tiny island at manageable levels by having every "second son" row out to sea upon reaching maturity. Although for most second sons this could be expected to be a death sentence, Atile'i unexpectedly stumbles unto the floating trash island just as his resources are about to be depleted and is able to ride the island until it reaches Taiwan's coastline. After the trash island deposits Atile'i on Taiwan's coast, Alice finds him, takes him in, and treats him, like Ohiyo, as a surrogate for her missing husband and son.

The novel's fictional trash island is inspired by a real-life oceanographic phenomenon known as the Pacific trash vortex in the North Pacific Gyre. Consisting of tens of thousands of metric tons of human debris, mostly non-biodegradable plastics, the North Pacific trash vortex covers an area of more than 1.5 million square kilometers, which is more than forty times the area of Taiwan itself. Containing mountains of debris originating from throughout the Pacific Rim—not to mention from countless ships and other vessels that pass through the Pacific—the vortex in many ways represents the direct antithesis of a conventional vision of a nation. Whereas most nations have a territory with borders, a citizenry, and a sovereign government, the Pacific trash vortex has no fixed territory, borders, or citizenry and is located in international waters outside of any state's jurisdiction. Instead, like a storm, the trash vortex is the product of a chaotic system shaped by a wide array of discrete human and natural forces.

In the novel, meanwhile, the trash island is both an autonomous world in its own right and a bridge between the radically isolated island community of Wayo Wayo and the more cosmopolitan island of Taiwan. Moreover, just as the trash island is literally a sedimentation of debris from many different earlier periods, the territory of Taiwan is also understood to be the product of many different waves of settlement. For instance, when "H County" is first introduced, the novel notes that Alice is very aware of the way that the region has been shaped by overlapping processes of habitation and political control:

> Originally, Alice reflected, this place had belonged to the Aborigines. Then it belonged to the Japanese, the Han people, and the tourists. Who did it belong to now? Maybe to those city folks who bought the homesteads, elected that slimeball of a mayor, and got the new highway approved.[25]

A similar acknowledgment of local difference even informs Alice's perception of the world itself. When chatting with Atile'i later in the novel, for instance, Alice at one point blows up an inflatable globe she had purchased for her son and remarks:

---

[24] Here, and in the following discussion, the spellings of the proper names that appear in the work are taken from Sterk's English translation of the work.
[25] Wu, *The Man*, 17–18.

You see this ball? It's the Earth, the planet we live on. No, no, it's not just mine, it's yours and mine. Look, the place we live is like a star in the sky, it's just that we call the star we live on Earth. This ball is a scale model of the Earth. I bought it for my son. It even glows in the dark! That's because it has a special night-shine coating. Some things in this world glow, some don't. Some are like the moon, others like the sun. What do you say for the moon? Nalusa? And the sun? The other one, the one that appears during the day? Yigasa?[26]

Even as Alice attempts to use the globe to share her understanding of the Earth, accordingly, she simultaneously acknowledges that Atile'i's understanding of the world is itself embedded within a different lexicon and corresponding conceptual framework. It is through this engagement with radically different understandings of the world, accordingly, that the novel offers a way of conceiving how localities are constituted and continually reimagined.

Near the end of the novel, meanwhile, there is a series of four short sections that belatedly recount the circumstances surrounding the death of Alice's husband, Thom, while also introducing the novel's mysterious titular figure: the man with the compound eyes. In particular, we learn that upon moving to Taiwan, Thom had become obsessed with mountain climbing, and eventually one night—for reasons that are never fully explained—he resolved to "blind climb" down a sheer cliff in the dark, without using any support equipment. Partway down, however, he lost his grip and fell, and after landing on the rocky ground far below, he was surprised to discover that he was still conscious but sensed that every bone in his body had been shattered. At this point there appeared a mysterious man with insect-like compound eyes:

> Though in general the man's head was no bigger than an average person's head, nor were his eyes larger than an average person's eyes, both of his compound eyes had at least tens of thousands of ommatidia, each so tiny as to be invisible to the naked eye. But if this was true, the man wondered, how could he himself be sure of what he was seeing?[27]

This man with compound eyes is presented as a human/animal hybrid who occupies a position of pure observation and becomes visible only at the border of life and death. Or, as the man with compound eyes himself puts it, "the only reason for my existence is that I can merely observe, not intervene."[28]

Mirroring the position of the man with the compound eyes as a figure of pure observation positioned at the border of life and death, the novel's conclusion reveals Alice herself to be a powerful creative force catalyzed by a similar encounter with death and loss. In particular, Alice is initially introduced as an aspiring author who pursued

---

[26] Wu, *The Man*, 176–77.
[27] Wu, *The Man*, 278.
[28] Wu, *The Man*, 282.

a doctorate in literature but who resigned her position at the university shortly before the novel begins. Near the end of the work, when the man with the compound eyes is speaking to Thom after his deadly fall from the cliff, the man reveals that Alice and Thom's son had died years earlier in a freak accident (a snake bite), but Alice, unable to accept his death, effectively wrote him back to life:

> It was your wife who kept the diary, did all the things only your son would have done. […] In fact, since then your son has only existed in her writing and daily activities, and you have been an accessory. You two have been the bearers of a traumatic memory, and its authors.[29]

It turns out, accordingly, that key elements of the novel's preceding plotline have been profoundly shaped by an unexpected contingency that not only has concrete consequences (resulting in the death of Alice and Thom's son) but also serves as the catalyst for an elaborate process of fabulation and world-making. To the extent that this process of fabulation may be viewed as a metonymic stand-in for the process of literary production itself, the novel's revelation that Alice has been compulsively and unconsciously reanimating her dead son points not only to the relationship between contingency and (literary) creativity but also to the way in which trauma and isolation may serve as catalysts for new forms of meaning-making.

The Butterfly Effect

Although in Wu Ming-yi's 2011 novel the titular character's eyes are clearly arthropodal in nature, they are not linked to any specific kind of insect in the novel. There is, however, one species of insect that is explicitly foregrounded in the original short story by Wu Ming-yi from which the novel takes inspiration. Also titled "The Man with the Compound Eyes," the 2003 short story features a researcher who has been hired to create a digital butterfly nature preserve using video feeds from countless video cameras positioned throughout an actual butterfly preserve. While walking through the preserve one day, the researcher encounters a man with compound eyes who asks him why he never thought of using his cameras to view the world from the butterflies' perspectives.[30]

Butterflies have been associated with everything from self-transformation (given their ability to metamorphose from caterpillars) and the limits of self-knowledge (encapsulated by the famous parable about Zhuang Zhou's uncertainty of whether he dreamed he was a butterfly or was a butterfly dreaming it was him), and more recently they have come to be inextricably linked to a popular metaphor for chaos theory. First

---

[29] Wu, *The Man*, 280.
[30] The untranslated story is included as an appendix at the end of the Chinese version of the novel. See Wu, "複眼人" [The Man with the Compound Eyes], in *Compound Eye Person*, 362–95.

introduced by meteorologist Edward Lorenz, the metaphor refers to the idea that tiny differences in the initial conditions of a complex dynamic system can end up having large-scale effects—or, as Lorenz memorably put the question in the title of a 1972 talk, "Does the flap of a butterfly's wings in Brazil set off a tornado in Texas?"[31] The idea, which Lorenz had been developing since the early 1960s, is that certain types of dynamic systems are very sensitive to changes in initial conditions, meaning that the ability to predict the system's future state decreases exponentially over time. Ironically, though, the paper title that generated chaos theory's most famous metaphor was not conceived by Lorenz himself but rather had been suggested by his panel's organizer, Philip Merilees. In an earlier paper, Lorenz had used a seagull to make a similar point, but Merilees felt that a butterfly would make the title more compelling.[32] One could say, accordingly, that the genesis and dissemination of the butterfly effect metaphor were shaped by the very sort of contingencies that the metaphor underscores.

Although Lorenz is currently best known for the notion that minute differences in initial conditions may end up having large effects, nevertheless his response to the rhetorical question in his original 1972 presentation was inconclusive. In the written version of his presentation, he notes that "Brazil and Texas lie in opposite hemispheres. [...] It seems entirely possible that an error might be able to spread many thousands of miles within the temperate latitudes of either hemisphere, while yet being unable to cross the equator."[33] The issue Lorenz raises here involves not so much the degree to which a certain system is or is not predictable but rather how one calculates the borders of the system itself. While many iterations of the butterfly wing metaphor treat the world's weather as a single system, Lorenz notes here that weather is more accurately understood as a set of overlapping subsystems—and that there may be more functional autonomy between these subsystems than there is within them.

Lorenz's speculation that different meteorological subsystems may be partially autonomous, meanwhile, has a correlate when it comes to literary fields, insofar as the functional distance between some literary fields and others means that there is a less reciprocal influence between them. In a recent discussion, for instance, Ng Kim Chew (黃錦樹), a Malaysian Chinese living in Taiwan, considers the relationship between Casanova's version of the field of world literature and what Ng proposes may be called a "republic of southern Chinese letters." Turning Casanova's premise that entry into a world republic of letters is always something to be welcomed, Ng instead proposes that there are certain advantages to the relative isolation of the field of southern Chinese letters:

> Whereas Casanova focuses on how authors from the periphery attempt to be accepted and recognized by the center, I am primarily interested not in narrative strategies of "entering the center," but rather in strategies of "being outside," even

---

[31] Edward Lorenz, "Predictability: Does the Flap of a Butterfly's Wings in Brazil Set Off a Tornado in Texas?" Paper presented at American Association for the Advancement of Science, December 1972.

[32] Peter Dizikes, "When the Butterfly Effect Took Flight," *MIT Technology Review*, February 22, 2011.

[33] Lorenz, "Predictability."

though this is not necessarily a question of "removing the center." Relevant writing strategies do not attempt to follow the "center" in establishing literary standards, nor are they constrained by the limits imposed by communist ideology or bound by its prohibitions. Accordingly, my phrase *Southern Chinese Republic of Letters* tropes ironically on Casanova's *World Republic of Letters* because what I am describing is actually a republic without a center and without borders.[34]

Comparing the South Seas Sinophone literary field to a figurative Galápagos archipelago, he concludes:

> Of course, our Galápagos archipelago is the product of a set of historical contingencies, including the collapse of the Chinese empire, the sealing off of the People's Republic, Hong Kong's colonization, the establishment of Taiwan's republic and the attendant suppression of nativist elements, and the status of *Huayu* within the Malayan emergency. It is within this set of unique historical circumstances that our Galápagos archipelago evolved, but eventually the day may come when these contingencies will disappear and these corresponding differences will fade away.[35]

In addition to emphasizing the various historical contingencies that have shaped Taiwan and other South Seas Sinophone regions, Ng also draws on the Darwinistic connotations of the Galápagos to suggest that it is precisely the relative isolation of the South Seas Sinophone literary field that has permitted it to "evolve" in interesting new directions:

> Comparatively speaking, the literary tradition of these regions was not severed as a result of political interference, but rather it continued to evolve at its own pace. This resulted in the production of some works that could not possibly have appeared in mainland China—including the multi-faceted works by Xi Xi and Yesi in Hong Kong, modernist works by poets like Ya Hsien, Yang Mu, and Hsia Yu in Taiwan, and the nearly untranslatable writings by Wang Wen-hsin and Wu He.[36]

Evolution, of course, is one of the most dramatic examples of the butterfly effect in action—wherein tiny changes in the structure of a stem cell's DNA can end up having vast consequences for the future development not only of a particular species but also for the entire ecosystem within which the species is positioned.

Moreover, just as Ng concludes his essay with a reflection on how the distinctive features that define the "Galápagos archipelago" of South Seas Sinophone literature may one day disappear, Wu Ming-yi's 2003 version of "The Man with the Compound

---

[34] Ng Kim Chew, "南方文學世界共和國" [The World Republic of Southern Letters]. Keynote address at a conference on "Sinophone Studies: New Directions," held at Harvard University on October 14–15, 2016. An English translation of this address is in *New World Orderings: China and the Global South*, ed. Lisa Rofel and Carlos Rojas (Durham: Duke University Press, 2023).
[35] Ng, "The World Republic of Southern Letters."
[36] Ng, "The World Republic of Southern Letters."

Eyes" similarly concludes with an apocalyptic twist. In an abrupt shift in narrative perspective, it is revealed that the first-person narrative that makes up the main body of the story is being related to a *different* narrator approximately twenty years in the future. The original narrator is now described as an "old man," and the new narrator listens attentively to the old man's nostalgic reminiscences ("they were not so much stories as they were fragmented remains of the past") and then goes home to record them ("piecing together the stories as though painstakingly reconstructing a shattered dish").[37] This emphasis on the fragmented quality of the old man's stories, meanwhile, resonates with the backdrop of the story's final futuristic frame—where it is revealed that the United States and Russia are about to finalize a twenty-year environmentally driven project to destroy the moon with a nuclear strike and shatter it into "countless fragments." Paralleling Ng's reflections on the implications of the future loss of the South Seas' "Galápagos archipelago," Wu's 2003 short story emphasizes that the moon's impending destruction will not only have global consequence but will also be felt particularly acutely by the young narrator, whose field of study is precisely "legends of the moon in folk literature."[38] At the same time, however, the conclusion of Wu's 2011 novel embeds a reversal within this reversal—in that it similarly concludes with a focus on loss (specifically Alice's earlier loss of her husband and son) but at the same time suggests that, for Alice, this loss resulted in a process of extraordinary creativity.

Coda: Stealing Bicycles and Identities

As noted above, in *What Is World Literature*, David Damrosch proposes a model of world literature that includes all works that circulate widely beyond their culture of origin. In *The World Republic of Letters* (which was released in English the year after Damrosch's book), meanwhile, Pascale Casanova proposes a narrower understanding that focuses on the subset of works that have been vetted by elite cultural institutions. Casanova emphasizes the role played by Western institutions, which means that her conception of world literature is disproportionately weighted toward Western texts. For instance, in the nearly five hundred pages of the original 1999 version of her book she doesn't mention any Chinese author by name, and she only added a short discussion of Gao Xingjian (高行健) to the updated versions of the study after Gao, in 2000, became the first ethnically Chinese author to win the Nobel Prize.[39]

The Nobel Prize for Literature is awarded in recognition of an author's entire oeuvre, rather than individual works. Among international literary prizes that recognize individual works, the International Booker Prize is currently among the

---

[37] Wu, "The Man with the Compound Eyes," 392.
[38] Wu, "The Man with the Compound Eyes," 393.
[39] Even in the 2004 English translation of Casanova's book, Gao is discussed exclusively in terms of his receipt of the Nobel. See Pascale Casanova, *La République mondiale des Lettres* (Paris: Editions du Seuil, 1999) and *The World Republic of Letters*, trans. M. B. Debevoise (Cambridge: Harvard University Press, 2004).

most prestigious. It was, accordingly, regarded as a significant achievement when, in 2018, the Booker Prize organizers announced that Darryl Sterk's translation of Wu Ming-yi's 2015 novel *The Stolen Bicycle* (單車失竊記) was one of thirteen titles longlisted for the prize, making Wu Ming-yi the first Taiwanese author to achieve this recognition.[40] When the organizers announced the longlist, however, they bowed to pressure from the Chinese embassy and changed Wu's nationality from "Taiwan" to "Taiwan, China."[41] After a wave of criticism, including pushback from Wu Ming-yi himself, the organizers quickly reversed course and switched back to identifying Wu with "Taiwan," though they specified that Wu and other authors would be identified not by their nationality but rather by their "country or territory." In a press release, the organizers explained, "The prize is not about defining nationality; all global citizens are eligible, provided they are published in translation in the UK."[42]

In a carefully worded April 4, 2018, Facebook post accompanying a photograph of a seascape, Wu Ming-yi responded in Chinese to the prize organization's decision to restore the designation of his affiliation as simply "Taiwan":

> After a few days the Man Booker International Prize has responded to my position—though I feel that this is not so much in response to my personal will, but rather to the will of literature. This decision means the Man Booker International Prize has affirmed that the will of literature is based on honesty and freedom.
>
> My literature derives from cultures all over the world, but it relies entirely on this land of "Taiwan" to sprout, grow, and evolve. Like my next book's description of the Taiwan clouded leopard, Taiwan hemlock, and the surrounding sea and more than two hundred mountains over 3,000 meters—if I were to abandon this land, this name, my work would have no basis.
>
> My works are written for readers who can read the language in which I write, and thanks to an excellent translator they have also been made available to readers who use other languages. They are written for those readers who agree with me, but also for those readers who do not agree with me. Readers awaken a work, and they have the power to interpret it. However, my "heart" will always belong to me.[43]

---

[40] Now known as the Booker International Prize, the Man Booker International Prize was established in 2004 to complement the Man Booker Prize (now known as the Booker Prize). At the time, the Man Booker Prize was limited to novels written in English by British authors, while from 2005 to 2015, the Man Booker International Prize was awarded on a biannual basis to an author of any nationality whose work is widely available in English. Since 2016, however, the latter has been awarded to an individual novel translated into English from a foreign language (and the prize is shared equally by the author and the translator).

[41] Lily Kuo, "Man Booker Criticized for Changing Taiwanese Author's Nationality," *The Guardian*, April 3, 2018.

[42] Alison Flood and Lisa Kuo, "Man Booker Prize Reverses Nationality Decision on Taiwanese Author," *The Guardian*, April 4, 2018.

[43] Wu Ming-yi, "我很喜歡的作家尼爾・蓋曼 (Neil Gaiman) 說" [My Favourite Writer Neil Gaiman Says], Facebook, April 4, 2018.

Wu Ming-yi concludes his post by quoting a short passage from Salman Rushdie's 1990 children's book *Haroun and the Sea of Stories*. Haroun's father is a famous storyteller who loses his ability to tell stories after his wife leaves him, whereupon Haroun embarks on a quest to recover his father's storytelling abilities and ultimately discovers that a demon called the Cultmaster is poisoning the Ocean of the Streams of Story. Haroun asks the Cultmaster (also known as Khattam-Shud) why he is doing this:

> "Why do you hate stories so much? ... Stories are fun ..."
> "The World, however, is not for Fun," Khattam-Shud replied. "The World is for Controlling."
> "Which world?" Haroun made himself ask.[44]

In his Facebook post, Wu Ming-yi skips this portion of the exchange but quotes the Cultmaster's response (in Chinese translation):

> "Your world, my world, all worlds," came the reply. "They are all there to be Ruled. And inside every single story, inside every Stream in the Ocean, there lies a world, a story-world, that I cannot Rule at all."[45]

Wu Ming-yi then adds in his own voice, "To be able to write freely, and not rule stories—this is writing's most fundamental significance."

Although Wu Ming-yi was attempting to be tactful, the allegorical implications of his allusion to Rushdie's book are clear. The first book Rushdie published after *Satanic Verses* (1988), *Haroun and the Sea of Stories* alludes to the censorship that the previous novel famously faced, and although the children's book critiques those sorts of political and institutional constraints, the book's existence is evidence of the degree to which these sorts of constraints may also be productive and generative. Wu Ming-yi, meanwhile, uses the Cultmaster to symbolize the external constraints against which his literary production is positioned, even as his own highly creative invocation of Rushdie's text illustrates how these constraints may also encourage new creativity. More generally, all literary and artistic creativity necessarily occurs under a set of constraints, ranging from the sort of overt political and institutional constraints Rushdie references in his book to a wide array of equally significant formal and practical constraints. But it is also the existence of these constraints that make creativity possible in the first place.

Perhaps more interesting is the way in which, embedded within this dialectic of freedom and constraint, there is a suggestive parallel point linking creativity not only to constraint but also to contingency. That is to say, Wu Ming-yi's allusion to the Cultmaster poisoning the ocean resonates with the focus in *The Man* on how the ocean itself has become literally poisoned by a mountain of floating debris. Moreover, just as in that earlier novel the pollution that yields the trash vortex ends up having a

---

[44] Salman Rushdie, *Haroun and the Sea of Stories* (London: Granta Books, 1990), 161.
[45] Wu's April 4, 2018, Facebook post; Salman Rushdie, *Haroun and the Sea of Stories*, 161.

productive dimension (in that it brings Atele'i to Taiwan and to Alice, thereby providing a key catalyst for the novel's subsequent plot development and for the two characters' ability to expand their respective horizons), the implication would appear to be that the disruptive forces to which Wu Ming-yi alludes in his Facebook post (be they the product of random contingencies or institutional constraints) may simultaneously be a productive, and even necessary, precondition for literary creativity itself.

3

Worlding Modalities of Taiwanese Literature: Family Saga, Autobiographical Narrative, and Bildungsroman

Pei-yin Lin

Taiwanese Literature in Border-Crossing Circuits

Since Goethe coined the term "world literature" (*Weltliteratur*) in 1827 to refer to the literary exchanges within Europe—particularly to how German literature was received in France, Italy, and Great Britain—the concept has received various definitions and has had its ebb and flow as a framework in comparative literary studies. Although Goethe demonstrated a transnational literary taste nearly two centuries ago, when considering Damrosch's approach to world literature as a "mode of circulation,"[1] the circulation of non-Western literatures in the English-speaking world or other major European-language zones remains limited to date. To tweak Immanuel Wallerstein's world-systems theory, the Western countries continue to be the center, whereas their non-Western counterparts constitute the periphery. This explains why major non-Western countries, such as China, have long yearned for a Nobel Laureate in Literature. As a small island often shadowed by China or blurred as a place of "Chinese" literature, Taiwan is even more invisible on the readership map of translated Sinophone literature.

This chapter explores Taiwanese literature as world literature from the perspective of circulation. It concentrates on the understudied dimensions of "reversed" circulation and "non-Western" circulation to address the Western-centric oversimplification according to which "international writers" usually mean writers enjoying recognition by the West. It also aspires to have an interlocution with Damrosch's emphasis on "writing that gains in translation,"[2] by asking whether in translation a literary work always "gains," meaning remaining a balanced text that can be appreciated by a wider audience, and by looking at the nontranslated works that get circulated in their original language. Before presenting my case studies, I would like to pose a fundamental and still valid question: What constitutes Taiwanese literature? The three conditions—language,

---

[1] David Damrosch, *What Is World Literature?* (Princeton: Princeton University Press, 2003), 5.
[2] Damrosch, *What Is World Literature*, 281.

content, and the writer's background—based on which contemporary Taiwanese Indigenous literature is habitually defined are useful for reconceptualizing what Taiwanese literature encompasses. Given Taiwan's multilingual and multiethnic nature, adopting a strict language-based or ethnicity-based criterion to define Taiwanese literature is likely to be counterproductive, albeit still legitimate. While the content-based principle may appear to be quite broad, it is fitting for this volume's goal of treating Taiwanese literature as world literature because it can incorporate a much greater diversity of Taiwanese literature. This article, therefore, includes works that fall under the usual definition: works by writers from Taiwan or books published in Taiwan, but also those *about* Taiwan produced elsewhere and in non-Sinitic languages. It is probably still true that Chinese remains the most dominant language for fiction from and about Taiwan. Nevertheless, with writers' increased mobility and migration experiences, it is only natural that in the years to come, Taiwanese literature will be written in different languages. In fact, it has commonly been written in English, like the works of Shawna Yang Ryan (楊小娜), Ed Lin (林景南), Tao Lin (林韜), and Livia Blackburne (金立葳), and in Japanese, such as the works of Chen Shunchen (陳舜臣), and newer-generation authors, including Akira Higashiyama (王震緒), Yuju Wen (溫又柔), and Kotomi Li (李琴峰).

Focusing on three cases—the California-born Taiwanese-American author Shawna Yang Ryan's English-language novel *Green Island* (2016), the Tao author Syaman Rapongan's (夏曼·藍波安) *Floating Dreams of the Sea* (大海浮夢, 2014; hereafter *Floating Dreams*), and the emerging Taiwanese writer Lien Ming-wei's (連明偉) *Tomato Street and Other Warzones* (番茄街游擊戰, 2015; hereafter *Tomato Street*)—this chapter demonstrates how Taiwanese literature can be seen as world literature. The first two novels have been translated: *Green Island* has been translated into Chinese and released in Taiwan, and *Floating Dreams* has been translated into Japanese. Ryan has received numerous accolades for *Green Island*, while the 2017 Japanese version of *Floating Dreams*, translated by Shimomura Sakujirō, won Japan's fifth Tekken (Iron Dog) Heterotopia Literary Prize in 2018. Both constitute straightforward examples for discussing the "circulation" of Taiwanese literature as world literature. Lien's novel about the Chinese population in the Philippines has not been fully translated into English. While it may appear "less-qualified" for Damrosch's definition of world literature, I wish to use it to propose that writers' transcultural imagination can be seen as an effort to engage with the world through literature and can be considered a dimension contributing to world literature.

As Kuei-fen Chiu points out in Chapter 1 of this volume, studying Taiwanese literature within the frameworks of Sinophone and world literature entails different sets of questions. The former risks narrowing the range of Taiwanese literature, as it is not applicable to works about Taiwan that are written in non-Sinitic languages. While the Sinophone model is valuable in considering Han settler colonialism versus Taiwan's Indigenous population, it somehow limits the transcultural archipelagic connection with other Indigenous cultures exhibited in Syaman Rapongan's work. Moreover, although Lien's novels have not been fully translated, they have circulated in their original language³ and fulfill some of the international recognition indicators proposed by Kuei-fen Chiu.⁴

In what follows, I will delve further into the process of circulation and modes of reading by examining each author's narrative strategies, as the genre, in my view, is a central factor in facilitating the global circulation of "minor" non-Western literature.⁵ *Green Island*, *Floating Dreams*, and *Tomato Street* employ family saga (though mixed with historical novel elements), autobiographical narrative, and bildungsroman, respectively. They also serve as instances of transpacific and intra-Asian (in both reality and potentiality) border-crossings. I will investigate the implications of these texts in translingual travels and within cross-cultural reflections. These texts were chosen primarily because they each exemplify distinct "worlding" modalities while illustrating three modes, or possibilities and barriers, of circulation. Ryan's work shows how Taiwanese literature, written in English, "flows back" to Taiwan in Chinese translation. Rapongan represents the recognition of Taiwan's Indigenous literature in Japan. Lien's novel, set in the Philippines, indicates the *potential* flow of Taiwanese literature to Southeast Asian Chinese-speaking communities.

Shawna Yang Ryan's Transnational Family Saga

Family saga has been an important genre in Taiwanese literature. After the lifting of martial law in 1987, several writers adopted this mode to represent Taiwan's postwar history, particularly the White Terror years. This trend of combining multigenerational family saga with Taiwan's wounded past is also seen in *Green Island* by Ryan, a Taiwanese-American novelist. Before her, Juan Huang (黃娟), a female Hakka Taiwanese-American author, had already dealt with Taiwan's White Terror period in her *Winter Cicadas* (寒蟬, 2003), the second volume of her Taiwan-dedicated "Yangmei Trilogy" (楊梅三部曲). However, perhaps because it was written in Chinese, its main readership is in Taiwan, unlike *Green Island*, which was written in English and first circulated in the United States.

Published in hardcover in 2016 by Knopf, a division of the multinational conglomerate publishing company Penguin Random House, and in paperback by Vintage in the following year, *Green Island* was in a privileged position for global circulation. It was recommended by Amazon and praised in various mainstream newspapers in the United States, such as the *Los Angeles Times*. It also won the 2017

---

³ Lien's *Mammon Bugs* (青蚨子, 2016) won the Jury's Award in the 2018 Hongloumeng Literary Prize competition, one of the most prestigious awards for full-length novels in Chinese. It was recommended by UCLA scholar Michael Berry.
⁴ See Chiu's chapter in this book. Lien was a writer-in-residence in Can Serrat in Barcelona from late July to late September 2019. He is featured in "Books from Taiwan," with a short English excerpt of his *Tomato Street and Other War Zones*.
⁵ Mariano Siskind has probed the role of magic realism in propelling Latin American literature to the global stage. See Mariano Siskind, *Cosmopolitan Desires: Global Modernity and World Literature in Latin America* (Evanston: Northwestern University Press, 2014).

American Book Award and the 2018 Association for Asian American Studies Book Award (for creative writing). With its Chinese translation made available in November 2016, *Green Island* reached Taiwanese readership nearly at the same time that the English original was circulating in North America. Copyright dealer Gray Tan was unsure about whether readers in Taiwan would be interested in *Green Island*, as they tended to be more eager to read about "foreign" things when reading translated works, but eventually thought that a February 28 Incident novel in English could find a niche readership.[6]

In *Green Island*, Ryan tells of how a Taiwanese family survives the February 28 Incident (1947) and the subsequent years of martial law rule.[7] The book title refers to a prison island (like South Africa's Robben Island) used by the Kuomintang (KMT) government to detain political dissidents. According to Ryan, it can also refer to Taiwan as a "verdant and beautiful" island, as its former name "Formosa" suggested.[8] The story is divided into four sections, each of which is named after a place, followed by specific periods. The basic structure—Taipei (1947–52), Taichung (1958–72), Berkeley (1979–80), and Taipei again (1982–2003)—not only sets the story's chronological flow but also gives readers a hint of the physical movement of the novel's narrator—the youngest daughter of a local physician surnamed Tsai. The novel opens with the narrator's mother's contractions before giving birth on February 27, 1947, the night before the February 28 Incident. This timing of the narrator's birth symbolizes the pain associated with the birth of Taiwan, a tactic also used in Hou Hsiao-hsien's February 28–related film *A City of Sadness* (1989). Throughout the novel, Ryan continuously stresses the relationship between the political and the domestic spheres. For instance, the narrator's eldest sister was born in 1937, the year of Japan's invasion of Nanjing. The novel's narrative focus, such as the female perspective and America's role in shaping postwar Taiwanese history, is laid out at the beginning. As an idealistic liberal intellectual, Doctor Tsai openly declares that the Taiwanese people are entitled to have their representatives in the new government if Generalissimo Chiang Kai-shek is truly pro-democracy. This leads to his detention and eleven-year disappearance (1947–58), ushering in the novel's distinct female narrative voice of Doctor Tsai's youngest daughter, born approximately two weeks after his arrest.

With the combination of the first-person narrative of Doctor Tsai's youngest daughter and the third-person narrative, Ryan presents the vivid personality of

---

[6] *Green Island* was recommended to Tan by his American fellow copyright dealer Daniel Lazar, whom he met in Israel. See Gray Tan, "《綠島》的版權故事" [The Copyright Story of *Green Island*], *Ink Literary Monthly*, no. 159 (November 2016): 59.

[7] On the evening of February 27, 1947, agents of Taiwan's Tobacco Monopoly Bureau seized contraband cigarettes from a widow and pistol-whipped her. An angry crowd formed, and an agent fired his gun and hit a bystander, who later died. People demanded the handover of the murderer, but Governor Chen I (陳儀) ignored it and considered the protests an uprising. The Nationalist troops arrived in early March and launched a crackdown, executing thousands of people. The purge was followed by a 38-year (1949–87) martial law rule in Taiwan.

[8] Shawna Yang Ryan, "Q. and A.: Shawna Yang Ryan on the 1947 Incident That Shaped Taiwan's Identity," interview by Didi Kirsten Tatlow, *New York Times*, January 22, 2016.

Doctor Tsai's wife as a self-reliant woman fond of French literature. Once Doctor Tsai returns home, he is subdued and remains under the surveillance of KMT secret agents. His reticence contrasts with his wife's Paris-yearning artistic personality. Behaving suspiciously alertly, he asks his wife to lower her voice even when she talks about nonpolitical issues. He releases the birds that his son raises as a passive pursuit of freedom. To save his family members, he agrees to draft a letter urging a political dissident friend of his to return to Taiwan. Unfortunately, most of his family members cannot forgive him for betraying his friend.

As the first third of the novel unfolds, it enters the 1970s and connects with American GI's presence in Taichung against the background of the ideological divide of the Cold War. The narrator's future husband, Lin Wei, a PhD student at UC Berkeley, is brought into the story for the first time. The narrator meets Lin during the latter's visit to his hometown, Taipei. Lin's Western-worshipping and progress-oriented attitude makes a stark contrast to the narrator's self-contained and more Taiwan-confident mentality; however, it turns out that Lin is, in fact, Taiwan-centric and highly critical of the KMT's authoritarianism. After a brief courtship, the narrator decides to join Lin in the United States. While she waits for her American visa, the novel contextualizes Taiwan's sports nationalism, the loss of its seat in the United Nations, and Nixon's 1972 visit to China, once more juxtaposing the personal with the political.

The novel's third section begins in 1979 when the US embassy in Taiwan was closed. This initiates the "American narrative" of *Green Island*. The narrator's "American dream"—a professor's wife living in a comfortable house with two children—seems perfect, but it becomes plain compared to Taiwan's demand for sociopolitical reforms in the late 1970s. The narrator is also sensitive to her American friends' racial stereotyping of Asian women as delicate, petite, and elegant. However, what surprises her the most is that her husband is a pro–Taiwan independence activist in the United States and even hosts a political dissident, Tang Jia Bao, wanted by the KMT.[9] Following Lin's association with Tang, the novel gradually turns into a detective story. The two men begin to organize political gatherings despite secret agents' warnings. However, the feminist aspect is sustained, as the narrator is discontented with being prevented from taking part in those male-only gatherings. Yet, a KMT agent surnamed Lu continues to try to extract information about the "males' meetings" from the narrator, asking her to assist them in dissuading Tang from publishing books critical of the KMT. The narrator is astonished when Lu informs her that Tang is receiving money from the KMT. Frustrated by her husband's political activism, the narrator confronts Tang but is dismissed. As Doctor Tsai is arrested in the 1980s, the narrator pleads with Lu to help and agrees to hand in Tang's manuscript as a condition. While Doctor Tsai is released, Tang is assassinated, with references to the death of Chen Wen-cheng in Taipei and the murder of Henry Liu in California, even though a police investigation concludes that Tang's assassination is not politically motivated.

---

[9] Ryan admits that the image of Tang is a mixture of Peng Ming-min (彭明敏), Henry Liu (劉宜良), and Chen Wen-cheng (陳文成). See *Green Island* (New York: Vintage, 2017), 384.

The fourth, and last, part of the book ends in Taipei, as Lin Wei and his wife bring Tang's ashes to his wife. This part serves an epiphanic function, as the protagonists navigate the changes in their personal lives and arrive at a new understanding of Taiwan's past, particularly the February 28 Incident. The narrator contemplates divorcing her husband when he confesses his affair after Tang's death but eventually decides to stay in the marriage after being interrogated in Taiwan and losing her unborn son. For her, this is what being a family is for—for "a shared experience, a shared history, a shared trauma" that others would not have been able to comprehend.[10] She also comes to understand why her mother made the same choice of staying in her own marriage, symbolizing to some extent an intergenerational reconciliation. This part ends in the SARS-ridden year 2003, in which the narrator loses her mother. In her bereavement, the narrator pays a visit to the February 28 Peace Park in Taipei and ponders her father's choice to survive at the cost of selling his soul. "The thousands who had disappeared over the years, stained as criminals [...] for nothing more than the desire to claim an island as their own. No memorial for the men more complicated than martyrs."[11]

The coda brings the story back to Berkeley. At fifty-six, the narrator finally digs out a surviving copy of Tang's manuscript and reads it. That past has been a haunting memory for her, but only her eldest daughter vaguely remembers Tang, signifying the generational gap in historical memory. Rather than hailing the February 28 Incident as the climax of the manifestation of Taiwanese identity, Ryan stresses how the authoritarian years have affected those who survived. By stating that Doctor Tsai is "not a saint, but a man,"[12] Ryan highlights the dilemma between survival and morality and even suggests that life is more precious than political ideals.

Ryan stated in an interview that she had two sets of readership in mind when composing *Green Island*. One was "the Taiwanese and Taiwanese-Americans, the generation who remembered it," and the other consisted of those "who did not know anything about Taiwan."[13] Her effort to straddle the two groups yielded mixed responses. While some from the first group were impressed by the story's "authenticity," the book received a negative review from a Reddit netizen who referred to Ryan as "just another Amy Tan wannabe, white-washed Asian woman."[14] This sort of remark, however, does not surprise Ryan. In the interview, she acknowledged that Amy Tan's writing had "laid a really important foundation" for the form of family epic.[15]

One can add another paradigmatic and hugely popular family saga—Jung Chang's *Wild Swans* (1991)—to the list of award-winning books by East Asian American and British-Chinese (female) writers. Perhaps certain Western readers have difficulty distinguishing between these writers. Even Amy Tan, mistaken by Margaret Thatcher for Jung Chang at a dinner at the British Embassy in Washington, amiably commented,

[10] Ryan, *Green Island*, 344.
[11] Ryan, *Green Island*, 377.
[12] Ryan, *Green Island*, 381.
[13] Ryan, "Interview: Shawna Yang Ryan," interview by Brian Hioe, *New Bloom*, June 20, 2016.
[14] Ryan, "Interview: Shawna Yang Ryan."
[15] Ryan, "Interview: Shawna Yang Ryan."

"Jung Chang, Maxine Hong Kingston, Iris Chang, even Lisa See [...] we all constantly get mixed up with each other."[16] This remark is interesting, as it indicates that family saga is already an established label attached to Chinese American writing. While some writers suffer from the anxiety of influence, the continuation of the same elements that have proven appealing, as in *Green Island*, is tangible. If we can detect the Maxine Hong Kingston–inspired ghost storytelling and the treatment of mother-daughter relationships in Amy Tan's *The Joy Luck Club* (1989), we can also draw similarities between Tan and Ryan, such as their common interest in a haunted past. Ryan is adroit in weaving together history and personal stories. In her debut work, initially titled *Locke 1928* (2007), Ryan tells of Chinese immigrants' life against the backdrop of the real-life Californian mining town Locke. In *Green Island*, she narrates Taiwan's undemocratic national past from an ordinary woman's perspective.

The reviews of *Green Island* inside and outside Taiwan differ. In Taiwan, Su Shuo-pin praised the fact that Ryan, through her nameless heroine, "sets out a feminine disposition as opposed to the revolutionary masculinity,"[17] offering us a new perspective for rethinking what happiness we could pursue in the dark years of authoritarianism. Chen Fang-ming, Wang Yi-huei, and Weng Chi-an all noted Ryan's individual and female-centric angle. Chen referred to the novel as a "female-centered postwar Taiwanese history from within (裡面史)."[18] Wang emphasized the literary form's value in "disrupt[ing] the history-based perspective in Taiwanese literature" and especially appreciated Ryan's "activating women's agency through the narrative in postcolonial Taiwan."[19] On the other hand, for Weng, a historian himself, Ryan's depiction of the survivors is unsophisticated. Some characters appear stereotypical, and the general plotline is predictable. Weng concludes that *Green Island* at best reveals "necessary banality," which refers to the ordinary people's seeking to survive, and does not contribute to the writing of postwar Taiwanese history, although he adds that this remark is probably too strict, for an author who "grew up overseas and wrote for the readers outside of Taiwan."[20] These reviews indicate that critics notice Ryan's attempt to tell Taiwan's postwar history through a combination of "a feminist, domestic novel" and "a political thriller."[21] While Su, Chen, and Wang welcome the former as destabilizing hardcore politics, this destabilizing in Weng's view has diluted the novel's historical depth.

When a Chinese excerpt from the novel initially appeared in *Ink Literary Monthly*, the first chapter was selected. While this seems natural, the section focusing on the

---

[16] See Amy Tan's interview by Lisa Allardice, "All about Her Mother," *The Guardian*, December 5, 2005.
[17] Su Shuo-pin, "婆娑海洋上的綠島，平凡人的白色恐怖故事" [The Green Island on the Whirling Ocean, and the White Terror of the Ordinary People], *Open Book*, February 14, 2017.
[18] Chen Fang-ming, "未亡人的未亡史：《綠島》讀後" [Survivors' Survival History: After Reading *Green Island*], *Ink Literary Monthly*, no. 159 (November 2016): 28.
[19] Wang Yi-huei, "Writing beyond History: Literature as Form in *Green Island*, Shawna Yang Ryan (2016)," *East Asian Journal of Popular Culture* 3, no. 2 (2017): 249–54.
[20] Weng Chi-an, "必要的平庸：讀楊小娜《綠島》" [The Necessary Banality: Reading Shawna Yang's *Green Island*], *The News Lens*, February 25, 2017.
[21] Ryan, "Interview: Shawna Yang Ryan."

February 28 Incident, quoting the Japanese-era critic Huang Shih-hui's (黃石輝) notion that "You are Taiwanese and thus should write about Taiwan," can be taken as a hint encouraging Taiwanese identity. The issue featuring Ryan on the cover is a special issue on February 28 literature. With a story about the Green Island prisoners by Lan Po-chou (藍博洲) and an informative piece by Lin Shu-chih (林樹枝), a political victim detained in Green Island in 1972, and a two-page bibliography on literary works concerning the White Terror, it facilitates a human rights–centered reading. A slightly different interpretation accentuating the palimpsestic aspect of Taiwanese history is offered by Yang Chao,[22] who urges people to continue rescuing the excluded voices in historiography.

English-language reviews tend to applaud Yang's treatment of Taiwan's political past but have reservations about the personal plot thread. According to the *Los Angeles Times*, this novel "is less successful on a granular level. The personal moments lack the power of the political. [...] [T]he narrator's marriage [...] invites little emotional investment,"[23] suggesting that the individual perspective valued by Taiwanese critics is deemed imperfect. A similar reception was also published in *The New York Times*. The review focuses mostly on what happened in Taiwan during the years of Chiang Kai-shek's rule and what the February 28 Incident means for Taiwanese identity.[24] Ryan acknowledges that this part of Taiwanese history is little known in the United States, as people there often "grew up thinking Chiang was one of the good guys."[25] On the book's Australian Penguin website, *Green Island* is praised for its "epic story" and as "a historical novel [that will] educate many."[26] While few comments notice the novel's synthesis of history and individual (female-centric) family story, the epic part and instructive function of *Green Island* are almost unanimously recognized. English-speaking readers in general care for "the nuances of complicity and survival" captured by Ryan. *Green Island*'s different receptions inside and outside Taiwan are anticipatable. It seems that the epic part impresses those who know little about Taiwan, and those readers feel that the novel's personal level is less convincing. Contrarily, for Taiwanese readers, the novel's merit lies in Ryan's treatment of survivors' personal lives rather than in the formulaic "epic" part.

Syaman Ropangan's Autobiographical Narrative

Like *Green Island*, Rapongan's *Floating Dreams* is an award-winning work that has enjoyed transnational circulation through translation. However, unlike the former's transpacific circulation, *Floating Dreams* reaches an East Asian (Japanese) readership.

---

[22] Yang Chao, "台灣的歷史大過於台灣人的歷史" [Taiwan's History Is Larger Than That of Taiwanese People], *Ink Literary Monthly*, no. 159 (November 2016): 29–31.
[23] Steph Cha, "Review: In Her Novel *Green Island*, Shawna Yang Ryan Explores Taiwan under Authoritarian Rule," *Los Angeles Times*, February 29, 2016.
[24] See Didi Kirsten Tatlow's interview in fn. 8.
[25] Ryan's interview by Paul Farrelly, *Modern Chinese Literature and Culture*, June 23, 2016.
[26] See the book description on the web page, "Green Island: A Novel," *Penguin Books Australia*.

Rapongan's work began to travel to Japan after the publication of the Japanese version of *The Black Wings* (黑色的翅膀, 1999) in 2003, translated by Uozumi Etuko. As for Shimomura Sakujiro, the translator of Rapongan's *The Sky's Eyes* (天空的眼睛, 2012) and *Floating Dreams*, he is a renowned scholar of Taiwanese, especially Indigenous, literature. When releasing the translation of *Floating Dreams*, Shimomura commented that Taiwan should be proud to have a writer like Rapongan, as his works are "a miracle of the world," and expressed the hope that his literature could "travel toward world literature from Japan."[27] While it is difficult to tell how effective the Japanese literary world could be as a transit to accelerate the circulation of Taiwanese literature to a global readership, intra-Asian circulation is likely conducive to the "worlding" ideal of Taiwanese literature.

Employing the genre of autobiographical narrative, which makes the novel intimate and more realistic, the four-chapter *Floating Dreams* details Rapongan's negotiation between the modern, represented by the Han society, and his Tao tribal tradition. It covers Rapongan's departure from Orchid Island for senior high school education in Taitung, his sailing trip to the Southern Pacific Ocean, his expedition to Moluccas with a Japanese adventurer, and his life in Taiwan prior to university until his return to Orchid Island in 1989. The tension between modern and traditional ways of living is the kernel of the novel, a recurrent theme in Rapongan's writing. In *Floating Dreams*, Rapongan, through an I-narrator, is stuck between two value systems—either the traditional Tao way that entails not aiming to make money or the "modern" lifestyle that means getting a "normal" job despite the reduced intimacy with the sea.[28] His dream of "encountering all other island peoples" is continuously ridiculed by his wife, creating a tension between the tradition-inclined narrator and his modernity-preferring wife.

Rapongan does not merely hope to follow the Tao practice in daily life but also yearns for a restoration of "native science," which is the ocean-centric Tao epistemology constructed upon his tribe's oral stories that the elders pass down to the younger generations. However, the more he wishes to return to the tradition, the more he becomes aware of the challenge. This concern over the Tao's cultural survival has much to do with the dominance of Han culture. The narrator grows up in the Han-centric education in which only the Han people's expression is considered "correct." Although he is alert about Han cultural hegemony, he is eager to learn more about Han culture. He is not against civilization itself but against stronger cultures' exploitation and coercive assimilation of weaker ones. In his view, people of diverse cultures should treat each other with respect. Rapongan's contemplation of interethnic relations is not limited to Han-Indigenous relations in Taiwan but encompasses the tragedies of

---

[27] See the news about the forum that marked the launch of the novel's Japanese version: "蘭嶼達悟族文化跨越土地藩籬：夏曼·藍波安《大海浮夢》日譯本發表座談會" [Tao Culture of Orchid Island's Crossing the Territorial Barriers: Symposium on the Publication of the Japanese Translation of Syaman Rapongan's *Floating Dreams of the Sea*], *Ministry of Culture*, November 1, 2017.

[28] Syaman Rapongan, 大海浮夢 [*Floating Dreams of the Sea*] (Taipei: Linking, 2014), 250.

"the weaker people's encounter with colonizers" in general.²⁹ In *Floating Dreams*, in addition to Han's cultural bigotry, he criticizes other forms of hegemony, including Malinowski's continent-centric anthropological knowledge, Christian evangelism, in which the local beliefs are deemed "backward," and the exploitative behavior of people toward their environment.

Rapongan identifies with all marginalized people in narrating his sailing experience. In *Floating Dreams*, Mr. Brat, Captain Chen, and the Chinese *Qiang*-tribe (羌族) teenagers who become crewmen hoping to lift themselves out of poverty are collectively seen as valuable encounters bound by their common oceanic wisdom. This transcultural alliance makes Rapongan blend in well in the South Pacific, as he and the local people are "similar culturally, linguistically, and blood lineage-wise."³⁰ On several occasions, Rapongan unveils an intimate linkage between the Tao and other Indigenous peoples of Southeast Asia and Oceania. This alliance, consisting of marginalized and introspective people and united by a shared respect for the ocean, makes Rapongan's sailing trip not just a personal self-exilic adventure but simultaneously a reconfirmation of an oceanic cultural subjectivity upheld by the Tao and other island peoples. However, he does not view Western colonizers monolithically. Those who are self-reflective can potentially become his trans-Indigenous allies.

The last two chapters continue to explore the possibility of a symbiosis between Tao roots and modernity. To maintain the Tao lifestyle, skills like fishing, felling, and boatbuilding are required, as they are important Tao codes. A Tao mind guided by animism and ecological belief is also needed. Moreover, Rapongan repeatedly underlines a mutual understanding between cultures. He attributes the survival of Tao culture to its "anti-hegemonic" strength. However, no cultural roots can be truly intact; they are constantly being renewed. As the novel concerns reclaiming the Tao cultural code, Rapongan's use of the first person in this work is particularly meaningful. From the outset, it offers intimate personal documentation of his life experience. It is also simultaneously political, inviting Han readers to mull over their domination over the Indigenous population. In this regard, this work can be aptly analyzed within the Sinophone framework. However, Rapongan is sensitive enough to draw a demarcation line between his literature and Han Taiwanese literature. He considers himself a "colonial" sea-writing author, as Orchid Island has been "colonized" by various foreign powers. The Sinophone lens seems to risk co-opting works by Rapongan and others to celebrate the multiculturalism of Taiwanese literature. This does not sit well with Rapongan's self-positioning, as he explicates that his literature, using cuisines as a simile, "does not belong to Chinese cuisine. Nor is it the same as Taiwanese dishes. It has its own Tao flavors."³¹

Reading *Floating Dreams* as world literature can redress this potential limit. According to a report, Rapongan was awarded the fifth Tekken Heterotopia Literary

---

²⁹ Rapongan, *Floating Dreams*, 135.
³⁰ Rapongan, *Floating Dreams*, 153.
³¹ Chiang Chao-lun, "大海之眼：夏曼・藍波安的異托邦作家宣言" [The Eye of the Sea: Syaman Rapongan's Declaration of Heterotopia], *Radio Taiwan International*, December 3, 2018.

Prize purely because of his "bold and intellectual" depiction of important content in this autobiographical work, which won unanimous support, and it was the first time that the award was given to a translated work.³² In short, Rapongan was praised for not compromising with a powerful society and instead presenting his island's voice to the world. This sense of "resistance" would enable his works to shine in world literature. From the Japanese jurors' remarks, we can deduce that they appreciated the resistance of a minor culture in a broad sense and did not necessarily highlight the Taiwan-specific Han-Indigenous relations. It is this more general struggle of minor cultures against dominant cultures in all aspects where the "heterotopic" of the novel lies.

In an interview, Rapongan expressed his appreciation for the Foucault-inspired prize name,³³ claiming that the Japanese judges truly understood his novel. He went on to explain that "heterotopia as a non-hegemonic place, regardless of whether it is a library or a museum. For me, I made this space wild (野性化). My island is a museum, and my ocean, too."³⁴ Contextualizing Rapongan's remark with the prize committee's report, it seems that retaining one's own cultural characteristics is the way to world literature. Rapongan, however, did not comment on whether these characteristics must be narrated by an Indigenous person. If *Floating Dreams* were not autobiographical and were not even written by a Tao author, would its authenticity be discounted (though I do not mean to take Indigenous writers' "authenticity" for granted)? While Indigenous culture does not always need to be narrated by an Indigenous writer, in my view, the use of autobiographical form does enable Rapongan to personalize the important and meaningful process of his re-Tao-ization. The many firsthand accounts, including the Tao legends that he learned from his paternal elders, also make his book less abstract, allowing him to explain concretely the effect of cultural assimilation, such as that of the Han people, on his own life.

Lien Ming-wei's Bildungsroman

Lien Ming-wei's *Tomato Street* illustrates a different take on cultural representation. Published after Lien's one-year sojourn in the Philippines, where he worked as a Chinese-language teacher, *Tomato Street* is a unique work not only because it is about the Philippines but also because it is unlike the works of the Sinophone Malaysian literature in Taiwan, which are not the mainstream either in Malaysia or in Taiwan.³⁵ To be precise, this novel is a result not of diaspora but of the author's voluntary

---

³² See the award's web page, "Announcement of the 5th Tekken Heterotopia Literary Award," *Sunny Boy Books*, August 5, 2018.

³³ The term "heterotopia," coined by Foucault, refers to "simultaneously mythic and real contestation of the space in which we live." See Michel Foucault, "Of Other Spaces: Utopias and Heterotopias," trans. Jay Miskowiec, *Diacritics* 16, no. 1 (1986): 24.

³⁴ Chiang, "The Eye of the Sea."

³⁵ While writers like Li Yung-ping, Chang Kuei-hsing (張貴興), and Ng Kim Chew (黃錦樹) enjoy high "symbolic" capital having won a few awards, after all, they are relatively marginalized compared to native Taiwanese authors.

global mobility. Yet, interestingly, Lien engages with the issue of Chineseness, like the preceding Sinophone Malaysian writers in Taiwan, including Lien's late teacher Li Yung-ping (李永平). *Tomato Street* consists of three short stories—each of which begins with a young male narrator telling readers his name, family background, and life experience. The three narrators are all minors, but of a successively older age along the book structure. The book begins with an elementary schoolboy in the first story, continues with a junior high school boy in the second story, and ends with a nearly eighteen-year-old sexually precocious narrator. Each story is a tale of growth, and it is also possible to read the three stories as one entity dealing with the development of subjectivity among Chinese males in the Philippines. Although *Tomato Street* is a Sinophone novel, viewing it within the Sinophone framework does not account for Lien's aspiration to get to know the world (of others).

Indeed, the reason Lien chooses the Philippines as the setting of his novel is that he wants to experiment with writing about other cultures. He notes that the three stories in the novel share the same motif: "Who am I?" And "[i]f not choosing [to write about] the Philippines but other places, would the questions of 'Who am I?' be responded differently? Thinking of this, I seem to have seen the Chinese population in Taiwan and those Chinese who roam around and multiply in different places becoming crystalized in front of me."[36] Hence, although *Tomato Street* has not been fully translated, and therefore its mode of circulation and reading outside Taiwan is unknown, it opens up the possibility for Chinese people in the Philippines and their identity issues to be understood by readers outside of the Philippines. To facilitate Taiwanese readers' foreign cultural imagination and convey his global ideas, Lien employs a fairly popular genre, the bildungsroman. This offers another angle, enabling us to approach *Tomato Street* as world literature, in addition to its authorial effort to translate the (Chinese) culture of foreign countries.

Originating in eighteenth-century Germany, bildungsroman, which is usually credited to Goethe's *Wilhelm Meister's Apprenticeship*, traveled to the Anglo-American world during the nineteenth century, yielding well-known works, such as Charles Dickens's *Great Expectations* and Mark Twain's *Adventures of Huckleberry Finn*. Since the twentieth century, writers from former colonies across the world have deployed bildungsroman as a platform for exploring issues surrounding class, identity, or self-determination. An exemplar of postcolonial bildungsroman can be found in *Weep Not, Child* (1964) by Ngũgĩ wa Thiong'o, in which the growth of the education-thirsty young male protagonist Njoroge is delineated against the backdrop of the Mau Mau Uprising in the British Kenyan Colony. As it ends with the Njoroge's feeling of hopelessness rather than developing more maturely by being integrated into mainstream society, as seen in classical European bildungsroman, the genre proves to be flexible and cosmopolitan in representing the colonial past on the heavy side and personal formation on the light side.

---

[36] Chen Po-ching, "最遠又最近的飛躍：連明偉與他的番茄街游擊戰" [A Leap That Is Furthest but Also Closest: Lien Ming-wei and His *Tomato Street and Other Warzones*], *China Times*, August 29, 2015.

Like Ngũgĩ's "re-invention" of bildungsroman with East African characteristics, Lien adopts this genre to communicate his observation of the Chinese community in the contemporary Philippines. When Lien submitted this work for the TSMC (台積電) Literary Award, a biennial award for Sinophone novella writing, judge Leung Man-tao, a Hong Kong writer, remarked that the first story, "Tomato Street and Other Warzones," resembles Twain's *Adventures of Huckleberry Finn*.[37] Narrated by Wu Yao-kuo, a sixth-grade elementary schoolboy born to a Taiwanese father and a Filipino mother, it is an account of a summer of Wu in the Philippines. As expected, Wu's "Chineseness" is a hybrid constituent, as he would "translate Chinese into English and the local language for his classmates."[38] The Chinese teacher at Wu's school is from Gansu Province, the center of Chinese civilization, but ironically, he cannot speak standard Mandarin. Wu's reception of "Chinese" culture is also heavily synthesized. It includes *Students' Rules* (弟子規) from the Qing dynasty, popular Hong Kong films, and occasional Bible psalm recitations.

If fatherhood is a symbol of Wu's Chineseness, then his father's long absence and local surrogate father, Uncle Chen—who turns out to be a pedophile—signify the dysfunction or degeneration of Wu's Chinese affiliation. Neither the school nor the family can provide him with the love that he needs. Unsurprisingly, he develops his own, much more interesting, life outside of school. He enjoys wandering on the streets with his classmates, as well as drifting on the river in a simple canoe that they build. However, this carefree time is marred by Wu's first real encounter with poverty. He discovers that his affluent Korean classmate Seung-seon's family chauffeur has kidnapped Seung-seon and demanded ransom out of poverty, whereas the girl he is fond of, Arisa, has been abandoned by her mother and is living on her own. As summer comes to an end, Seung-seon's family settles back in Korea, and Arisa goes to live with her aunt. Wu finds himself "becoming a small boat without knowing where to go."[39] His continued wanderings on the streets symbolize his resistance against the ugly adult world.

The novel's other stories explore the class issues and gender confusion of the Chinese protagonists. The sense of Chineseness continues to be ridiculed. The middle story, titled "My Yellow-skinned Brother" (我的黃皮膚哥哥), questions the myth of ethnic purity, as the protagonist, a local boy named Su Hsiao-chu, is proud to be raised as a Chinese boy (after being sold to the affluent Su family), but his brother, whom Hsiao-chu believes to be purely Chinese, is half Chinese–half Filipino. Actually, Su is not the true family name of the grandfather of the two non-blood-related boys. In addition to destructing the necessity of a primordial link, confused male "Chinese" subjectivity is depicted as nobler than the locals' non-Chineseness. A local female helper named Jane, in particular, is placed at the bottom of the racial/gender/class hierarchy. Interestingly, Hsiao-chu's adoptive father's two girlfriends correspond to two

---

[37] See Leung's comment in the "Final Review Judges' Meeting" minute, *Ink*, no. 100 (December 2011): 223.

[38] Lien Ming-wei, 番茄街游擊戰 [*Tomato Street and Other Warzones*] (Taipei: Ink, 2015), 21.

[39] Lien, *Tomato Street*, 143.

different attitudes toward the Chinese. His Filipino lover yearns to become Chinese, as she is obsessed with Chinese furniture and porcelain. His Hong Kong girlfriend, on the other hand, is westernized and considers China "uncultured" and Hong Kong too money-worshipping.

The subversion in "Lovers" (情人們), the last story of the novel, is most radical. It focuses on a nonbinary boy named Huang An-lu, who goes so far as to cross-dress to seduce his brothel-owning grandmother's senile lovers. Huang's androgyny can be taken as a metaphor for celebrating hybridity, as opposed to any clearly defined identity, be it a gender or nationality choice. Running a brothel is described as "an alternative way of rejuvenating traditional Chinese culture," and the pain of war-escaping Chinese refugees' journey becomes "a penetration [of the female's body] by history."[40] Obviously, Chineseness is not only secularized but also sexualized.

The male protagonists in the three stories seek to find their position in the (adult) world by different means of rebellion. This world, as mediated by Lien through bildungsroman, seems to be a world with rather rigid racial and gender hierarchies. Despite the ambiguity of male "Chinese" subjectivity, it is perceived as superior to local female subjectivity. Lien claimed that his motivation to write about the Filipino Chinese is an "anthropological" attempt to probe different possibilities of the Chinese population. In other words, the work's mode of reading encourages readers in Taiwan, the novel's main readership, to reflect on their perspective of receiving those stories about other Chinese people. What are the limits of perceiving others in literature? Can Lien's novel have an impact on the community that it describes—in this case, the Philippines, where Filipino and English are designated as official languages? How can Lien's "worlding" of Taiwanese literature be related to Chinese writing in the Philippines? As Ng Kim Chew, a Taiwan-based Sinophone Malaysian writer, anticipated, it is most likely an "interesting expansion of Taiwanese literature instead of being considered Chinese Filipino (菲華) literature."[41] Only time can tell whether this cross-cultural thematic experiment can help strengthen the connections in the intra-Asian literary world.

Conclusion

This chapter discussed three cases of how Taiwanese literature can be seen as world literature. This does not mean that world literature is the only feasible explanatory model for Taiwanese literature. On the contrary, critics can pick an analytical framework that best matches their research agenda. The language-based Sinophone framework is tenable in marking Taiwan's distinct literary characteristics, insightful in singling out the settler colonialism in Raponan's work, and beneficial for exploring the

---

[40] Lien, *Tomato Street*, 299 and 316.
[41] Ng Kim Chew, "柳丁與番茄" [Oranges and Tomatoes], foreword to Lien Ming-wei's *Tomato Street*, (Taipei: Ink, 2014), 4.

relationship between Taiwanese literature and Sinophone writing outside of Taiwan. However, it disqualifies works in non-Sinitic languages, leaving other issues tackled by *Floating Dreams*, such as trans-Indigenous connection, insufficiently accounted for. To approach the three novels as world literature, understood as ways of reading and circulation, and of taking readers to unfamiliar parts of the world, Ryan and Rapongan propose different perceptions during circulation, as the targeted readership comes to appreciate translated works against their own cultural backgrounds and in specific sociohistorical contexts. To what extent the new understanding developed in translation is meaningful, and whether this "gain" of audience entails a potential "loss" in which a text might become homogenized, warrants further thoughts.

Although *Tomato Street* has yet to be translated and its circulation outside of Taiwan remains impossible to evaluate, it is possibly a great unread, and Lien's interest in the other can be taken as a well-intended tactic of "worlding" Taiwanese literature. That is to say, the thematic capacity of Taiwanese literature does not need to be limited to Taiwan per se. This closely mirrors Goethe's cosmopolitan statement about the "unmeaning" of national literature and echoes Venkat Mani's claim that the origin of a text does not automatically determine its cultural or national context.[42] The question "Who am I?" addressed by Lien's novel is far more universal than national. However, if world literature is defined as a mode of circulation, then scholars and readers of world literature should treat this as a starting point to do more—either enable more texts to be translated or explore wider-ranging and lesser-known writers and aim to read as extensively as possible in the languages that they know.

This chapter also investigated the role of the genre in making a literary work global. The three novels showcase three popular worlding modalities—family saga, autobiographical narrative, and bildungsroman. Bearing two groups of readers in mind, Ryan's family saga is tinted with historical fiction, and this synthesized genre is relevant and useful for explaining the diverse interpretations that *Green Island* has generated. While Western critics value Ryan's grasp of Taiwan's sociopolitical history and appreciate less the novel's personal parts, Taiwanese readers expect a more nuanced survivors' portrayal or view Ryan's ordinary female-centric narrative positively as a subversion of oft-masculine official historiography. Rapongan's autobiographical narrative makes his ocean-centric writing personal, as readers can learn the actual impact of a stronger culture on a minor one. Japanese critics have applauded Rapongan's adherence to his ethnic dignity in present-day capitalist societies. His case demonstrates that returning to one's Indigenous culture, albeit not without difficulty due to Han cultural assimilation, is an advantageous step toward a world readership. Lien's writing about non-Taiwanese topics is itself an experimental practice that probes the interests of his target readership, mainly in Taiwan. "World literature" here is best comprehended not as a global flow of texts via translation but as curiosity and appreciation of the world of one's cultural alterity within the often still nationalist literary boundaries, in which

---

[42] Venkat Mani, "A Pact with Books: The Public Life of World Literature," *Global E-Journal* 8, no. 1 (2014).

writing about Others remains a rarity. The bildungsroman genre that Lien employs is not only suitable for highlighting the precariousness of identity but can also be a reader-friendly form with the potential for smoother border-crossing in the years to come.

If going beyond Western-centrism is a scholarly objective for current studies of world literature, then we can explore gaining recognition, or even arousing controversy, in the non-Western world. In this regard, the three cases, with their "reversed" flow and intra–East Asian circulation and imagination, create new possibilities for approaching Taiwanese literature as world literature in addition to the conventional unidirectional attention to the export of Taiwanese literature. We should also transcend the national boundaries of literature by including the "hyphenated" literatures, such as Taiwanese-American literature, in our scope of inquiry. Moreover, if *Green Island* serves as a mnemonic of Taiwan's past and the multilingualism of its literature, the other two novels prompt us to act on some of the burning global issues, such as habitat destruction, poverty, and layers of inequality.

Part Two

Bringing the World Home: Transcultural Practice in Taiwanese Literature

4

Reading Taiwan through Japanese and French Literatures: The Surrealism of *Le Moulin* Poetry Society

Yi-chen Liu (translated by Blake Brownrigg)

Le Moulin and "Surrealism"

The documentary *Le Moulin* (日曜日式散步者), directed by Huang Ya-li (黃亞歷), was released in Taiwan in September 2016. Prompted by the artistic pursuit of Lin Hsui-erh (林修二), a young poet of colonial Taiwan who had met Jean Cocteau in Japan and written enthusiastically about him, Huang developed the idea of making a documentary about Le Moulin Poetry Society,[1] to which Lin belonged. The society was founded by Yang Chih-chang (楊熾昌), together with six other poets,[2] in Tainan in October 1933, during the height of the Japanese occupation. The history recounted in the film, which received only sporadic attention when it was released,[3] has recently been subjected to much greater attention in both Japan and Taiwan. Subsequent exhibitions about the society, such as the 2019 "Synchronic Constellation" (共時的星叢) at the National Taiwan Museum of Fine Arts, have intensified this new interest.[4] Much of the ensuing discussion of the society has centered on the notion of surrealism.

---

[1] In 2011, Huang came across Lin Chen-hua's (林政華) article "日政時期詩人林修二及其作品研究" [A Study on the Poet Lin Hsiu-erh and His Works under Japanese rule], 通識研究集刊 [*Journal of the Chinese for General Education*] 1 (June 2002): 17–32, which prompted him to make the film. See the interview "30年代的風車詩人, 改寫我們對台灣現代詩對認知：專訪《日曜日式散步者》編者陳允元、黃亞歷" [Le Moulin Poets of the 1930s Changed Our Understanding of Modern Taiwanese Poetry: An Interview with Le Moulin editors Chen Yu-yuan and Huang Ya-li], *Okapi*, September 21, 2016.

[2] They are Li Chang-jui (李張瑞), Chang Liang-tien (張良典), Lin Hsiu-erh, and three Japanese poets—Toda Fusako (戶田房子), Kishi Reiko (岸麗子), and Shimamoto Teppei (島元鉄平).

[3] The publication of Yang's poetry collection 水蔭萍作品集 [*Selected Poems of Shui Ying-ping*] in 1995 facilitated the research on Yang. Scholars have tackled his literary achievements in Taiwanese literary history to date. See Lin Chi-yang (林淇瀁), ed., 臺灣現當代作家研究資料彙05楊熾昌 [*Yang Chih-chang*, vol. 5 of *A Compilation of the Research on Contemporary Taiwanese Writers*] (Tainan: National Museum of Taiwan Literature, 2011).

[4] The exhibition was held in the National Taiwan Museum of Fine Arts from June 29 to September 15, 2019. An eponymous edited volume, *Synchronic Constellation*, was published by the Museum in June 2019.

A plethora of comments have referred to the works of Le Moulin poets as part of a Taiwanese version of surrealism or declared that the poetic style of Le Moulin Poetry Society is surrealism. While such comments acknowledge the creative absorption of world literature by these poets,[5] a good deal of ambiguity surrounds scholars' and commentators' use of the term *surrealism*. What exactly is meant by the term? Has it been deployed merely as a synonym for "modernism"? How did the poets themselves understand this concept and style that was transmitted to them from the West through Japan as an intermediary? And in their actual use of surrealism in their poetry, what changes occurred to transform Western and Japanese surrealism into what we now recognize as a local hybrid literature? These issues require clarification if we are to understand the place of Le Moulin poets within modern Taiwanese literature.

In his postscript to *Paper Fish* (紙の魚, 1985), a collection of literary commentaries, Yang Chih-chang makes a straightforward reference to Le Moulin as a surrealist movement.

> I have transplanted surrealism from Japan to Taiwan. In *Le Moulin*, the magazine founded by just seven individuals, we tried to introduce this new style [...] and turn this genealogy of surrealism presented in the four issues of *Le Moulin* into a source for intellectualism (主知主義) and new objectivity (*Neue Sachlichkeit*).[6]

In the postscript to his postwar collection *Burning Cheeks* (燃える頬, 1979), Yang provides more detail on this "genealogy" by linking it to surrealism's predecessor Dadaism and the works of Japanese modernists.

> The poetic circle that concerned me about that time was the Dadaism of Tsuji Jun (辻潤) and Takahashi Shinkichi (高橋新吉). It was a movement that sought to destroy the form of a poem and deny the status quo. It blossomed in the surrealist *Poetry and Poetics* (詩と詩論) genealogy of Haruyama Yukio (春山行夫), Anzai Fuyue (安西冬衛), and Nishiwaki Junzaburō (西脇順三郎), and created a modernist poetic style with new categories of imagery and form.[7]

The "new style"—which was a mixture of the Dadaism of Tsuji Jun and Takahashi Shinkichi, as well as poets of the surrealist genealogy, such as Haruyama Yukio, Anzai Fuyue, and Nishiwaki Junzaburō—points to a rich and poetic image or form that also possesses "intellectual" characteristics. Yang considers himself a Promethean figure who brought the surrealist fire from Japan to Taiwan and, in doing so, launched a

---

[5] Kuei-fen Chiu, "From Postcolonial Literature to World Literature: Performative Historiography and the Reinvention of Taiwan Literature in a New Age," *Journal of World Literature* 4, no. 4 (December 2019): 467–87.

[6] Yang, "《紙魚》後記" [Afterword of *Paper Fish*], in *Paper Fish* (Tokyo: Kappa Shobo, 1985), 635–36.

[7] Yang, 燃える頬 [*Burning Cheeks*] (Tokyo: Hetonglang Maoshe, 1979), 61.

form of Taiwanese modernism that has fueled the growth of a new intellectualism and objectivity in Taiwanese literature. This leaves open the question of the relationship between Taiwanese surrealism and its Japanese forebear as well as the broader relationship between surrealism and modernism.

Questioning Japanese and Taiwanese "Surrealism"

Japanese scholar Ōhigashi Kazushige (大東和重), in his analysis of the works of Tainan-based Le Moulin poets Yang Chih-chang and Li Chang-jui during the Japanese occupation, argues that Yang's apparent focus on personal emotions in his surrealist poems causes many contemporary readers to miss the allusions to anticolonial resistance and grievances.[8] When reading against the grain of the colonial history of Tainan or Taiwan, however, one can notice that the implications of the repeated image of the "girl" or "prostitute" become inescapable. She is a device that enables Yang to convey obliquely the aversion to colonial rule.[9] In the discussion of Yang's "The Ruined Street: Tainan Qui Dort" (毀壞的市街 Tainan Qui Dort), another Japanese scholar, Matsuura Tsuneo (松浦恆雄), claims that it was Yang's creative assimilation of the indirect strategies of Japanese and Western modernism that enabled him to publish poetry fiercely critical of Japanese rule.[10] Taiwanese critic Chen Yun-yuan (陳允元), on the other hand, maintains that the adoption of modernist techniques by Le Moulin poets Yang Chih-chang and Li Chang-jui, who drew from Haruyama Yukio's intellectualism, led them to mount an attack against any literature in Taiwan that they saw as left-wing realist and sentimentalist.[11]

If Yang's practice of adapting Nishiwaki Junzaburō's Japanese poetics for Taiwanese poetry gives his Taiwanese surrealism a distinctly Japanese flavor, several questions concerning localization arise. What precisely did *modernism* (モダニズム) and *surrealism* (シュルレアリスム) mean for Le Moulin poets? What sort of surrealism did Yang and Li absorb while studying in Tokyo? Was it *truly* surrealism? Was the theory of imagination advocated by Nishiwaki, an avant-garde approach that deeply influenced Yang, truly a part of surrealism? To date, scholars have largely chosen to repeat these key terms without interrogating them. Without exploring the meanings

---

[8] Ōhigashi Kazushige, "古都で芸術の風車を廻す: 日本統治下の台南における楊熾昌と李張瑞の文学活動" [Turning the Windmill of Art in the Old City: The Literary Activities of Yang Chih-chang and Li Chang-jui in Tainan under Japanese Rule], 中国学志 [*Chinese Study Journal*] 28 (2013): 51–52.

[9] Ōhigashi, "Turning the Windmill of Art in the Old City," 51–52.

[10] Matsuura Tsuneo, "台湾的蝶: 代後記" [A Postscript of the Butterfly Generation in Taiwan], in 越境するテクスト: 東アジア文化. 文学の新しい試み [*Cross-Border Text: A New Attempt in East Asian Culture and Literature*], ed. Tsuneo Matsuura et al. (Tokyo: Kenbun Shuppan, 2008), 426.

[11] Chen Yun-yuan, "殖民地前衛: 現代主義詩學在戰前台灣的傳播與再生產" [Colonial Avant-Garde: The Spread and Transformation of Modernist Poetics in Prewar Taiwan] (PhD diss., National Chengchi University, 2017).

and uses of these terms, however, it is not possible to comprehend the place of Le Moulin Poetry Society in Taiwanese literary history.

To evaluate the "modernism" of Le Moulin Poetry Society, one must first investigate the Japanese context, as Iwaya Kunio (巖谷国士), the cocurator of the "Synchronic Constellation" exhibition, has pointed out.[12] In doing so, two factors should be considered. First, postwar "modernism" promoted by Chinese mainlander poets in Taiwan is not the same as the prewar "modernism" endorsed by Le Moulin poets who translated directly from Japanese (モダニズム *modanizumu*) to Chinese (現代主義 *xiandaizhuyi*). Second, there are at least two expressions of surrealism in Japanese: the katakana forms *surrealism* (シュルレアリスム) and *sur-realism* (シュル・レアリスム) and the single Kanji form (超現実主義).

The Kanji term—which is the linguistic source for the Chinese translation of *surrealism*—immediately reminds one of Nishiwaki *Surrealist Poetics* (超現実主義詩論, 1929), a study greatly admired by Yang. Ironically, in the 1954 republished version, Nishiwaki admitted that the book's title was changed from the original *Supernaturalism* (超自然主義) at the request of the editor Haruyama Yukio.[13] Indeed, Nishiwaki's poetics is deeply indebted to the European discussion of truth and realism in poetry that can be traced from the "mimetic" poetics of Renaissance philosopher Francis Bacon up to the "supernaturalism" of Charles Baudelaire. Because the renaming of the book revealed a discrepancy between the content (supernaturalism) and the title (surrealism), Nishiwaki invited his student Takiguchi Shuzo (瀧口修造) to contribute an article "From Dadaism to Surrealism" as a postscript to justify the new title. Differing from his mentor—who saw surrealism and Dadaism solely as forms of poetry and did not contribute to any related discourse—Takiguchi was not only actively engaged in the surrealist representation of automatic writing, one of the most important features of surrealism, but also translated André Breton's *Surrealism and Painting* (*Le surréalisme et la peinture*), the earliest Japanese translated book on surrealism as well as the only translation of its kind to appear before the war.

If Yang, as stated in his postscript to *Burning Cheeks*, admired Nishiwaki, how did he view Breton's surrealism, which Nishiwaki opposed? What stance did he take with respect to surrealist practices such as automatic writing and object-making via estrangement (*dépayesment*)? Moreover, if Yang's concept of "intellectual" literary technique was influenced by Nishiwaki, who changed the book title at the suggestion of Haruyama, how did Yang perceive the trend of irrationality that was widely used to oppose the modern civilization after the First World War? How did Yang view the contradictions between a European surrealism that valued irrational expression and rejected the logic, reason, and aesthetics of modern capitalist society and a Japanese version that celebrated the exercise of intellect and reason?

---

[12] Huang Ya-li and Chen Yun-yuan, eds., 共時的星叢：風車詩社與新精神的跨界域流動 [*Synchronic Constellation: The Cross-boundary Flow of Le Moulin Poetry Society and Its New Spirit*] (Taipei: Yuandian, 2020).

[13] See Nishiwaki Junzaburō, vol. 4 of 西脇順三郎全集 [*The Complete Collection of Nishiwaki Junzaburō*] (Tokyo: Chikuma Shobō, 1971), 468.

While comprehending various related literary movements in France, Japan, and Taiwan, one must notice that transcultural practice—while crossing borders—always needs time and the content is always transformed. The time difference between the emergence of surrealism in Europe and Japan and the "practice of localization" (or appropriation) by Taiwanese writers is admittedly an important dimension for understanding Le Moulin poets. To answer the question of how poets such as Yang Chih-chang, Li Chang-jui, and Lin Hsui-erh received the Japanese modernist movement from its emergence in the Taishō period (especially after the Great Kantō earthquake) to its subsequent flourishing in the early Showa period, one needs to examine the channels through which both Japanese and Western European surrealism were transmitted to them. By doing so, we may be able to determine the reasons for Le Moulin Poetry Society's deviations from the models it appropriated, especially those of the original French surrealists.

Nishiwaki's Theory of Imagination as the First Literary Source

To examine why the modernism practiced by Le Moulin poets differs from French surrealism, one must address two key interpretive lenses of the movement: Nishiwaki Junzaburō's theory of imagination and Hori Tatsuo's reading of Jean Cocteau.

Nishiwaki was a pivotal participant in *Poetry and Poetics*, the magazine that first expressly advocated the values of poetic thinking, or *poésie*, in Japanese literary culture. It set a milestone for modern Japanese poetry and was much appreciated by Le Moulin poets. Although poets such as Nishiwaki Junzaburō, Takiguchi Shuzo, Hori Tatsuo (堀辰雄), and Haruyama Yukio may have taken different routes, they all arrived at an "intellectual" stance in their poetry. In particular, Nishiwaki's emphasis on the power of imagination and the agency of a poet in the process of composing a work is a sort of "intellectualism" that Yang Chih-chang, the founder of Le Moulin Poetry Society, appreciated. However, this form of intellectualism is quite distinct from that of French surrealism. Nishiwaki's understanding of the term *surrealism*, as many commentators have pointed out—and as Nishiwaki himself expressly states in the preface to his 1954 republished *Surrealist Poetics*—is not equivalent to André Breton's. Instead, it is inspired by the poetics of Yvan Goll and the "supernaturalism" of Charles Baudelaire. The main purpose of the imagination theory, as the critic Asabuki Ryoji (朝吹亮二) states, is to "connect opposite elements to reconcile them—that is the essence of poetry."[14]

Although Nishiwaki in *Surrealist Poetics* constantly alludes to the supernaturalism described in Baudelaire's *Intimate Journals* (内面の日記) and does not acknowledge the influence of Breton, Asabuki argues that regardless of terminology, whether the "supernaturalism" lauded by Baudelaire and then Nishiwaki or the "surrealism" spoken of by Breton, both terms celebrate the faculty of "imagination."[15] However, there may

---

[14] Asabuki Ryoji, "西脇順三郎のシュルレアリスム" [*The Surrealism of Nishiwaki Junzaburō*] (Tokyo: Keio University Art Center, 2013), 92–100.
[15] Asabuki, "The Surrealism of Nishiwaki Junzaburō," 96.

be another thread that connects Nishiwaki and Breton. Pierre Reverdy was a French poet, whose work both influenced and was inspired by surrealism and Dadaism. In his *Surrealist Manifesto* (*Manifeste du surréalisme*), Breton, as Asabuki points out, not only emphasizes automatic writing as a way to escape the constraints of reason but also praises Pierre Reverdy's concept of imagination as a "spiritual" force that brings disparate realities together.

Breton and Reverdy differ markedly, however, in their understanding of the imagination's role in connecting dissimilar objects. Breton maintains that the poet is purely a recorder. Reverdy, by contrast, argues that, just as automatic writing cannot be entirely automatic, the act of connecting "two realities" in a poem should involve some form of conscious intervention. Poets, in other words, can go beyond mere recording. They can use their imagination to create a sense of the relation between two realities. Thus, the poet is not merely a creator but also a conscious agent in the act of literary creation. This view is closer to Nishiwaki's theory than Breton's poetics. In "Surrealism as a Literary Movement" (文学運動としてのシュルレアリスム), for example, Nishiwaki criticizes Breton's mistakenly taking "dreams" and the "unconscious" as bases for poetry. A poetic image, Nishiwaki asserts, is neither a metaphor nor an allegory.

> The real world is nothing but the brain. To destroy this brain is the purpose of surrealism. The forms of noble art are all surrealist. That being so, sublime poetry is also surrealist poetry. Poetry builds an intangible desert in the brain, in which all feelings of the body, all sensations, and all thoughts connected to real experiences are screened out, and that is one method by which the brain may be made pure. Therein lies pure poetry.[16]

For Nishiwaki, the goal of surrealism is to undermine the sense of a "real" world in its place and construct a world of imagination estranged from material reality. At the moment of this imaginative creation, a "pure" work of poetry is produced that is both surrealist (that is, literally *beyond* reality) and lofty. In addition, for Nishiwaki, "surrealism" in this sense is an approach or strategy that cannot be understood or evaluated outside the social and historical context of the creative act. Under the guidance of Nishiwaki at Keio University, both Yang Chih-chang and Lin Hsui-erh studied Western literature from the same perspective. Le Moulin's approach, vision, and assimilation of French literature—particularly the works of Jean Cocteau—strongly reflect the influence of these two founding members' Japanese mentor.

---

[16] Qtd. from Nikky Lin, "主知、現實、超現實:超現實主義在戰前台灣的實踐" [Intellectualism, Realism, and Surrealism: Surrealism in Prewar Taiwan], 台灣文學學報 [*Bulletin of Taiwanese Literature*], no. 15 (December 2009): 89.

Hori's Reading of Cocteau as the Second Literary Source

Hori Tatsuo's translations of Jean Cocteau's works are the second source for the literary aesthetics of Le Moulin poets and the *Poetry and Poetics* writers. Examining these translations and Hori's commentaries on them, as well as how they intertextualize and relate to the works of Le Moulin poets, reveals the multiplicity of the "modernism" that they have imbibed and its deviation from French surrealism.

Of primary importance is the defense of surrealism in Yang's frequently cited article "Burnt Hair: A Ceremony for Poetry" (炎える頭髮: 詩の祭典のために, 1934), which he published in the newspaper *Tainan Shimpō* under the pen name "Shui Yin-ping" (水蔭萍) as well as in the third issue of *Le Moulin*:

> A black-gloved hand can catch something more realistic than reality. However, the way of encountering this "something more realistic than reality" can only be done through a surrealist work. I believe that this is a new development—no, it is key to furthering the continually evolving insights into art. However, whether it can lead the development of all art in a new direction remains questionable.[17]

Nikky Lin argues that Yang's view of surrealism as "more realistic than reality" is fabricated from the French surrealist tradition, which holds that external reality is always constrained by stale ideas and ideologies, so the path to freedom can only be found through the subconscious or dreams.[18] However, my research suggests that Yang's account of surrealism in "Burnt Hair" comes from Cocteau's *Professional Secrets* via Hori Tatsuo's translation in his *Jean Cocteau Collection* (考克多抄, 1929). *Jean Cocteau Collection* is the first volume of the "Collection of Modern Art and Criticism" (現代の芸術と批評叢書), a series arranged by Haruyama Yukio, the principal behind *Poetry and Poetics*. Contemporaneous literary critics, including Haruyama himself, often cited Hori's translations in their articles, among which *Professional Secrets* attracted the most attention; its words were also frequently quoted in Haruyama's *The Study of Poetry* (詩の研究).

The most important clue to the source of Yang's surrealism is the following passage in "Burnt Hair." Yang's account of the distinction between reality and a literary work does not come directly from Cocteau but rather from an article on Cocteau by Hori Tatsuo. The key is the "red balloon" (紅氣球) image.

> Beauty, sensation, fear, etc., that are based in reality.... I feel that these flames are extremely inferior. I believe that a poet should create a "red balloon," cut its thread, and let it rise from the ground. The spiritual floating is a ceremony of literature. If

---

[17] Shui Yin-ping [Yang Chih-chang], "炎える頭髮: 詩の祭典のために" [Burnt Hair: A Ceremony for Poetry], 台南新報 [*Tainan Shimpō*], April 18 & 19, 1934.
[18] Nikky Lin, "Intellectualism, Realism, and Surrealism," 84. See also Michelle Yeh's "燃燒與飛躍：一九三零年代台灣的超現實詩" [Burning and Flying: Surrealists in Taiwan in the 1930s], *Bulletin of Taiwanese Literature*, no. 11 (December 2007): 75–107.

a literary work falls into the trap of simple romanticism and confessional writing, I think it is because the writer has confused a "work" with "reality."[19]

Based on my investigations, Yang had likely read Hori's essay "Slightly Arbitrary" (少し 独断的), published in 1929.[20] In that article, Hori borrows Cocteau's balloon parable[21] to emphasize that cutting a work off from external reality gives the work more beauty. But not long after making this point, Hori states that, whereas writers who want to make their pain move their readers must let that pain go far away from their hearts, romanticism, by confusing the work and reality, falls to the level of confessional writing. Yang's statement at the end of "Burnt Hair" that "a literary work falls into the trap of simple romanticism and confessional writing" due to the mix of a literary work and reality clearly comes from Hori's interpretation of Cocteau. Moreover, this view of the interplay between imagination and reality and between a literary work and reality prefigures the alternative approach to realism that Yang Chih-chang and Li Chang-jui were striving to realize in opposition to what they saw as the "sentimentality" of conventional Taiwanese modernism. Yang's conception of realism could scarcely be more different from that of mainstream left-wing Taiwanese modernists such as Yang Kuei (楊逵) and Lōa Hô (賴和), but it also differs from those French surrealists who believed dreams to be surrealistic.

Hori argues that when literature borrows images from dreams, those images are used to see social reality from new angles. Whether in his view of realism or his use of the parable of the red balloon, there are many clear consonances between Hori's ideas and the ideas he encountered by translating Cocteau. These consonances, through Japanese translation, continued to be seen in Yang Chih-chang and other Le Moulin poets. More important, though, is that the views of Hori and Yang differ from those of French surrealism. Hori believes that although surrealism can change our conception of art, its methods are unable to produce new art. Throughout his life, his position was that poetry should be rooted in reality and aim toward a "new realism," that is, building a world cut off from ordinary reality. In "Surrealism," an article published in *Literature* (文学, the literary descendant of *Poetry and Poetics*), Hori points out:

> Many people have thought that our movement is toward surrealism and felt regret for it. The direction in which we are heading is a new form of realism. [...] As Cocteau has said, genuine realism is to present the things we encounter, things that have nearly slipped into our mechanical reaction, from new angles and with new speeds. In contrast with the French surrealists who regard "dreams" as something

---

[19] Yang, "Burnt Hair: A Ceremony for Poetry."
[20] Hori, "少し 独断的" [Slightly Arbitrary], originally published in 帝国大学新聞 [*Imperial University Newspaper*], April 28, 1929. It was republished in vol. 2 of 堀辰雄全集 [*Complete Works of Hori Tatsuo*] (Tokyo: Kadokawa Shoten, 1964), 104.
[21] The original reads: "A balloon. A string ties it to the ground, and with that, it cannot move us much. But when that line is cut, then the balloon will then rise into the air alone and beautiful. At that time, we will be deeply moved. That contains in it our principles of classicism. When a work is tied to reality by a string, it is not beautiful. To make it more beautiful, that string must be cut."

beyond "reality," we do not regard "dreams" as outside "reality." And "dreams" do not add anything to "reality"—dreams just stir it.[22]

The point is, for Hori, to draw a clear line with surrealism. He agrees with Cocteau in the idea that true realism enables writers to perceive things from fresh perspectives. This attitude may be similar to a surrealist practice, but it is essentially different.

In Yang's poetics, as we saw above, his idea is borrowed from Hori's translations of Cocteau or Hori himself. But in the article "The Dawn of Poetics," Yang carves out a poetics from Cocteau's position that is more his own.[23] He makes it clear that, in his view, the *reality* that a poet intends to depict should not be the mundane social reality but rather the *reality* that can be universal. This universality can be achieved only through a poet's use of reason, intellect, and calculation during the act of creation. By digging deep into *social* reality to meditate on a new *literary* reality, a poet can create fresh expressions, orders, and things in the works. In other words, the use of intellect and mental calculation gives birth to poetic authenticity, and such a poet is a sculptor of language.

In "The Dawn of Poetics," Yang repeatedly refers to Cocteau, particularly Cocteau's view that "poetry is a kind of calculation," resonating with Hori's reflection on poetry in relation to social reality in his articles on Cocteau's surrealism. The reason for Yang's emphasis on Cocteau is that, in addition to being influenced by the translations and commentaries of Hori Tatsuo and others, Nishiwaki Junzaburō, whom Yang respects, also respects Cocteau, which may also be a clue. Nishiwaki comments that he is not interested in the methods of Stéphane Mallarmé, Pablo Picasso, or some French surrealists, and is methodologically closer to Cocteau, that is, to the goal of transforming general relationships to discover new ones through sensory faculties and mental calculation.[24] Moreover, Nishiwaki regards Cocteau as the greatest poet since Rimbaud precisely because Cocteau's poetry, in his view, expresses the poetic abstraction that corresponds to contemporaneous abstract visual art. Paradoxically, for Nishiwaki, Cocteau at the same time comes close to the Romantic worship of infinity but, by abandoning sentimentality, reveals the halo of intellect and reason as in most modern artistic works.[25] The desire to eschew sentimentality while using the imagination—regarded by Nishiwaki as the highest human power of intellect and reason—to reshape reality by combining dissimilar mental images into new, strange, and mesmerizing forms of beauty can be felt throughout the works of both Nishiwaki and Cocteau.

---

[22] "Surrealism," originally published in *Literature*, no. 3 (December 1929). Qtd. from 2 vol. of *Complete Works of Hori Tatsuo*, 49.
[23] Yang Chih-chang's article on poetic criticism "The Dawn of Poetics" (詩論の夜明け) was published in three parts (A, B, and C) in the *Tainan Shimpō*, on November 19 and 25 and December 22, 1934, respectively.
[24] Nishiwaki Junzaburō, "詩の幽玄" [The Subtlety and Profundity of Poetry], in 西脇順三郎詩論集 [*Collected Poetry Criticism of Nishiwaki Junzaburō*] (Tokyo: Shichōsha, 1964), 210–11.
[25] Nishiwaki, "近代芸術とコクトー" [Modern Art and Cocteau], vol. 6 of 定本西脇順三郎全集 [*Complete Works of Nishiwaki Junzaburō. Final Version*] (Tokyo: Chikuma Shobō, 1994), 341.

Yang Chih-chang and his fellow Le Moulin poet Lin Hsui-erh also present their appreciation of Cocteau in their articles; by virtue of this, we may say that they were influenced by the translations of Hori Tatsuo and Horiguchi Daigaku (堀口大学).[26] Horiguchi and Hori translated Cocteau, and Hori translated the poems and ventured into translating the novels. Their translations encompassed not only Cocteau but also work by Cocteau's friend Raymond Radiguet, who became another important influence on Le Moulin Poetry Society. Radiguet's poetry collection *Cheeks on Fire* (*Les Joues en feu*), published in his youth, was introduced to Japan through Horiguchi's collection of translated poetry *Poets under the Moon* (月下の一群). Hori greatly admired Radiguet, frequently praising his work in literary magazines and even naming his own novel *Burning Cheeks* after Radiguet's youthful collection. After the war, Yang Chih-chang collected the work written before the war and published it as *Burning Cheeks* (1979). Yang also mentioned Radiguet in an article included in the third issue of *Le Moulin*.

In summary, we know that Hori Tatsuo's translations of Cocteau, and of writers respected by Cocteau, together with Hori's pronouncements on poetry, reality, and the imagination, deeply impressed the members of Le Moulin Poetry Society. Nishiwaki's theory of imagination was another powerful influence. Consequently, Le Moulin poets' "surrealism" deviated from what is generally recognized as French surrealism. Although later generations have come to regard the "surrealism" of Le Moulin Poetry Society as a local practice of Taiwanese literature, we owe it to these pioneers of Taiwanese surrealism to acknowledge the world literature that they absorbed during the Japanese colonial period. Le Moulin poets read not only Hori's translations of Cocteau but also Hori's novels and commentaries, and they were also familiar with *The Complete Works of Ryūnosuke Akutagawa* (芥川龍之介全集), which Hori had edited. In other words, when later generations question whether the modernism of Le Moulin Poetry Society is the same as French surrealism or wonder why it deviates from French surrealism, it is very important to clarify the sources of their poetics and give due attention to the Japanese paths by which they absorbed and interpreted their sources.

Conclusion

Le Moulin poets were modernists who, unlike the French surrealists, believed that poetry must be founded on reason and intellect and pay heed to literary representation in relation to social reality, and they were less politically radical than French surrealists who expressed aversion to the war and how it damaged the bodies of its victims. They are seen as outside the Taiwanese literary establishment of the 1930s not because they were surrealists but because the mainstream of literature in Taiwan at that time was

---

[26] Horiguchi Daigaku successfully transformed Jean Cocteau's poem "My ear is a hell who loves the sound of the sea" into Japanese using the seven-five meter of Japanese poetry, making it more pleasant to the Japanese ear.

occupied by "proletarian" writing. The seemingly apolitical Le Moulin poets' literary notions were thus at odds with the prevailing ideas of other Taiwanese literary societies.

Le Moulin poets' engagement with foreign modernism, in my view, clearly indicates a preference, when facing the choice between "art for life's sake" and "art for art's sake." Although the former has been implicitly conveyed in their works and poetics, they mostly agree with the latter, putting emphasis on the intrinsic value of art, separating literary works from any political, didactic, and utilitarian function. Li Chang-jui, for example, advocated that literature should be a completely independent art with no ulterior purpose: "We do not write about injustice or resistance, themes tackled by your side of people; we deliberately do not write them."[27] This does not mean, however, that Li and other Le Moulin poets sought poetry as an escape from reality. Rather, writers should skillfully use literary techniques to depict Taiwan's reality. What he and Yang questioned was the definition of "new" in the New Taiwanese Literary Movement of that time, which focused on conspicuously literary rebellion against Japanese rule. Lin and Yang wondered whether there could be different types of "new" writing. With a desire to develop an alternative way of writing that promoted the use of rationality and intellect, they criticized what they saw as the sentimentality of most Taiwanese literature in the mid-1930s and stressed that their objection was about style rather than content. As Li put it, "it is not that the object of writing should not be sentimental. Instead, it is the way of expression that should not be sentimental."[28]

The aesthetic inspiration of Le Moulin poets was drawn, as we have seen, mainly from the Japanese teacher and critic Nishiwaki Junzaburō and the French author whom Nishiwaki admired most, Jean Cocteau, especially Cocteau as translated by Hori Tatsuo. The writings of Li Chang-jui and Yang Chih-chang are deemed "surrealism" in the eyes of most contemporary scholars. Taking their sources from Cocteau and Nishiwaki into consideration, however, makes it clear that Le Moulin poets departed significantly from the surrealism prevalent in Europe at that time. They believed that authors can exert their mental and sensory faculties in creative writing, a credo very close to Japanese surrealism but different from French surrealism's faith in automatism. Moreover, they hoped to employ this aesthetic credo to move Taiwanese literature as a whole in a new direction in the mid-1930s when Li and Yang returned to Taiwan.[29] For Li and Yang, the "newness" of new Taiwanese literature should come from its methods, not its content. These methods, as well as the new spirit that informed them, were intimately associated with their reception of world literature.

In 1946, at the symposium "Speaking about the Future Path for Taiwanese Culture" organized by Taipei's monthly newspaper *Xinxin* (新新), attendees discussed how Taiwan's future cultural development took into account both "globalization" and

---

[27] Li Chang-jui, "詩人的貧血：這個島的文學" [The Anemia of Poets: Literature of This Island], 台灣新聞 [*Taiwan Shimbun*], February 20, 1935.

[28] Li, "The Anemia of Poets: Literature of this Island."

[29] Li returned to Taiwan in 1933 and joined Le Moulin Poetry Society soon afterward. Yang settled back in Taiwan in 1934 due to his father's death and was invited to work as acting editor-in-chief for *Tainan shimpō*'s literary supplement.

"Sinicization." For them, Taiwanese artists and intellectuals, after a half-century of Japanese rule, were eager to rebut the criticism that the Taiwanese people lacked a culture of their own. They argued that under Japanese rule, Taiwanese culture had kept pace with many foreign cultures and in no way lagged in the reception of classic works of world literature. The Taiwanese people felt disgusted at how the KMT saw them as "enslaved" by the Japanese Empire just because of their willingness to use the Japanese language. To shake off the ideologic discourse of Sinicization imposed by the KMT, they sought to reconsider the issue of what made Taiwan distinctive from the perspective of "globalization" and how postwar Taiwan might assert its difference from the past.[30]

What was it that enabled intellectuals at that time to hold that Taiwan under Japanese rule had culturally kept pace with the Global North, such as France and Japan? I would argue that a study of the world literature absorbed by Le Moulin Poetry Society provides a small part of the answer. In suggesting why the "surrealism" of the society deviated from French surrealism, I have argued that Cocteau, Hori, and the other artists that Le Moulin poets admired differed from many surrealists who excluded the use of reason, instead insisting that literature requires rigorous mental and sensory faculties. In incorporating the literary trends of the time, be they from world literature or from Japanese literature, Le Moulin Poetry Society pursued poetics in an alternative way. This enabled them to reflect on Taiwan's distinctiveness and address the pressing issues facing their new nation.

---

[30] Ying-che Huang, 「去日本化」「再中國化」：戰後台灣文化重建 (1945-1947) [*Uprooting Japan and Implanting China: Cultural Reconstruction in Postwar Taiwan 1945-1947*] (Taipei: Rye Field, 2007), 213.

5

Responsible Primitivism: Wu Ming-yi's *The Man with the Compound Eyes* as Indigenous-Themed Environmental World Literature

Darryl Sterk

Wu Ming-yi's (吳明益) novel *The Man with the Compound Eyes* (hereafter *The Man*) features apparently idealized Indigenous characters.[1] Atile'i is preternaturally sensitive to and knowledgeable about nature, both on and around his Pacific Island home and later in Taiwan. Hafay runs a café at which she serves traditional Pangcah cuisine made with wild greens she has gathered herself on the coastal hills along Taiwan's east coast. Dahu is the son of a Bunun hunter who has spent his life getting to know the mountains in his way. Chief Anu is a Bunun hunter who is running an ethnic ecotourism operation on a mountain in southeastern Taiwan, a place that heals urbanites' wounded souls. As Atile'i puts it, "the mountain will cure you."[2]

Why would Wu create Indigenous characters like these? Given that Taiwan is a settler society, one might wonder if Wu is a Taiwanese nationalist, because nationalists in settler societies like Taiwan often idealize and identify with their Indigenous heritage.[3] Yet Wu has never made a claim to indigeneity, nor has any non-Indigenous Han Taiwanese character in his fiction. Rather than a nationalist, Wu is better described as a "primitivist," someone who sees in "primitive" Indigenous cultures solutions to "modern" problems, particularly degradation of and alienation from the natural environment. But he is not a simplistic or naive primitivist. His primitivism is tempered by knowledge of Indigenous cultures and histories and acquaintance with Indigenous individuals and lifeways in Taiwan.

Nonetheless, Wu's primitivism is part of the secret of his success as a writer of "environmental world literature," in that the perspectives of his Indigenous characters contribute to his novel's appealing "ecocosmopolitanism." As defined by Ursula Heise, ecocosmopolitanism is "an attempt to envision individuals and groups as

---

[1] Wu Ming-yi, 複眼人 [*Compound Eye Person*] (Taipei: Summer Festival, 2011), translated by Darryl Sterk, as *The Man with the Compound Eyes* (London: Harvill Secker, 2013).
[2] Wu, *The Man*, 270.
[3] Laura Jane Murray, "Going Native, Becoming American: Colonialism, Identity, and American Writing, 1760–1820" (PhD diss., Cornell University, 1993).

part of planetary 'imagined communities' of both human and nonhuman kinds."[4] The formation of the real-life Great Pacific Garbage Patch into the Trash Vortex, a fictional floating mountain of trash, is a speculative scenario that sounds archetypally ecocosmopolitan, because it is a mess all the world's people created and are responsible for cleaning up, whatever imagined community they happen to be part of. The imagined community in the novel is a transnational group of trash-clearing scientists from Germany and Norway and Indigenous activists like Hafay and Dahu.[5] Given that so many of the characters in the novel are Indigenous, one wonders if it can be considered not just environmental world literature but also Indigenous world literature.

Indigenous World Literature

The scholars' names to reckon with today in world literature studies are Damrosch, Moretti, Casanova, and Apter, but before they started publishing, Native American literary critic Arnold Krupat had considered the possibility of Indigenous world literature.[6] However, his book was mainly about Native American literature as a part of the American national canon. The first book-length scholarly work to focus on "Indigenous world literature" is the 2018 collection *Indigenous Transnationalism*, devoted to Australian Indigenous writer Alexis Wright's 2006 novel *Carpentaria*.[7] Editor Lynda Ng and the chapter contributors point out that while we typically associate "Indigenous" peoples with temporal and spatial roots to a local landscape, which would seem to be the antithesis of worldliness, in fact, as a modern identity and status category, "Indigenous" has been international from the start. In Ronald Niezen's influential 2003 account, "global indigenism" dates to the 1960s, when Indigenous activists joined forces in their struggles for sovereignty and cultural and linguistic rights in settler states around the world.[8]

Carpentaria is not about activists at government functions or United Nations gatherings but about ordinary Indigenous people who do not have passports but are as aware as anyone of the globally interrelated character of modern life, particularly in its environmental dimensions. One way of reading Wright's novel is as an Indigenous response to a fictitious multinational corporation's mining project, which of course can

---

[4] Ursula K. Heise, *Sense of Place and Sense of Planet: The Environmental Imagination of the Global* (Oxford: Oxford University Press, 2008), 61.

[5] You-ting Chen argues that Wu's *The Stolen Bicycle* is ecocosmopolitan. See his "Compound Eyes and Limited Visions: Wu Ming-yi's 'Weak Anthropocentric' Gaze for World Literature," *Ex-position*, no. 41 (2019): 33–52. *The Man with the Compound Eyes* is more explicitly so, but it is not my purpose to compare the two novels.

[6] Arnold Krupat, *The Voice in the Margin: Native American Literature and the Canon* (Berkeley: University of California Press, 1989).

[7] Lynda Ng, ed., *Indigenous Transnationalism: Alexis Wright's "Carpentaria"* (Sydney: Giramondo Publishing, 2018).

[8] Ronald Niezen, *The Origins of Indigenism: Human Rights and the Politics of Identity* (Berkeley: University of California Press, 2003).

only proceed with the permission of the Australian government because the project aligns with the state or national development policy. Indigenous Australians have different values from a multinational corporation and the government, values that they might today express in terms of environmentalism, even ecocosmopolitanism. Alexis Wright's characters do not use such sophisticated terminology, but they appear to be feeling their way toward an Indigenous ecocosmopolitanism. Adapting Heise slightly, Indigenous ecocosmopolitanism could be defined as culturally specific attempts by Indigenous people to imagine themselves as members of *glocal* ecocommunities, like the one that attempts to clean up the shores of eastern Taiwan after the trash tsunami hits in *The Man*.

The study of the significance of Wright's novel's travels beyond Australia's borders would have to contextualize recent efforts in Australia at reconciliation with Indigenous peoples, if not historical justice let alone contemporary equality. A prominent Australian Indigenous writer's reflection on Indigenous Australians' place in Australia is a part of this larger process. A year after the publication of *Carpentaria* in 2007, the year of the passage of the United Nations Declaration of the Rights of Indigenous Peoples (UNDRIP), then prime minister Kevin Rudd made his historic apology to Indigenous peoples, in February 2008. His national apology must be seen in both local and global context, as should be unsurprising to anyone who has accepted the basic tenet of world literature that the nation-state is ultimately an inadequate container for literature or anything else for that matter. When Rudd made his apology, other countries with similar demographics as a result of similar histories of settlement were watching. Then prime minister of Canada Stephen Harper made his apology to the First Nations four months later in June. While neither country had endorsed UNDRIP, an apology is a start.

Taiwanese Cultural Production in a "Settler Society" Context

Nearly ten years later on August 1, 2016, Taiwan's President Tsai Ing-wen made an apology to the Indigenous people as one of the first acts of her presidency.[9] Why it made sense for her to make one is complicated. She was surely differentiating herself from the previous president, Ma Ying-jeou, whose party, the Kuomintang (KMT), had always enjoyed (and continues to enjoy) Indigenous political support.[10] Beyond the motive of peeling away Indigenous voters from the KMT, Tsai sincerely hoped to further the reconciliation process, and five years on some progress has been made, particularly with the passage of a national languages act in 2017 that made sixteen of Taiwan's Indigenous languages national languages and quintupled funding for Indigenous language revitalization.[11] But to most Indigenous activists and their

---

[9] Linda van der Horst, "Taiwan's President Offers Apology to Indigenous People," *The Diplomat*, August 3, 2016.
[10] Eric Hale, "'Always Campaign Time': Why Taiwan's Indigenous People Back KMT," *Aljazeera*, January 9, 2020.
[11] Gareth Price, *Language, Society, and State: From Colonization to Globalization in Taiwan* (Amsterdam: Mouton de Gruyter, 2018).

supporters, not enough progress has been made toward addressing past injustices and realizing some form of Indigenous sovereignty.[12]

It should be noted that the KMT got the ball rolling by recognizing Taiwan's Indigenous people as such in the 1990s. The KMT recognized Indigenous people for two main reasons. First, to distinguish Taiwan from China, which has a "national minority policy" that was imported from the USSR and modified to reduce local autonomy in the 1950s. Having indigenes, specifically Austronesian indigenes, Taiwan could reach out through global Indigenous, in particular Austronesian, networks.[13] Second, to pivot to democratic politics. The old monolingual, monocultural, Mandarin-only, Chinese-only language and culture policy would not play well to minorities in a democracy. The KMT recognized them as Indigenous to keep their support.

A bottom-up account, at least at the level of Indigenous elites, who might try to share their visions with ordinary Indigenous people, would be that the KMT was also responding to Indigenous activists, who took up the term "Indigenous," translated as *yuanzhumin* (原住民, literally "the people who lived here first"), around 1984, at the beginning of the local Indigenous movement. The activists could plausibly claim to be Indigenous because their Austronesian ancestors had settled Taiwan over five thousand years before Han Chinese began to migrate to Taiwan in the seventeenth century.[14] As Alice explains to Atile'i in *The Man*, "people like [the Han Taiwanese] are latecomers," and the ancestors of people like Hafay and Dahu came earlier.[15] As a result of this history, Taiwan can be compared to Australia and other settler states like New Zealand, Canada, and the United States.[16] The comparison to the United States is particularly compelling because of the time frame of settlement (starting in the seventeenth century) and the resulting demographic profile (both countries have an Indigenous population of under 5 percent).[17] In my previous research, I attempted a discussion of Taiwan's Indigenous-themed literature (and film) in terms of the concept of the settler state.[18] The year after a book chapter of mine on the topic was published, along came Wu Ming-yi's *Fuyanren* (複眼人), literally "compound eye person," in 2011, which I would go on to translate as *The Man with the Compound Eyes*.

---

[12] Awi Mona, "Conceptualizing Indigenous Historical Justice toward a Mutual Recognition with State in Taiwan," *Washington International Law Review* 28, no. 3 (2019): 654–76.

[13] Scott Simon, "From the Village to the United Nations and Back Again: Aboriginal Taiwan and International Indigenism," *Taiwan Journal of Indigenous Studies* 9, no. 3 (2016): 49–89.

[14] Robert Blust, "Austronesian Culture History: The Window of Language," *Transactions of the American Philosophical Society* 86, no. 5 (1996): 28–35.

[15] Wu, *The Man*, 175.

[16] Benedict Anderson, "Western Nationalism and Eastern Nationalism: Is There a Difference That Matters?" *New Left Review* 9 (2001). https://newleftreview.org/issues/ii9/articles/benedict-anderson-western-nationalism-and-eastern-nationalism.

[17] John R. Shepherd, *Statecraft and Political Economy on the Taiwan Frontier, 1600–1800* (Stanford: Stanford University Press, 1994).

[18] Darryl Sterk, "Romancing the Formosan Aborigine: Colonial Interethnic Romance and Its Democratic Revision in Postwar Film and Fiction," in *Becoming Taiwan: From Colonialism to Democracy*, ed. Ann Heylen and Scott Sommers (Wiesbaden: Harrassowitz Verlag, 2010), 49–62.

Indigenous-Themed Environmental World Literature

Kuei-fen Chiu has offered an insightful analysis of the secrets of *The Man*'s global success, in other words, the ways Wu overcame barriers to entry to world literature: by signing with the literary agent and publishing expert Gray Tan, by employing magic realism, a genre with which readers around the world are familiar, and by foregrounding his scientific knowledge, especially about the environment and his environmental concern, in that environmental issues are global in scope and matter to a great many readers.[19] In this way Wu has made it into some echelon of environmental world literature, where he remains. May he have a long "shelf life."

I argue that Indigenous content is a part of *The Man*'s appeal as a work of environmental world literature. I describe it as "Indigenous-themed" rather than Indigenous because, unlike Alexis Wright, Wu Ming-yi is not himself Indigenous, even though Indigenous characters figure prominently in the main plot and the subplots. Although the main plot is about a Han Taiwanese professor of literature named Alice, her Indigenous friends have their own subplots. One of these friends is an Indigenous youth, though not a Taiwanese one, named Atile'i. The first substantial chapter in the novel is about Atile'i. In chapter two, Atile'i leaves the imaginary island of Wayo Wayo (which was Woenesia, island of woe, in an early version of the sample translation). Wayo Wayo was partly inspired by Orchid Island as represented by the noted Tao writer Syaman Rapongan (夏曼·藍波安). Atile'i later lands on a floating trash island he calls Gesi Gesi. Gesi Gesi carries Atile'i onto the shores of eastern Taiwan, where he befriends Alice and accompanies her on a trip into the island's alpine interior to try to find her lost son and husband. Atile'i is introduced before Alice, who does not appear until chapter three. In the sample translation, chapters two and three, which was submitted by Wu Ming-yi's literary agent Gray Tan to Harvill Secker, the novel's eventual English publisher, Atile'i was given as much space as Alice. When a selection was made from this sample for *Asymptote*, a website that (cl)aims to be "the premier site for world literature in translation," chapter two about Atile'i was chosen over chapter three about Alice. In other words, *The Man*'s initial appeal to world literature readers was through its indigeneity. When Ursula Le Guin commented, "We haven't read anything like this novel. Ever. South America gave us magical realism—what is Taiwan giving us? A new way of telling our new reality, beautiful, entertaining, frightening, preposterous, true," she may have been responding to the Indigenous story of Wayo Wayo and Atile'i.[20]

---

[19] Kuei-fen Chiu, "The Making of Small Literature as World Literature: Taiwanese writer Wu Ming-yi," forthcoming in *Modern Chinese Literature and Culture*.

[20] Gray Tan, "Ursula K. Le Guin Recommends Wu Ming-yi's *The Man with Compound Eyes*," The Grayhawk Agency (blog), July 16, 2013.

Research Question and Literature Review

To argue that indigeneity is an inseparable part of *The Man*'s appeal to ecocosmopolitan readers, which is to say, consumers of environmental world literature, I would have to present evidence about both production and reception, in other words, how the book was written, pitched, and marketed and then how it was read and received by professional and non-professional readers alike. In recent literary reception research, reviews left by non-professional readers on Amazon and Goodreads have become grist for the mill. Kuei-fen Chiu has used such evidence as one "indicator" of *The Man*'s global visibility.[21] But I shall not marshal such evidence because the main goal of this chapter is not to prove the thesis that Indigenous content increased *The Man*'s appeal (though I assume that thesis is correct).

The main goal is rather to answer the following research question: In idealizing Indigenous characters, did Wu Ming-yi represent Taiwan's Indigenous heritage, particularly in its environmental dimensions, responsibly? I ask this question because Wu is not himself Indigenous and may be more prone to distortion or misunderstanding of Indigenous issues. This is not to say that Indigenous writers' representations should be taken at face value or that *The Man* should be automatically dismissed as cultural appropriation. I cannot imagine that Indigenous writers would want their representations to be taken at face value; and if we outlaw writing about the other, ultimately the only one a writer will be allowed to write about is himself or herself.

What would a responsible representation of Indigenous peoples by a non-Indigenous writer like Wu be like? It should be based on a hard-nosed, realistic understanding of historical subjugation and contemporary inequality; and yet realism is not the only principle of responsible representation because representation can be both of reality and of possibility. Hence, an honest representation may partake of "primitivism," the modern idealization of Indigenous peoples who might have answers to modern problems like our degradation of and alienation from the environment. As Indigenous peoples are at a distance from their cultural "traditions," as they have been formulated in modern times, they may idealize themselves, hence "Indigenous primitivism." For Indigenous or any other kind of primitivism to have any depth and complexity, it should be "ironic" not naive.[22]

So, what kind of Taiwanese indigeneity does Wu give readers of environmental world literature in *The Man*? Before trying to answer this question myself, I should first make sure I am not reinventing the wheel.

There is now a substantial critical literature on the environmental dimensions of *The Man*, for instance about Wu's localization of Western nature writing and his vision of nature.[23] Regarding Indigenous representation, Corey Byrnes writes:

---

[21] Kuei-fen Chiu, "'Worlding' World Literature from the Literary Periphery: Four Taiwanese Models," *Modern Chinese Literature and Culture* 30, no. 1 (2018): 13–41.

[22] Darryl Sterk, "Ironic Indigenous Primitivism: Taiwan's First 'Native Feature' in an Era of Ethnic Tourism," *Journal of Chinese Cinemas* 8, no. 3 (2014): 209–25.

[23] See Serena Shiuhhuah Chou, "Sense of Wilderness, Sense of Time: Mingyi Wu's Nature Writing and the Aesthetics of Change," in *East Asian Ecocriticisms: A Critical Reader*, ed. Simon C. Estok and Won-chung Kim (New York: Palgrave Macmillan, 2013), 145–63 and Dingru Huang, "Compound Eyes and Limited Visions: Wu Ming-yi's 'Weak Anthropocentric' Gaze for World Literature," *Ex-position*, 41 (2019): 53–70.

Wu's portrait of the people and traditions of the fictional Wayo Wayo is lovingly detailed, but it also bears the mark of a primitive romanticism so retrograde as to seem almost ironic. Do the islanders represent an ecological alternative to the death-drive of global capitalism as embodied by the ethnically Han Taiwanese, or are they a knowing allusion to a Western literary tradition fraught with racist and imperialist origins?[24]

Presenting the counter thesis, Kathryn Chang claims that Wu is "far from idealizing or romanticizing the Taiwanese Aboriginals because he perceives their vulnerability and victimization by colonialism and global climate change."[25] Byrnes's and Chang's criticisms are actually not mutually incompatible because Byrnes is commenting on Atile'i, while Chang is commenting on Hafay and Dahu. While she is well aware of Hafay and Dahu, Rose Juan argues that Atile'i and Alice's friendship represents an encounter between oral and literate, premodern and modern.[26]

Wayo Wayo is ironic primitive romanticism, and that is a good thing. Not all primitive romanticisms are indelibly stained by their racist and imperialist origins. Wayo Wayo is ironic in the sense that it is, as Rose Juan puts it, a "fable" and a "floating signifier."[27] Atile'i and his people may offer an ecological alternative to modernity, but it is hardly feasible in a world of nearly eight billion people, nor is it one that any modern person, including any modern Indigenous person, could accept. Environmentally salient aspects of the Austronesian culture of Wayo Wayo that modern people might be able to accept are explored in Taiwan after Atile'i arrives and makes contact with Alice. Similar aspects of Formosan Austronesian cultures—cultures of the colonized Indigenous peoples of Taiwan—are explored through what Byrnes describes as "Wu's more well-rounded native Taiwanese characters." These Formosan Indigenous characters complicate Rose Juan's binaries, in that they are trying to make oral traditions relevant in modern or postmodern times. One alternative these characters explore is small-scale capitalism, which, as an approach to exchange and production, is not necessarily a force of destruction and death.

---

[24] Corey Byrnes, review of *The Man with the Compound Eyes*, by Wu Ming-yi, *MCLC Resource Center Publication*, October 2014.

[25] Kathryn Yalan Chang, "If Nature Had a Voice: A Material-Oriented Environmental Reading of *The Man with the Compound Eyes*," in *Ecocriticism in Taiwan: Identity, Environment, and the Arts*, ed. Chia-ju Chang and Scott Slovic (Lanham: Lexington Books, 2018), 104.

[26] Rose Hsiu-li Juan, "Imagining the Pacific Trash Vortex and the Spectacle of Environmental Disaster: Environmental Entanglement and Literary Engagement in Wu Ming-yi's *Fuyanren* (The Man with the Compound Eyes)," in *Ecocriticism in Taiwan: Identity, Environment, and the Arts*, ed. Chia-ju Chang and Scott Slovic (Lanham: Lexington Books, 2018), 79–94.

[27] Juan, "Imagining the Pacific Trash Vortex and the Spectacle of Environmental Disaster," 85 & 89. Juan's application of "floating signifier" to *The Man* is a stroke of brilliance. A translation of *signifiant flottant*, Lévi-Strauss's characterization of *mana* in Polynesian languages and cultures, "floating signifier" is particularly apt for Wayo Wayo because the island floats. What the island means is, similarly, open to interpretation, though its meaning may not be quite so hard to pin down as *mana*'s.

Ben Holgate and Christine Marran have placed *The Man* not in a Taiwanese or (in Byrnes's case) modern Chinese literary context but in a regional or global context. Holgate's book on magic realism in Austronesian and Australian nature writing ends with a chapter on Wu's novel. According to Holgate, this novel adopts a "conscious planetary perspective" that makes it a work of "environmental world literature."[28] Arguing that environmental world literature is constituted partly by intertextuality, Holgate compares *The Man* with works by Austronesian and Australian Indigenous writers. The Sea Sage in *The Man* reminds Holgate of the Māori elder Koro in Witi Ihimaera's *The Whale Rider*.[29] The floating island of trash on which Atile'i lands reminds him of the trash island Will Phantom lands on in *Carpentaria*.[30] I disagree, however, that "Atile'i represents spiritual communion with nature and a pristine environment."[31] I prefer Pei-yin Lin's qualifier in her description of Wayo Wayo as a *quasi*-utopian place.[32] I would also qualify Holgate's claim that "environmental knowledge is embodied in the Indigenous Taiwanese Bunun people."[33] Dahu has failed to inherit tradition but is nonetheless still trying to combine it with a modern scientific perspective, while Hafay's Amis tradition represents a different body of local knowledge of a different landscape, the coastal foothills.

Christine Marran's *Ecology without Culture* is global in purview. She takes *The Man* as exemplary of "texts that develop expansive ecological imaginaries that resist or explicitly dismiss exceptionalist claims made at the level of ethnicity, culture, and species in their critiques of industrial modernity."[34] But the fact that the trash cleanup effort in the novel is arguably "postnational" does not mean that the ethnic and cultural and national differences are irrelevant or unexceptional.[35] I argue that without essentializing anyone's culture, Wu develops several relevant and exceptional cultural contrasts, between Atile'i on the one hand and Hafay and Dahu the other and then further differentiating between Hafay and Dahu, who are learning from, and influencing, each other, in a process that might be described as Indigenous transculturation.[36] In developing these contrasts, Wu teaches lessons readers can apply wherever they live, both about Indigenous peoples and about ways of relating to nature.

---

[28] Ben Holgate, *Climate and Crises: Magical Realism as Environmental Discourse* (London: Routledge, 2019), 208.
[29] Holgate, *Climate and Crises*, 211.
[30] Holgate, *Climate and Crises*, 216.
[31] Holgate, *Climate and Crises*, 215.
[32] Pei-yin Lin, "Positioning 'Taiwanese Literature' to the World: Taiwan as Represented and Perceived in English Translation," in *Positioning Taiwan in a Global Context: Being and Becoming*, ed. Bi-yu Chang and Pei-yin Lin (London: Routledge, 2018), 22.
[33] Holgate, *Climate and Crises*, 213.
[34] Christine L. Marran, *Ecology without Culture: Aesthetics for a Toxic World* (Minneapolis: University of Minnesota Press, 2017), 3.
[35] Marran, *Ecology without Culture*, 2.
[36] Thanks to the editor Wen-chi Li for this insight.

Indigeneity in *The Man with the Compound Eyes*

Since Wu begins with Wayo Wayo, I will begin here, too. The initial impression one gets of Wayo Wayoan culture is of *difference*. One gets this impression through invented idioms that suggest alien approaches to orientation in space and time: Wayo Wayoans think in terms of facing the sea and facing the island's center.[37] Men calculate their ages in moons, women in the number of children. Shorter lengths of time are conveyed through idioms like "before a single fish was hooked."[38] Alice describes these metaphors skeptically as "overly poetic."[39] In creating them, Wu took inspiration from Syaman Rapongan's literal translations of Tao idioms.[40] He was probably also drawing on the findings of cognitive linguistics.[41]

Wayo Wayoans may inhabit a different cognitive world, but is Wayo Wayo a paradise? Not according to the narrator, who describes the looks on Wayo Wayoan fishermen's faces when they catch gulls with their *gawana*—a small hunting implement—as "cruel."[42] As a reader, I found the tradition of the second son's exile from the island when he turns a hundred and sixty moons to be cruel, even if a Malthusian justification could be attempted for it. The supposedly necessary cruelty of the Wayo Wayoans to themselves and other creatures is reflected in their underwater origin myth about the consequences of overconsumption.[43] They eat a certain shrimp that has been outlawed and are expelled from their watery Eden onto the shores of a tiny round island that has been painstakingly constructed by a certain bird out of grains of sand.[44] The caution against overconsumption in the myth has obvious relevance in their daily life. They are not allowed to overeat, for there is a shoal of fish called *asamu* that spy on the islanders to make sure they observe rules against eating certain things.[45] They are not allowed to cut down trees so that they can avoid the fate of Easter Island.[46] These overconsumption rules are spatialized in literal lines that the Wayo Wayoans are not allowed to cross.[47] Then Atile'i does cross the final frontier and discovers that he is no worse for it.

---

[37] Wu, *The Man*, 12.
[38] Wu, *The Man*, 37.
[39] Wu, *The Man*, 213.
[40] Kuei-fen Chiu, "The Production of Indigeneity: Contemporary Indigenous Literature in Taiwan and Trans-Cultural Inheritance," *The China Quarterly* 200 (2009): 1071–87.
[41] For examples of cognitive differences inscribed in language, see Nicholas Evans, *Dying Words: Endangered Languages and What They Have to Tell Us* (Hoboken, NJ: Wiley-Blackwell, 2009).
[42] Wu, *The Man*, 11.
[43] Wu, *The Man*, 165–66.
[44] Wu, *The Man*, 247. The Christian myth of Eden is also about overconsumption, where the apple represents the precious resource. The Wayo Wayoan mythology seems quite Christian to me, particularly when the word is made flesh: the creator god Kabang's words will become the spirits of the deep (Wu, *The Man*, 166).
[45] Wu, *The Man*, 10.
[46] Wu, *The Man*, 170. On the "collapse" of Easter Island, see Terry L. Hunt, "Rethinking the Fall of Easter Island," *American Scientist* 94, no. 5 (2006): 412. Wu Ming-yi possibly has sampled practices from around the Indigenous world for his fictional ethnography of Wayo Wayo. Another example is Atile'i's roaring rite, which sounds like a Māori haka. See also, Wu, *The Man*, 144.
[47] Wu, *The Man*, 29 & 33.

One might then wonder if the whole point of the second son rule is for the second sons to break it, to cross the line, explore new frontiers, and learn from the people who live on them. Indeed, Wayo Wayoan material culture has elements that make sense in a seafaring context, not just a context of insular autarky. Atile'i makes a *talawaka*, a kind of outrigger canoe.[48] He observes the elevations of the sun and the morning star.[49] He carries with him a speaking flute, his lover Rasula's last gift to him, a (cultural) translation device.[50] He plays it for Alice so that she and he can find common ground.[51]

When Atile'i lands on the trash island of Gesi Gesi, he fashions another *gawana*, though not in the traditional way.[52] (He uses makeshift tools and waste plastic.) After the trash island crashes onto Taiwan, Atile'i makes a new kind of boat according to a design in a book of a plank canoe with crude tools he finds at Alice's cabin.[53] In doing so, he is adapting his culturally specific skill to a new set of circumstances. He adapts himself mentally to changing circumstances as well. His terms for airplane and ocean liner are bird of hell and ghost ship.[54] He applies his concept of "reflection" to Alice's photographs, which indeed are reflections preserved for posterity.[55] And just as he tries to take in all the new modern things he is witnessing, so Alice tries to culturally translate what she learns from Atile'i of Wayo Wayoan ways. But the notion of cultural alterity and its translatability is not in my opinion the main lesson the novel teaches about Indigenous peoples.

Rather, its main lesson is that cultures are different repertoires, which every individual can inherit and contribute to, of mental and material strategies to survive in changing or new environments without degrading them over the long term. A given culture, it stands to reason, would be knowledge adapted to a certain environment, like Wayo Wayo, but to the extent that indigeneity as presented in the novel is generalizable, it would be in adaptiveness to natural environments. Alice observes Atile'i's incredible adaptiveness to his new natural surroundings in Taiwan. Soon he knows the terrain of Taiwan better than she does, as well as the flora and fauna.[56] He forages for plants around the cabin, discovering that certain ferns are not poisonous, with no need for tradition to teach him.[57] He imitates a thrush call, then the call of the green pigeon he is trying to hunt.[58] He teaches Alice to gather food plants and snails.[59] Borrowing from Aldo Leopold, Alice claims that the mountain knows Atile'i, who knows what it is

---

[48] Wu, *The Man*, 13.
[49] Wu, *The Man*, 38. On Austronesian astronomy and seafaring, see D. Lewis, "Voyaging Stars: Aspects of Polynesian and Micronesian Astronomy," *Philosophical Transactions of the Royal Society of London, Series A: Mathematical and Physical Sciences* 276, no. 1257 (1974): 133–48.
[50] Wu, *The Man*, 15.
[51] Wu, *The Man*, 211.
[52] Wu, *The Man*, 34–35.
[53] Wu, *The Man*, 291.
[54] Wu, *The Man*, 40.
[55] Wu, *The Man*, 164.
[56] Wu, *The Man*, 174.
[57] Wu, *The Man*, 213.
[58] Wu, *The Man*, 173.
[59] Wu, *The Man*, 213.

thinking.⁶⁰ Eventually, inspired by Atile'i's example, Alice renews her relationship with nature, which she expresses through personification or even deification.⁶¹ These are surely aspects of indigeneity that many readers of environmental world literature who live a relatively mediated, alienated existence would find compelling.

Though Rasula, Atile'i's lover, is a minor character, she is equally compelling. Much more than Atile'i, she represents an explicit questioning of tradition. When Rasula decides to make a *talawaka* and go off in search of Atile'i, her mother warns her that she might turn into a jellyfish if she disobeys the traditional sexual division of labor, according to which only men build *talawaka*. Rasula doubts the veracity of the belief about disobedient girls turning into jellyfish and does what she wants in secret.⁶² Although she does it for a clichéd reason—all for the love of her man—she represents not just the intergenerational innovation that keeps tradition relevant but also a Wayo Wayoan feminism. Atile'i fears he may not be able to become a man according to the traditional Wayo Wayo standards.⁶³ Rasula has no such worries about being a woman according to her own standards.

To make the fable of Wayo Wayo all the more compelling, Wu adds pathos by endangering the island. Its shores are lapped by plastic bags and bottles and have been visited by white men who studied the material culture, serving as the putative source of the ethnographic information in the novel, and who left behind children like Rasula.⁶⁴ At the end of the novel, Wayo Wayo is destroyed by a torpedo, and Atile'i along with it.⁶⁵ Scholars have associated its destruction with the nuclear tests on the Bikini Atoll, but it seems to me that the torpedo launch is an attempt to destroy the Trash Vortex. By this point Rasula, who has left the island in search of Atile'i, is safely out of range, but she dies after being found drifting in the Gulf of Mexico with a baby in her belly, the only hope for the future of the Wayo Wayoan people. As representatives of coastal foothill Pangcah and alpine Bunun culture, Hafay and Dahu offer a more hopeful alternative Austronesian future.⁶⁶

The first Formosan Indigenous character the reader meets is Hafay. Hafay is distant from her own tradition because she did not grow up in a Pangcah village. Having left her natal village when she was young, she has no memory of it besides the silver

---

⁶⁰ Wu, *The Man*, 214. See also Aldo Leopold, *A Sand County Almanac: And Sketches Here and There* (Oxford: Oxford University Press, 1949). See Darryl Sterk, "The Apotheosis of Montage: The Videomosaic in *The Man with the Compound Eyes* as a Postmodern Ecological Sublime," *Modern Chinese Literature and Culture* 28, no. 2 (2016): 183–222 for discussion of Wu's use of Leopold.

⁶¹ Wu, *The Man*, 246–47.
⁶² Wu, *The Man*, 85.
⁶³ Wu, *The Man*, 147.
⁶⁴ Wu, *The Man*, 10 & 83–84.
⁶⁵ Wu, *The Man*, 297–99.
⁶⁶ Wayo Wayo is clearly part of the same Austronesian family of cultures and languages as Pangcah and Bunun, as evidenced by pairs of cognates. *Yina*, the Wayo Wayo word for mother, is cognate with *Ina*, the word for mother in Pangcah. The *asamu* fish that enforces taboos on Wayo Wayo is cognate with the word for taboo in Bunun, *masamu*. Although it appears that the culture and language of Wayo Wayo should come earlier, based on the out of Taiwan hypothesis, the ancestors of Hafay and Dahu would have been in Taiwan before the ancestors of Atile'i set out from Taiwan.

flowers that grew there.⁶⁷ She initially went to live with her mother in a riverside squatter community in the city.⁶⁸ After her mother died, she had to fend for herself. After a period of time working as a "masseuse," a euphemism for sex worker, she built a café called the Seventh Sisid. There, she reconnected with her culture by globalizing it. Now, the *salama* coffee she serves is "a fusion of Brazilian beans with a dash of sorghum, and certain fragrant herbs picked wild in the hills."⁶⁹

Although her name means millet, suggesting autarkic Austronesian agriculture, Hafay's main culturally specific activity is not planting millet but rather gathering wild greens in the coastal foothills.⁷⁰ However, she would not be comfortable describing it as a "culturally specific activity" because she is critical of academic cultural study.⁷¹ An academic study of "Pangcah culture" might assume such a thing exists, when in fact there are multiple Pangcah cultures that have changed over time. The Pangcah origin song that Hafay sings implies not only a familial origin of the Pangcah people but also the ramifications of the culture.⁷² Any of these ramifications are at some kind of distance from any putative cultural source.

Hafay's critique of cultural objectification is a self-critique because she is, as the owner of the Seventh Sisid, engaged in the commodification of her culture. She gathers those herbs, the bounty of nature, to flavor the coffee and garnish the meals she sells to tourists. If they want souvenirs, Hafay sells them works by local Indigenous artists and bottles of millet wine in fancy boxes that she takes on consignment. She no doubt sells these things to help struggling local artists and entrepreneurs, and she views the art and the wine ironically: the artists had nothing better to do, and what is millet wine for outside of a ritual context?⁷³ As a self-critical capitalist, Hafay humanizes and localizes capitalism. Her self-criticism leads her to set clear limits. When tourists ask her to sing a song on request, she makes them an offer they are sure to refuse: a hundred dollars for *them* to sing a song for *her*.⁷⁴ Locals are welcome to come in at any time and pour themselves a free cup of coffee.⁷⁵

Unlike Hafay, whose mother never insisted that her daughter lead a traditional life, Dahu had to argue with his traditional father about how he lives his life. In a charming conversation with his father, he pointed out that his father was once a kid who had to listen to his own father.⁷⁶ Dahu listened to his father until he failed the test of manhood by shooting the ear of the wrong animal in the Bunun coming-of-age

---

⁶⁷ Wu, *The Man*, 89–90.
⁶⁸ Wu, *The Man*, 92. There are several such communities in and around Taipei. See Jin-yung Wu, "Amis Aborigine Migrants' Territorialization in Metropolitan Taipei," *Cross-Currents: East Asian History and Culture Review* 1, no. 1 (2012): 1–31.
⁶⁹ Wu, *The Man*, 66.
⁷⁰ Wu, *The Man*, 61.
⁷¹ Wu, *The Man*, 64.
⁷² Wu, *The Man*, 66–67.
⁷³ Wu, *The Man*, 61–62.
⁷⁴ Wu, *The Man*, 63.
⁷⁵ Wu, *The Man*, 64.
⁷⁶ Wu, *The Man*, 154.

ritual.⁷⁷ Following this failure, Dahu had to find his non-traditional way of being a man, like Atile'i. Dahu's father finally gave Dahu his approval on his deathbed, telling Dahu to become a man who knows the mountains in his way.⁷⁸ So Dahu became an ecologist instead of a hunter. As a scientist, he doubts whether the taboos his father taught him have any rational basis.⁷⁹ But he carries on respecting them, apparently out of reverence for his dead father's memory.

Like Hafay with her global fusion coffee, Dahu is cosmopolitan through his daughter Umav. Umav is taking piano lessons in which she learns German pieces. Dahu sees her as a "new breed of Bunun" because she has grown up on cultural influences from everywhere mediated through YouTube.⁸⁰ Umav, the next generation, will avoid replicating the socioeconomic subordination of her mother, who, like Hafay, worked as a "masseuse."

Dahu and Hafay are not romantically involved, but they have been hanging out so long that he feels half Amis.⁸¹ Surely, Hafay will feel partly Bunun if she settles down in the Bunun village introduced near the end of the novel.

After Hafay's café is devastated by the trash tsunami, Dahu proposes a trip for Hafay, Umav, and himself to stay with his Uncle Anu,⁸² who is running an ethnic ecotourist operation in a Bunun village on a mountain in Deer County.⁸³ Anu is given a colorful backstory. He went into debt to buy land to fend off a columbarium consortium and turned the land into a "forest church" formed by two weeping fig trees.⁸⁴ Hafay and Umav spend the night in the forest church.⁸⁵ Anu introduces them to the forest and instructs them in how to relate to it, starting with a prayer.⁸⁶ The creatures of the forest, for instance snakes, are addressed as family members. Actual family members have been absorbed into the forest, like Anu's late son Lien, who can be sensed by anyone who takes one of Anu's ecocultural tours. Anu's teaching has a lot in common with Atile'i's (and Aldo Leopold's)! But Anu has had longer than Atile'i to think about his relationship with modernity. His sense of humor plays around the fact that contemporary Bunun are as modern as anyone. He tells that being over 170 centimeters tall is considered "a disability" for a Bunun hunter and that if you surprise a bear, he will take you to the police station. The mountain huts made of bamboo on a stone foundation are like "a five-star hotel."⁸⁷ Like Hafay and Dahu, Anu tries to

---

⁷⁷ Wu, *The Man*, 184.
⁷⁸ Wu, *The Man*, 187.
⁷⁹ Wu, *The Man*, 101. Dahu could have argued that the taboos help ensure the sustainable use of resources. For an argument along these lines about the Rukai, see Kurtis Pei's 1999 conference paper "Hunting System of the Rukai Tribe in Taiwan, Republic of China," in *Proceedings of the International Union of Game Biologists XXIV Congress*, Thessaloniki, Greece.
⁸⁰ Wu, *The Man*, 120.
⁸¹ Wu, *The Man*, 155.
⁸² Wu, *The Man*, 149.
⁸³ Wu, *The Man*, 150.
⁸⁴ Wu, *The Man*, 52.
⁸⁵ Wu, *The Man*, 259.
⁸⁶ Wu, *The Man*, 259–60.
⁸⁷ Wu, *The Man*, 261, 268.

establish a new relationship between modernity, his tribe, and his tradition in order to survive and even thrive in the age of capitalism.

The village Sazasa that is running the ecotours under Chief Anu's leadership is the most romanticized element of *The Man*. It is described in glowing terms as "a place where sugar cane grows tall, animals leap, folks grow."[88] When Hafay goes on an ecocultural hike with Anu, she feels like a hermit crab that has found a shell or like she has returned to nature's womb.[89] In this way, she seems to have forgotten her earlier critique of cultural commodification.

Anu's operation was based on an actual operation run by a Bunun chief called Aliman (阿力曼) in Luye Township (鹿野鄉, literally "Deer Country Township"), located southern Hualian County, that operated (and continues to operate) on a surprising scale: when I dropped in on my literary tour of the east coast, Aliman told me that he sometimes got two hundred visitors per day on weekends.[90] He was hardly in debt when I met him; though this is only hearsay, he was reputed to have gotten extremely rich. I doubt that most of the hundreds of visitors who go on his tours got as much bang for their buck as Hafay. Then again, it is hard to say how transformative an experience, even one you pay for, might be.

This is not to criticize Wu for not accurately representing Aliman's operation; as a writer, he does not have to represent anything realistically. He represented Aliman's operation idealistically because this kind of enterprise is potentially a source of income for Indigenous people and a way for them to contribute to society by offering a kind of environmental education to non-Indigenous urbanites who are alienated from nature.

Discussion

Does Wu's representation responsibly reflect the realities and possibilities of Indigenous peoples in Taiwan? My answer is a mostly unqualified yes. *The Man* may verge into primitivism at times, but it is also responsibly ironic and realist.

Wayo Wayo may initially seem to be a piece of romantic primitivism, but a close reading reveals that the Wayo Wayoans are not entirely in harmony with their environment: their relations with the creatures they consume are not presented as benign, and their mythology suggests they have the same problem of overconsumption as any other human community. The culture that orients them in this environment is not a body of unquestioned belief but a guide to survival that can be questioned and adapted through the generational, sexual, and cultural conflicts that take Rasula to the Bermuda Triangle and Atile'i to Taiwan. In Taiwan, Atile'i begins to question aspects of his own tradition.[91] Wu cuts his self-questioning process short with the destruction

---

[88] Wu, *The Man*, 268.
[89] Wu, *The Man*, 262.
[90] Darryl Sterk, "What I Learned Translating Wu Ming-yi's *The Man with the Compound Eyes*," *Compilation and Translation Review* 6, no. 2 (2013): 253–61.
[91] Wu, *The Man*, 271.

of Wayo Wayo and the deaths of Atile'i and Rasula but shows where it might lead in Taiwan.

Wu cites Pangcah and Bunun cultures as examples of coastal foothill and alpine Formosan Indigenous cultures that, similarly, are not cultural essences but guides to survival to be adapted through the same kinds of conflicts. In a modern context, Hafay and Dahu have become detached from, and critical of, their cultural traditions, and in reconnecting with those traditions they have recreated them in order to address contemporary problems: their own socioeconomic subordination, extreme overconsumption, and the sense of alienation from the natural environment that many modern people suffer from, be they Indigenous, Han, or members of other ethnic groups or nationalities. In *The Man*, Indigenous people help themselves through humanized small-scale capitalism, and in helping themselves, they help non-Indigenous people. Wu believes that this is a role for Indigenous leaders like Aliman to play as they try to provide opportunities for their communities by helping alienated non-Indigenous urbanites. I imagine Aliman thinks so, too.

Two comparisons to films, one local and one global, can highlight *The Man*'s responsible, ironic approach to the representation of Indigenous peoples. The first comparison is to *Fishing Luck* (等待飛魚, 2005). As Anita Chang argues, the Indigenous setting for the film, Orchid Island, is presented for the consumption of a tourist, a young woman in search of authentic experience, which she finds scuba diving and in the arms of a young Tao man.[92] To me, *Fishing Luck* is like a tourist brochure. Parts of *The Man* read like descriptions in a tourist brochure for Indigenous areas in eastern Taiwan, but then, except for Anu's village Sazasa, which is garbage-free in the novel and blighted by roadside litter in real life, Wu Ming-yi undermines his descriptions by covering the places in garbage. There is even plastic litter on Wayo Wayo, which is reminiscent of Orchid Island. Unlike Orchid Island, Wayo Wayo is a place that only anthropologists have visited, not a place that tourists could visit. As for romance, Wu Ming-yi uses romance to motivate Atile'i and Rasula, but he undermines it in Taiwan: Alice does not find anyone to take her late husband Thom's place, and Dahu and Hafay remain friends to the end. Finally, Sazasa does seem to be a site of authentic experience, but after going on a nature walk with Chief Anu, Sara decides to stay and study the place as a scientist, not as a tourist.[93] I imagine she will behave more responsibly than the anthropologists who sired children on Wayo Wayo.

The second comparison is to James Cameron's *Avatar*. As Slavoj Žižek argues, *Avatar* adapts a "racist" white-savior romance-and-violence formula for an audience of consumers of MMORPGs.[94] Racist romantic primitivism is a highly marketable commodity, and not just among gamers: *Avatar* reclaimed the highest-grossing film title in March 2020.[95] *The Man* arguably rode the *Avatar* wave in its passage to world

---

[92] Anita Chang, "In the Realm of the Indigenous: Local, National, and Global Articulations in *Fishing Luck*," *Positions: East Asia Cultures Critique* 17, no. 3 (2009): 643–53.

[93] Wu, *The Man*, 289.

[94] An avatar is an identity in a massively multiplayer online game (MMORPG). See Slavoj Žižek, "Avatar: Return of the Natives," *New Statesman*, March 4, 2010.

[95] "Avatar Reclaims Title as Highest Grossing Film," *BBC*, March 15, 2021.

literature, but Wu Ming-yi offers a much more sophisticated treatment of Indigenous peoples than James Cameron. I have shown how Wu undermines reader expectations of romance, and the only violence in *The Man* is the "slow violence" of gradual environmental degradation, which Wu speeds up in the most dramatic scene in the novel when a tidal wave of trash crashes into Taiwan's east coast.[96] *The Man* also undermines expectations of outside salvation. The foreign experts, Detlef the German engineer and Sara the Norwegian marine biologist, who visit Taiwan after the trash wave hits, might be expected to play the role of a savior or leader, but they do not end up saving anyone or leading anything. Instead, they work alongside Taiwanese experts and volunteers, both Han and Indigenous.

A final comparison might help spotlight Wu Ming-yi's position as a writer with the opportunity to represent Taiwan to the world, including Indigenous Taiwan. This comparison is between Taiwan and Australia. In his introduction to the second edition of his magisterial monograph on the representation of Australian Indigenous peoples in Australian literature at a time when Indigenous Australians like Alexis Wright were beginning to publish, J. J. Healy wrote that perhaps it was time for white authors to fall into silence about the "blackfellow" and let him speak for himself (or her for herself).[97] Non-Indigenous Han Taiwanese writers reached a similar moment in the 1980s, at the beginning of the Indigenous literary movement, but they have hardly fallen into silence. High-profile non-Indigenous writers like Wu Ming-yi continue to write about Formosan Indigenous peoples, crowding out Indigenous writers, both at home and abroad. When *The Man* was published, no book by an Indigenous Taiwanese writer had been translated into English, though John Balcom had translated short pieces by many authors for *Indigenous Writers of Taiwan*.[98] To date, Husluman Vava's (霍斯陸曼·伐伐) *The Soul of Jade Mountain* (玉山的生命精靈, originally published in 1997) and Sakinu Ahronglong's (亞榮隆·撒可努) *Hunter School* have appeared in English translation.[99] Readers of environmental world literature should all welcome such works and read them alongside novels by the likes of Wu Ming-yi. I hope that someday soon an Indigenous Taiwanese writer will have a contribution to make to the canon of environmental world literature. Or rather, writers like Sakinu Ahronglong, Husluman Vava, and the soon-to-be-translated Syaman Rapongan have *already* started to make contributions, and it is now up to literary critics to acknowledge and discuss them.

---

[96] Wu, *The Man*, 129–31. On the "slow violence" that Wu speeds up, see Rob Nixon, *Slow Violence and the Environmentalism of the Poor* (Boston: Harvard University Press, 2011).
[97] J. J. Healy, *Literature and the Aborigine in Australia* (St. Lucia: University of Queensland Press, 1989).
[98] John Balcom and Yingtish Balcom, eds., *Indigenous Writers of Taiwan: An Anthology of Stories, Essays, and Poems* (New York: Columbia University Press, 2005).
[99] See Husluman Vava, *The Soul of Jade Mountain*, trans. Terence Russell (Amherst: Cambria, 2020) and Sakinu Ahronglong, *Hunter School*, trans. Darryl Sterk (London: Honford Star, 2020). Sakinu Ahronglong's hunter school is similar to Aliman's ethnic ecotourism operation.

6

The Foreign at Home: World Literature, Viral Postmodernism, and *Notes of a Desolate Man*

Nicholas A. Kaldis

The 1994 publication of Chu T'ien-wen's (朱天文) novel *Notes of a Desolate Man* (荒人手記; hereafter also referred to as *Notes*) was a literary phenomenon, precipitating considerable discussion and debate.[1] Whether hailing *Notes* as a rare literary achievement, disparaging its challenging style and content (both negatively characterized as "westernized"), or criticizing its representation of gay culture in Taiwan, fans and detractors alike observed the meticulously wrought postmodern features of the novel, and the literary world conferred recognition upon it with such awards as the prestigious *China Times* Novel Prize.[2]

The novel reads as an autobiographical quasi-bildungsroman of a forty-year-old gay Taiwanese man referred to only as "Shao."[3] In a rambling first-person narrative, constantly self-interrupted by tangential discussions, Shao describes selected events from his past, mostly related to love, sex, friendship, and family. His reflections are prompted by the recent death from AIDS of his best friend Ah Yao (full name Huang Shuyao), whom he helped care for during the latter's final agonizing days in a Japanese clinic.

I argue that *Notes of a Desolate Man*'s postmodern content and form work in tandem to insinuate the idea of a Western-originating, debauched, and contagious *lifestyle* and *literature* that are implicitly infecting Taiwan society and culture. The portrayal of a cosmopolitan gay yuppie protagonist, characters, and lifestyle exposes a hidden but

---

[1] Chu T'ien-wen, 荒人手記 [*Notes of a Desolate Man*] (Taipei: China Times, 1997). The work was later translated by Howard Goldblatt and Sylvia Li-chun Lin (New York: Columbia University Press, 1999).

[2] A discussion of the discourse surrounding this controversial text can be found in Nicholas A. Kaldis, "Infectious Postmodernism in/as *Notes of a Desolate Man*," 臺灣東亞文明研究學刊 [*Taiwan Journal of East Asian Studies*] 9, no. 1 (2012): 47–78. For a concise summary of the socioeconomic history of the era of the novel's writing and contents, see June Yip, *Envisioning Taiwan: Fiction, Cinema, and the Nation in the Cultural Imaginary* (Durham: Duke University Press, 2004), especially 211–15. Although Yip presents cogent discussions of globalization and postmodernity in Taiwan, curiously, no mention is made of *Notes of a Desolate Man*.

[3] In the Chinese original, this reference is to "little Shao" (小韶), during a phone call in which a friend of the character prefixes the familiarizing particle.

seemingly ubiquitous mutation in familiar heteronormativity, a male homosexual subculture surreptitiously spreading across the island—introduced into the social system via newly forming pathways, such as the underground urban network of "secret portals" (祕口) used by gay culture insiders in the novel. Formally, *Notes* instantiates a distilled and dizzying example of postmodern narrative, most notable in its I-narrator's stream-of-consciousness non sequitur ramblings, many of which are comprised of seemingly inexhaustible Western cultural references.

Owing to the ubiquity of these dual features of its style and content, the novel seems destined to compel Taiwanese readers to conflate its negatively inflected (self-loathing, exhibitionistic, lubricious, superficial) gay male characters (not infrequently stereotypes) and their social microcosm with the exhibitionistic postmodern narrative technique through which they are brought to life. This, I argue, provokes a paranoid revulsion toward both the perceived foreign mutation of local literary traditions and the invasive infection's alien lifestyle.

Notes of a Desolate Man as World Literature

Ubiquitous world cultural references—to an astonishing variety of things American, Japanese, PRC, Indian, Egyptian, French, Italian, Russian, biblical, and others—are the major constituents from which the I-narrator protagonist and his peers form their identities. They visit (mostly as tourists) and/or identify with these places and their cultural products, which they have thoroughly incorporated into their worldview, social interactions, and self-positioning (i.e., their Bourdieusian *habitus*). Their cosmopolitanism is mirrored in the (sub)theme of domestic exile and foreignness with which the narrator associates Taiwanese homosexual identity. To be gay in Taiwan is, for Shao and his cohort, to be socially ostracized ("desolate"), inextricably bound up with feelings of self-loathing, loneliness, marginalization, and degradation.

This compounded sense of foreignness marks *Notes* as a work of world literature. It does so, I would argue, in a unique (or less-frequently observed) way. *Prior* to its translation into English and other foreign languages, *Notes* could be described in terms identical to those used to map the unique features constituting world literature; it is, for example, "predicated on cultural heterogeneity. It maps a space where works from diverse cultures and literary traditions engage in dialogues with one another while competing for recognition."[4] It also incorporates an abundance of "unsettling foreign textual knowledge that destabilize[s]" the reading experience, which can

---

[4] Kuei-fen Chiu and Táňa Dluhošová, "Introduction: East Asian and Southeast Asian Literature in the World Literary Space," *Archiv Orientální* 89, no. 2 (2021): 225. Echoing the work of David Damrosch, Chiu, and Dluhošová present a concise distillation of concepts concerning the mix of "commonalities" and "differences" we encounter in literature from other cultures, how a writer or work can serve as a conduit or locus of negotiation between different cultures, the incorporation of foreign knowledge into a literary agenda for transforming domestic culture and society, and so on. See David Damrosch, *How to Read World Literature* (Malden, MA: Wiley-Blackwell, 2009), 23; "World Literature, National Contexts," *Modern Philology* 100, no. 4 (May 2003): 514.

unsettle readers "in new and surprising ways," expanding their "field of vision" as they experience "the shock of the new."[5] This is to say that, for Taiwanese readers encountering *Notes* in its source language (Chinese), the novel consistently destabilizes "prior experience, [...] the fund of knowledge and expectations developed within the home tradition," catalyzing what David Damrosch identifies as a—or *the*—key event marking a text as world literature, in which the reader gains access to "resources and aesthetic experiences beyond what is available at home."[6]

In other words, *Notes* is foreign and exoticizing *from its source-language inception* and *within* its domestic social and linguistic community, owing to such features as the narrator's use of Western-language words, which appear without glosses to assist domestic readers, the narrative's "often idiosyncratic semantics and grammatical structure," and the overall "intentional opacity of the text."[7] That opacity includes a nonlinear narrative replete with non sequitur tangents, a panoply of non-Taiwanese images, personages, and cultural and intellectual references, all conveyed through a perspective of limited affinity with its readership, that is, the point of view of a member of a marginalized subaltern minority whose experiences would be utterly unfamiliar to the majority of local readers.[8] However, contrary to the conventional argument that world literature expands the experiential horizons of its readers in edifying ways, *Notes* stigmatizes both the alien subculture it explores on the margins of (or hidden within) local readers' familiar domestic environment and the cultures outside of Taiwan's borders that readers encounter in its pages. This impels a kneejerk, antagonistic reaction to both domestic and foreign otherness, rather than sympathetic identification or empathetic unsettlement in the encounter with the other.[9]

In what follows, I will elaborate on the postmodern features of the novel which, intentionally or not, produce an unsettling reading experience that is arguably less edifying than it is antagonistic or even hostile.

---

[5] David Damrosch, "Frames for World Literature," in *Grenzen der Literatur. Zu Begriff und Phänomen des Literarischen*, ed. Simone Winko, Fotis Jannidis, and Gerhard Lauer (Berlin: De Gruyter, 2009), 505; Damrosch, *How to Read World Literature*, 3.

[6] Damrosch, "Frames for World Literature," 513. The novel's sense of foreignness in the Taiwanese context, especially its many Western words and ubiquitous cultural references, is not diluted much in translation. The English translators begin their brief preface by recalling how they had to embark on many a "treasure hunt" through books and video resources in the process of translating *Notes*, which is only partially represented by their far-from-exhaustive appendix of some two-dozen or more explanatory notes for English language readers. See *Notes*, 167–69.

[7] Goldblatt and Lin, "Translator's Preface," in *Notes of a Desolate Man*, vii–viii.

[8] This perhaps fits within or expands Damrosch's argument concerning the "multiple senses" and "frames of reference" within which "world literature is continually formed and reformed." See Damrosch, "Frames for World Literature," 96.

[9] This does in fact fit within one of David Damrosch's descriptions of a work that "profoundly challenges home-country values" and finds many readers abroad. See Damrosch, "Frames for World Literature," 497.

Postmodern Features

Notes is a thoroughly postmodern text in its characters, style, form, and content. The I-narrator protagonist, Shao, is an exceedingly erudite, widely traveled, cosmopolitan, hip, effeminate,[10] metro/homosexual man with a PhD in some sort of cultural studies and contemporary academic theory. Leaving aside for the moment Shao's characterization, some of the novel's prominent postmodern features include, among other things:

1. The leveling of "high and low" culture that is a trademark of postmodernity;[11] I argue that in this novel, such a leveling renders psychological depth indistinguishable from superficiality.
2. The celebratory representation of a consumer-flâneur lifestyle, reflected in a cosmopolitan acquisitiveness that constantly places the narrative in the service of a sojourning connoisseur's exhaustive inventories of commodities, tastes, and encounters. As Ban Wang observes, Shao and his companions are "set adrift on a consumerist spree of 'cultural and historical goods,'" blind to each object's "origin or context of acquisition."[12]
3. The third, and perhaps most pronounced, indicator of the novel's postmodernity is its nonlinear, frequently non sequitur narration that freely leaps from high to low cultural references in passages that dizzy the reader with their astonishing miscellanies. As Carlos Rojas has noted, "The 'postmodern' quality of *Notes of a Desolate Man* not only is exemplified by the lack of a unitary linear narrative at the level of the novel's plot but also is visible in the complex pastiche of allusions making up the work."[13]

---

[10] Shao repeatedly describes gay men as belonging to the category of the "feminine" (陰 or 雌). Chapter Eight, for example, contains an extensive elaboration of the feminine qualities of gay men.

[11] In addition to David Harvey, *The Condition of Postmodernity: An Enquiry into the Origins of Social Change* (Oxford: Blackwell, 1990), the essays collected in *Post-Ality: Marxism and Postmodernism*, issue I of *Transformation: Marxist Boundary Work in Theory, Economics, Politics, and Culture*, ed. Mas'ud Zavarzadeh, Teresa L. Ebert, and Donald Morton (Washington, DC: Maisonneuve Press, 1995), and other well-known analyses of postmodernism, see also Jameson's summary of theories of the postmodern in his foreword to *The Postmodern Condition: A Report on Knowledge*, by Jean-François Lyotard, trans. Geoff Bennington and Brian Massumi (Minneapolis: University of Minnesota Press, 1991). Among the best summaries of postmodernity in the PRC are Xiaobing Tang, "The Function of New Theory: What Does It Mean to Talk about Postmodernism in China?" in *Politics, Ideology, and Literary Discourse in Modern China: Theoretical Interventions and Cultural Critique*, ed. Xiaobing Tang and Kang Liu (Durham: Duke University Press, 1993), 278–99, and Xiaobing Yang, *The Chinese Postmodern: Trauma and Irony in Chinese Avant-Garde Fiction* (Ann Arbor: The University of Michigan Press, 2002).

[12] Ban Wang, "Reenchanting the Image in Global Culture: Reification and Nostalgia in Zhu Tianwen's Fiction," in *Writing Taiwan: A New Literary History*, ed. David Der-wei Wang and Carlos Rojas (Durham: Duke University Press, 2007), 382–3.

[13] See Carlos Rojas, "Chu T'ien-wen and Cinematic Shadows," in *The Naked Gaze: Reflections on Chinese Modernity* (Cambridge, MA: Harvard University Asia Center, 2008), 288. See Kaldis, "Infectious Postmodernism," 53, for a contrast of narratives between the postmodern *Notes of a Desolate Man* and Wang Wen-hsing's (王文興) modernist *Family Catastrophe* (家變).

Upon closer inspection, the rambling narrative is an accumulation of seemingly random tangential references around solemn topics. In recurring instances, Shao's meditations on somber themes such as disease, death, AIDS, sorrow, loneliness, suffering, and alienation are undermined and overwhelmed by the ease and rapidity with which he consistently veers away from any serious probing of these issues into prolix pop culture panoplies and turgid quasi-intellectual treatises. For example, the twelve-line first chapter opens: "This is an age of decadence. This is an age of prophecy. I am securely bonded with it, sinking to the bottom, the very bottom."[14] After touching upon other weighty matters concerning sexual depravity, the Bible, heaven, hell, eternity, and Buddhism, the chapter concludes with a portentous existential declaration: "[l]iving and dying serenely with [...] loneliness, looking death straight in the eye, I am no longer afraid."[15] Chapter Two continues in this dour vein for a short while, as Shao describes his last conversations with Ah Yao as the latter was in the final throes of AIDS. Yet here, but a few pages into the novel, the capricious postmodern bricolage of Shao's narration already begins to overwhelm the ponderous issues and language with which the novel opened. Chapter Two references include: Act Up, Greta Garbo, octopi, the Ganges river, New York, San Francisco, Tokyo, the Shifen Waterfall of Taiwan, Brian de Palma, *Man of La Mancha* with Peter O'Toole and Sophia Loren, Tony Orlando and Dawn's "Tie a Yellow Ribbon," Spanish, English, and Japanese words in the Chinese text, Fellini, the wife of Rhodes, Lord Jesus, Noh Drama, Japanese tea ritual, the Epistle of Jude, Ozu Yasujiro, details of Tokyo's geography and train lines, Eliot's "The Waste Land," Daoism, Kaposi's sarcomas, the New Testament, the Japanese Festival of the Dead, and more, all within the space of ten pages. Chapter Two ends with the narrator mourning the death of his best friend, crying out, "'*People, people who need people*,' as Barbra Streisand sang [...]. My tears were falling; as the wind and rain died out, then returned, I wailed in agony. Ah Yao, he was already gone!"[16]

Oblivious to the awkward or inappropriate nature of associating Barbra Streisand's melodramatic song with the tragedy of his best friend's death, Shao begins Chapter Three thusly: "Ah Yao was gone. Cold, hard reality confronted me. Gone, what does it mean to be gone? [...] Michael Jackson said, I was born to be immortal. This resilient moonwalker from the West [...]."[17] This is followed by an extended discussion of Michael Jackson, with diversions into Rider Haggard, the film *Home Alone*, an abrupt discussion of Ingmar Bergman, Luis Buñuel, Mel Gibson, eternal signifiers, and so on. These passages from the first three (of fifteen) chapters exemplify much of the novel's structure. Here and throughout, postmodern bricolage and pastiche[18] drown out the gravitas associated with the themes of grief, loneliness, personal loss, mourning, and

---

[14] Chu, *Notes*, 1.
[15] Chu, *Notes*, 2.
[16] Chu, *Notes*, 12.
[17] Chu, *Notes*, 13.
[18] J. A. Cuddon counts among the key features of postmodern writing, "an eclectic approach [...] and pastiche." See *The Penguin Dictionary of Literary Terms and Literary Theory* (London: Penguin Books, 1999), 690.

AIDS ravaging the gay community—themes which the narrator on several occasions proclaims to be the impetus for his writing.[19]

Postmodern (In-)alienation

The immediacy of events, the sensationalism of the spectacle (political, scientific, military, as well as those of entertainment), become the stuff of which consciousness is forged.

—David Harvey[20]

In an insightful essay on the novel, Carlos Rojas takes at face value the invocation of serious themes in *Notes* while downplaying how those themes are undermined by the superficial rhetorical style within which they are couched: "[T]he 'desolate man' […] cloaks himself in cultural and philosophical allusions in order to fend off and contain the specters of 'desolation' and 'death.'"[21] Where Rojas sees Shao's utterances as strategically designed to "cloak" and "fend off" these specters, desolation and death are in fact consistently and thoroughly undermined at the structural level of the text, evoked by the narrator only to be quickly dissipated via a narcissistic and magisterial display of an astonishing amount of trivial and scholarly information (knowledge), only some of which can be characterized as philosophical allusions.[22]

Rojas's reading of the novel's postmodern "pastiche of allusions" as reflective of the protagonist's genuine psychological struggle with the "specters" of desolation and death is generous. Many critical appraisals of the same postmodern narrative techniques identified by Rojas attribute such features to an ideological disavowal of both class inequalities and alienation in postmodern theory and art. Postmodern (fictional) narrative, as characterized in these appraisals, deconstructs subjectivity in ways that untether it from overarching discursive frameworks which might otherwise provide a critical perspective on the subject's ideological and concrete subjection

---

[19] We can assume that many Taiwanese readers might find the postmodern levelling of difference between the solemn and the silly particularly offensive in passages such as that in which Shao recalls his lack of feeling over his father's death from stomach cancer (after seeing him in the hospital "with tubes sticking out of nearly every orifice of his body"), which didn't affect him nearly as deeply as his "lost [first] love"—a torrid superficial affair with a gorgeous dancer that ended with the revelation of the latter's infidelity (Chu, *Notes*, 133). Where readers would expect some expression of filial grief, Shao invokes Western pop culture in the image and upbeat singing and whistling of Walt Disney's Jiminy Cricket. See Kaldis, "Infectious Postmodernism," 55, for a contrast of Shao's breezy, ludic, postmodern rejection of traditional Chinese familial bonds to Pai Hsien-yung's treatment of filiality and family/clan in his modernist novel *Crystal Boys*.

[20] Harvey, *The Condition of Postmodernity*, 54.

[21] See Rojas, "Chu T'ien-wen and Cinematic Shadows," 290.

[22] Drawing on the work of Xudong Zhang, Xiaobing Yang's analysis of narratorial manifestations of "indeterminate history and memory" in the postmodern works of PRC author Ge Fei points to a similar "constant dissemination[s] of meaning, without reaching an absolute, self-sufficient knowledge that might otherwise confirm his historical identity." Yang, *The Chinese Postmodern*, 183.

within the economy of global capital and its local cultural variations. Postmodern narrative presents, in this scenario, "a world free from any imposed scheme of meaning or extracted pattern of significance."[23] Such incisive critiques expose how traumatic encounters with pivotal experiences—such as desolation and death—in a postmodern novel like *Notes* are consistently deprived of their existential import by being evoked only to be immediately deprived of significance through dissociation into precisely the type of pastiche of allusions found throughout Chu's novel, that is, iterations of astonishing catalogs of information—both trifling and weighty—from characters who are little more than acquisitive consumer-beings reveling in (fantasies of) constant plenitude.[24] Rather than being prompted by his loneliness and despair to undertake introspection or self-analysis, Shao instead seeks haven in emotionally nonthreatening clinical narrative taxonomies.

In breaching and overwhelming any clear demarcations between the profound and the petty, *Notes* thereby succeeds in foreclosing on an alienated gay identity whose encounters with AIDS-related premature death, loneliness, and exclusion from mainstream heterosexual society and the Confucian family system might otherwise enunciate a subjectivity that is excruciatingly aware of its estrangement. In its eschewal of alienation, the novel is thoroughly postmodern. To borrow from Terry Eagleton's dissection of postmodernism, characters in *Notes* are neither "agonizedly caught up in metaphysical depth" nor "able to experience psychic fragmentation and social alienation as spiritually wounding," for they have outlived "all that fantasy of interiority" and abandoned "epistemological paranoia" for the "brute objectivity of random subjectivity."[25]

Eagleton's views resonate with Ban Wang's analysis of the "evaporation of subjectivity" in Chu T'ien-wen's fiction.[26] Much like Eagleton, Wang observes "the consumer of 'cultural goods' is less a subject, possessing a complex internal life and rich experience, than a particle adrift with the fashions of the moment in the stream of circumstances. The inner, integrated consciousness is erased."[27] This link between "the

---

[23] Zavarzadeh, qtd. in Paul Maltby, "Excerpts from *Dissident Postmodernists*," in *A Postmodern Reader*, ed. Joseph Natoli and Linda Hutcheon (Albany: State University of New York Press, 1993), 520.

[24] This chapter is by no means an attempt to dismiss all postmodernist fiction as unethical or amoral. I intend rather to expose a problematically conservative bias underlying the structure and content of *Notes of a Desolate Man*. Some postmodern authors whose novels do *not* glibly elide the distinction between serious existential probing of subjectivity, elitist/high and popular/low culture would, in my estimation, include Thomas Pynchon, Haruki Murakami, Don DeLillo, Toni Morrison, William Gass, William Gaddis, and Martin Amis, to mention a few.

[25] See Terry Eagleton, "Capitalism, Modernism, and Postmodernism," in *Modern Criticism and Theory: A Reader*, ed. David Lodge (London: Longman, 1988), 394–5.

[26] While Eagleton and Wang launch Marxist or quasi-Marxist assaults on many features of postmodernism, for the most rigorous, sustained, and implacable discursive pillorying of all things postmodern, see the prolific writings of Mas'ud Zavarzadeh. See also Peter Nicholls's excellent, nuanced efforts to formulate "an alternative postmodernism [...] which is fully historical," grounded in his careful readings of Toni Morrison's fiction, for an entirely different version of the postmodern in the article "The Belated Postmodern: History, Phantoms, and Toni Morrison," in *Psychoanalytic Criticism: A Reader*, ed. Sue Vice (Cambridge: Polity Press, 1996), 50–74.

[27] See Ban Wang, "Reenchanting the Image in Global Culture," 380. Xudong Zhang likewise connects (Ge Fei's) postmodern narrative's figuration of "the abandoned self in objects" to "an alienated relationship to the world." See Zhang, *Chinese Modernism in the Era of Reforms* (Durham: Duke University Press, 1997), 194.

theater of consumption" and identity, so integral to *Notes of a Desolate Man*, is one of the dominant features of "post-al" society, a term coined by Mas'ud Zavarzadeh in his effort to expose how the ideologically cultivated illusion of "[c]hoice in consumption, lifestyle, sexuality" asserts a sense of self that stymies collective politics by encouraging individuals to equate pathological acquisitiveness with identity, so they can "assert their difference from others."[28]

Eagleton, Wang, and Zavarzadeh share common critical ground in their vision of the "randomness" and "non-interiority" of the postmodern subject whose inner world is "complex" only in the *quantity* of its accretions—precisely the type of interiority found in Shao's narrative.[29] For Zavarzadeh, the postmodern worldview is thoroughly "ludic" in its eschewal of metanarratives such as humanism, Hegelian history, or Marxism. Consequently, the postmodern individual experiences a world leveled, "socially flat," where "everything affects everything else without anyone having (explanatory) priority over the others. Each social entity has its own immanent laws of intelligibility and is self-determining."[30] It is not coincidental that Zavarzadeh frequently points to the works of Foucault—one of Shao's heroes—as exemplifying postmodernism's "ludic deconstruction of binaries" such as "powerful-powerless, dominant-dominated, subjugating-subjugated, and above all [...] (social) 'class' (ruling-ruled).'"[31]

Class is in fact effectively absent from *Notes of a Desolate Man*. The rendering of gay male subculture in the novel reifies the notion of "an incommensurable [social] 'inside'" and disavows "an 'outside' such as class or economics."[32] The non-alienated uber-consumerist middle- and upper-middle-class gay Taiwanese characters presented in

---

[28] Mas'ud Zavarzadeh, "Post-Ality: The (Dis)Simulations of Cybercapitalism," in *Post-Ality: Marxism and Postmodernism*, 13.

[29] While definitions of postmodernity largely agree that it is a global phenomenon, many scholars have discussed the phenomenon in terms specific to Taiwan and/or PRC culture. See, e.g., Sung-sheng Yvonne Chang for a brief but rigorous analysis of literary and socio-political postmodernist discourse in Taiwan in *Literary Culture in Taiwan: Martial Law to Market Law* (New York: Columbia University Press, 2004), 183–86 & 193–99; *Modernism and the Nativist Resistance: Contemporary Chinese Fiction from Taiwan* (Durham: Duke University Press, 1993), 179–80; and June Yip for a more nuanced and upbeat take on postmodern Taiwan cosmopolitanism in *Envisioning Taiwan: Fiction, Cinema, and the Nation in the Cultural Imaginary* (Durham: Duke University Press, 2004), 211–48. For a thoroughgoing definition and sustained rooting out of all things Chinese (PRC) postmodern, see Yang, *The Chinese Postmodern*; Liu Kang provides an analysis of both the larger general and specific local-historical conditions of postmodernity in the PRC, with careful attention to the latter in *Globalization and Cultural Trends in China* (Honolulu: University of Hawai'i Press, 2004).

[30] Mas'ud Zavarzadeh, *Seeing Films Politically* (Albany: State University of New York Press, 1991), 35.

[31] Zavarzadeh, *Seeing Films Politically*, 34. See Jason McGrath for some insightful comments on the appearance of ludic "postmodern irony" in some of Feng Xiaogang's New Year's films, within a larger argument linking twenty-first-century PRC postmodernity to "the fundamental dynamics of capitalist modernity itself" in *Postsocial Modernity: Chinese Cinema, Literature, and Criticism in the Market Age* (Stanford: Stanford University Press, 2008), 7. Arif Dirlik and Xudong Zhang, a decade earlier, problematized the notion of PRC postmodernism on the basis of the "coexistence of the precapitalist, the capitalist, and the postsocialist economic, political, and social forms" in their "Introduction: Postmodernism and China," *Boundary 2*, vol. 24, no. 3 (1997): 3; see also the many excellent essays collected in their edited volume on the topic.

[32] Zavarzadeh, *Seeing Films Politically*, 40.

Chu T'ien-wen's novel, ensconced as they are in the "cozy affluence of [a] closeted yuppie gay" life, I would argue, are rendered incapable of authentic political empowerment.[33] Additionally, the novel's incessant indulgence in detailing their superficial pseudo-intellectualizing and narcissistic concerns disavows any "outside" perspective necessary for oppositional political practices based in ostracism from mainstream society (which Shao frequently laments) or forged through solidarity with other classes. In the world of Chu's sybaritic gay characters, you are what you can purchase, whether it be high-end antiaging skincare products and rituals or the memories and mementos of leisurely, sex-filled holidays in Rome, Rimini, New Orleans, San Francisco, and so on.[34] Acquisitiveness rather than "consumption" is the proper word for their postmodern (self-)branding, for they accessorize themselves both literally and figuratively, showing off a Dead Sea mineral mud mask in the same fashion as recounting a trip to Fellini's hometown. Their identity is bolstered by constant reiterations of the objects and experiences they have acquired. These hysterical displays of plenitude are a type of dissociation, a defense mechanism that diverts awareness away from traumas such as societal alienation. Furthermore, the aggregative nature of the characters' acquisitive consumerist lifestyle is inseparable from the novel's postmodern narrative technique (e.g., its pastiche of allusions), both functioning defensively to, as Rojas phrases it, "cloak" and "fend off" alienation, isolation, and mortality.

The potential for oppositional politics—in this case, for imagining alternatives to the consumerist and heterosexist status quos (Shao notably wails only against the latter)—depends on the subject experiencing alienation from the mainstream social order. The potential for such awareness is rendered moot by the permanent orchestrated distraction of the characters' acquisitive lifestyle and the narrative's cumulative prose. The spokesman for a self-described subaltern class, Shao habitually inscribes his experience into encyclopedic laundry lists (both erudite and facile), overwhelming with volubility a sustained reckoning with his suffering. This conflation of high and low culture into a potpourri of self-distraction, rather than questioning the function of either or the

---

[33] Liang-ya Liou, "在全球化與在地化的交錯之中 ： 白先勇、李昂、朱天文與紀大偉小說中的男同性戀呈現" [At the Intersection of the Global and the Local: Representations of Male Homosexuality in Fictions by Pai Hsien-yung, Li Ang, Chu T'ien-wen, and Chi Ta-wei], *Chung-Wai Literary Quarterly* 32, no. 3 (2003): 15–16.

[34] It is notable that the novel's only character to invoke PRC/Maoist class politics is neither gay nor from Taiwan. In Chapter Six, a honeymooning Shao and his partner Yongjie stay at the Rome apartment of their friend Momo, depicted as a heterosexual, blue-eyed, gesticulating ethnic Italian. Shao recalls that, in 1974, inspired by Cultural Revolution era Maoism (as opposed to tourism), Momo left Italy to attend Liaoning University and worked in the Northern Wasteland (agriculturally barren region of Heilongjiang Province). In the present-day of the novel (c. early 1990s), a drunken Momo enthusiastically sings "Chairman Mao is the helmsman of our proletarian homeland," which Shao and Yongjie find "totally absurd," scoffing at Momo's "naïve infatuation with China" (Chu, *Notes*, 52–53). The sole character speaking for an identity grounded in class politics is depicted as a dilettantish Western Sinophile foolishly brainwashed by Maoism. There is no irony to this scene; that is, the narrative does not in any way frame Momo as speaking truths the other characters refuse to acknowledge. Momo, a straight European with PRC-inspired leftist politics who only briefly appears during Shao and Yongjie's hedonistic Roman holiday, is constructed and singled out as an aberration in *Notes*; no person or ideology similar to that represented by Momo appears elsewhere in the novel.

distinction between the two, dissolves the possibility of heteroglossic tension between the serious and the superficial and deprives subjects marginalized by heteronormativity an oppositional perspective on the center/mainstream. Otherness sans alienation is the result.

A reader could, on the other hand, choose to overlook this criticism of the novel's postmodernism and celebrate instead how *Notes of a Desolate Man* promotes awareness of the serious themes confronting gay subjects in Taiwan. Indeed, at first blush, the events and many characters in the novel do seem to be affirmatively inscribing images of gay subjectivity into Taiwan's cultural imagination, bolstering the social visibility, viability, contributions, and legitimacy of a minority group that is frequently marginalized in mainstream society.[35] In addition, the narrative sympathetically manipulates the traumatic experiences of loss, ostracism, internalized homophobia,[36] and AIDS endured by Taiwan's gay community, which might be seen as deterring potential critique of this marginalized subculture. But, while the content of the novel does indeed portray many events that could have evoked empathy and erected a bulwark against homophobic censure, the opposite is in fact the case, owing to the rhetorical excess of the novel's narrative style. The formal properties of the narration— the protagonist's effusive, logorrheic monologue with its ludic undertones, prolix self-interruptions, exhausting laundry lists of cultural acquisitions and academic references, and so on—accrue to all but guarantee that even the most sympathetic reader is positioned to find the traumas of desolate loneliness, AIDS, familial ostracism, and so on either entirely drowned out or mutating into mere melodramatic tropes, foreclosing on empathetic reader engagement.

To restate, *Notes of a Desolate Man*, rather than intervening into or disrupting the artistic and social centers from the margins, conversely incites readers to side with conservative mainstream cultural attitudes and close ranks against a perplexing nontraditional literary form and an unfamiliar peripheral minority subculture.[37] It does so via the uniform deployment of an off-putting postmodern narrative style

---

[35] My interpretation here draws from Rey Chow's analysis of the "global visibility" or lack thereof of (Chinese) local cultural products and identity (in film), vis-a-vis globalization, in *Sentimental Fabulations, Contemporary Chinese Films: Attachment in the Age of Global Visibility* (New York: Columbia University Press, 2007), and from Shu-mei Shih's critical parsing of the function of homosexual characters in Taiwanese films as "marker[s] of advanced civilization [akin to that found] in the West," the viewing of which makes a Taiwanese filmgoer "qualified to become a global citizen," imparting a sense of "Taiwan's successful globalization," and enhancing the fantasy of "the international image of Taiwan." See Shu-mei Shih, "Globalization and Minoritization: Ang Lee and the Politics of Flexibility," *New Formations: A Journal of Culture/Theory/Politics* 40 (Spring 2000): 94. To the insights of Chow and Shih, I hope to add an awareness of the more conservative, even potentially reactionary, literary, and cinematic representations of phenomena such as ("Western") homosexuality and postmodernity that may be operative within local cultural products and/or resonant with mainstream audience biases.

[36] But one example of this self-hatred can be found near the end of Chapter Eight, where Shao refers to himself, Ah Yao, and his lover Yan Yongjie as "sexual deviants who have exiled ourselves to the margins of society, [and] generally come to grief because of the wasteland inside us […]" (Chu, *Notes*, 87).

[37] Drawing from the work of Todd McGowan, I believe that fictional texts "internally posit their own [readers]," responding to and (re-)structuring collective fantasies and desires, and that the main "task of interpretation" is to reveal the ideological imperatives and contradictions underlying the text and develop an appropriate interpretation in response. See Todd McGowan, *The Impossible David Lynch* (New York: Columbia University Press, 2007), 23.

and repellant figurations of homosexuality as a social, psychological, and corporeal contagion. This corroborates the negative assessments of postmodern logic found in Eagleton, Wang, Zavarzadeh, and others.[38] Counterintuitively, Chu T'ien-wen's presentation of a subculture unfamiliar and liable to be perceived as threatening to the local status quo, couched in a deliberately opaque logorrheic rhetoric, creates a reading experience that is a hallmark of world literature—it is both unsettling and "foreign." In this instance, however, it is foreign and disturbing for its *domestic* readership.

Fran Martin presents a nuanced reading of *Notes* that might for some readers—both domestic and foreign—mark an edifying encounter with the novel that would place it more squarely within conventional definitions of world literature. Martin offers a "resistant, *tongzhi*-affirmative" interventionist reading of the novel's grim specters of AIDS-related death and desolation, in which Shao is figured as a postmodern flâneur in *tongzhi* Taipei.[39] Martin proposes that *Notes* reappropriates AIDS and "viral *tongxinglian*" (homosexuality 同性戀, literally "same-sex love") as a trope for the way that homosexuality "infects" straight (urban) cultural spaces via a kind of "homosexualized, anal penetration."[40] Martin argues that the entry points for this homosexualizing penetration are what the narrator coins "secret entryway[s]" (祕口)—mostly boutiques and nightspots[41]—that are paradigmatic of Taiwan's postmodern consumer culture. By penetrating—that is patronizing—these secret entryways, a wandering gay urban subclass appropriates rampant commodification, taking over the city, using their "virally structured homosexuality to infect the city in general."[42] In Martin's reading, this subversive butting in on the dominant social order by the gay subculture allows readers to imagine Taipei and Taiwan as "an 'other' kind of [non-heterosexual] social space, neither purely familial nor purely national."[43]

---

[38] This includes leftist critics' reactions to Jean-François Lyotard's well-known highlighting of the postmodern "incredulity toward metanarratives." See Lyotard's *The Postmodern Condition*, xxiv. Zavarzadeh, for example, faults Lyotard (and others) for making "the structures of post-capitalism" appear "so layered, complex and abstract that one cannot locate a single fixed center from which power issues." See Zavarzadeh, "Post-Ality: The (Dis)Simulations of Cybercapitalism," 19.

[39] *Tongzhi* (同志, literally "comrade") is a term that "appeared originally in Taiwan Mandarin, via Hong Kong, as a translation of the English term 'queer,' [...] it was soon recognized that *tongzhi* approximated more closely something like 'lesbian/gay' identity than queer." See Fran Martin, introduction to *Situating Sexualities: Queer Representation in Taiwanese Fiction, Film, and Public Culture* (Hong Kong: Hong Kong University Press, 2003), 3–4. See also Liang-ya Liou, "Queer Theory and Politics in Taiwan: The Cultural Translation and (Re)Production of Queerness in and beyond Taiwan Lesbian/Gay/Queer Activism," *NTU Studies in Language and Literature*, no.14 (2005): 135–42, Chi Ta-wei's edited volume 酷兒啟示錄：台灣當代 Queer 論述讀本 [*Queer Archipelago: A Reader in Taiwan Queer Discourses*] (Taipei: Yuanzun, 1997), and the essays collected in *Chung-Wai Literary Monthly* 25, no. 1 (1996) and 26, no. 12 (1998).

[40] Fran Martin, "Postmodern Cities and Viral Subjects: *Notes of a Desolate Man*," in *Situating Sexualities: Queer Representation in Taiwanese Fiction, Film, and Public Culture*, 109–12.

[41] Namely *gexingdian* (個性店), self-styled "quirky" boutiques, bars, and restaurants. Some forty-odd such businesses are listed in the last segment of Chapter Eleven.

[42] See Martin, "Postmodern Cities and Viral Subjects," 104 & 107. Terry Eagleton might identify as reactionary the same passages of the novel that Martin figures as subversive when he decries how postmodern subjectivity "become[s] coextensive with ordinary commodified life itself, whose *ceaseless exchanges and mutation* [...] recognize no [...] borders." See Eagleton, "Capitalism, Modernism, and Postmodernism," 393.

[43] Martin, "Postmodern Cities and Viral Subjects," 104.

This argument for the novel's defamiliarization of mainstream notions of cosmopolitan consumer culture imagines a reading experience that is more soundly within the parameters of world literature.

I would, however, significantly qualify Martin's reading by noting that the novel's geographic imaginary, its "map of the city" (城市版圖, literally "urban territory/domain") as Shao calls it, doesn't allow readers to cognitively gain purchase in the streets, spaces, entryways, or elsewhere from which to imaginatively intervene in its negative representation of homosexuality and envision a more liberating kind of social space.[44] Conversely, *Notes* merely superimposes images of a profligate gay social sphere rife with anonymous couplings and predatory cruising of public spaces atop mainstream versions of a (relatively) sanitary and decorous heterosexual Taipei. The cartographic result is a prurient anatomical-*cum*-topographical map of a Taipei that is *disturbingly* (de-hetero)sexualized via the "anal penetration" through said "secret portals." At one point, the narrator even paints a lurid mirror image of his own sexual experiences in Taiwan and Ah Yao's in New York City, where the latter was living when he contracted AIDS. Shao imagines Ah Yao's weekend bar-hopping followed by musical chairs with a dozen or more men in a steam bath. He comments on Ah Yao as follows:

> I knew only too well the frenzied rites of sucking and touching after spitting on your palms and getting down on your knees [...]. All those merging fluids sucked out of other bodies to smear on their own bodies, and on his, congealing to form a veil that smelled like foul mud in a ditch, impossible to get rid of, entangling him like a spiderweb.[45]

Here, Shao's self-description overlaps with Ah Yao's, conflating Taiwan and American gay subcultures in the repugnant image of a frenzied gay male subject trapped in a web of anal sexual filth, which is itself plotted onto superimposed maps of homosexual urban spaces accessed via secret (anal) portals. While the complex, tour de force imagery and allusions are powerful, it takes some interpretive gymnastics to bend this into a *tongzhi*-affirmative reading.

Thus, it seems to me that, while Martin's reading may be "resistant" and "interventionist" and while it does indeed imagine an alternative "social space, neither purely familial nor purely national," it is not plausibly "*tongzhi*-affirmative." That said, although Martin's "interventionist" reading imposes an ill-fitting utopian *tongzhi* aesthetic on Chu T'ien-wen's narrative, it does indeed foreground world literature features of the novel, in that readers sympathetic to such an approach can immerse

[44] Chu, *Notes*, 121.
[45] Chu, *Notes*, 29. Ah Yao is more precisely said to have been splitting his time between New York City and San Francisco when he was diagnosed with AIDS, which adds to the implied superimposition of Taiwan and Western urban spaces. Daniel Mendelsohn's unique and engaging work, *The Elusive Embrace*, combines theorizing of male homosexuality, etymology, gay mapping of NYC urban space, the AIDS epidemic, and more. While outside the scope of the present study, reading *Notes* alongside Mendelsohn's book leads to several productive and insightful avenues of inquiry. See Daniel Mendelsohn, *The Elusive Embrace: Desire and the Riddle of Identity* (New York: Knopf, 1999).

themselves in a defamiliarizing experience of the other that is both unsettling and redemptive, even perhaps empowering.

To recap, *Notes of a Desolate Man*'s representation of a nontraditional (esp. non-Confucian, nonreproductive) debauched gay male culture associated with AIDS, elaborated via a postmodern narrative replete with confusing semantics and grammar, intentional opacity, and panoplies of global cultural references, encourages (Taiwanese) readers to conflate a degenerate and contagious Western-originating *lifestyle* with a foreign and objectionable *literary style*. This provokes a reactive paranoia against the alien corruption of both local culture (namely literature) and society.[46] Such a text establishes a complicated and arguably novel addition to the world literature canon. From the perspective of a local reader in Taiwan, *Notes of a Desolate Man* is demonstrably "foreign" from the outset. While the work's source language and culture of origin are ostensibly identical to those of the reader, and, although it is read (and set) in "an elliptical space bounded by […] the reader's own culture," it paradoxically falls outside the experiences of most local readers' "own home tradition," in light of its westernized postmodern narrative style, (secret/hidden) local subculture settings, non-mainstream characters, ubiquitous foreign references, and other aspects of style and content remote from the reader's "fund of knowledge and expectations developed within the home tradition."[47]

While this foreignizing reading process for the local reader is, as I have argued, likely to invoke a negative reaction toward the alien content and westernized style that the novel represents and manifests as infecting Taiwan, we cannot entirely rule out more sanguine possibilities counter to the interpretation I have offered. A local Taiwan reader's experience of *Notes of a Desolate Man* may draw him or her out of a reactionary conservative kneejerk response to this text, for "[t]he ultimate boundary of world literature is found in the interplay of works in a reader's mind, reshaped anew whenever a reader picks up one book in place of another, begins to read, and is drawn irresistibly into a new world."[48]

---

[46] Homosexuality is frequently figured by Shao as the demise of Taiwan's traditional kinship system, contributing to popular fear of this Western-associated "illness" with which the novel easily aligns.
[47] Damrosch, "Frames for World Literature," 513.
[48] Damrosch, "Frames for World Literature," 513–14.

Part Three

Bringing Taiwan to the World: Taiwanese Literature in Translation

7

Anthologizing Taiwan: Taiwanese Literature toward the Anglophone World

John Balcom

In *Translation, Rewriting, and the Manipulation of Literary Fame*, André Lefevere argues that rewriting—including translation, criticism, historiography, as well as anthologizing and editing—plays a critical role in the dissemination, acceptance, and canonization of literature and shapes the foreign perception of authors, cultures, and societies. This sort of rewriting, usually manipulated by the specific ideologies or poetics of translators, critics, reviewers, teachers, and institutions, constitutes forms of mediation that determine and manipulate the image of literary works for particular audiences. The process of anthologizing, to illustrate, is usually undertaken through the poetics and ideologies of patrons, publishers, and editors who decide to include and exclude certain works and express a specific literary simulacrum at a historical moment.[1] While editing anthologies, they may have numerous rationales that affect their selections. These can be philosophical considerations, political declaration, or an intention to express a fresh exploration of language, link to the literary tradition of the source country, emphasize the role of writers in society, or, particularly for the Global South, articulate struggles against colonial authorities.[2] When certain works are introduced and canonized through earlier anthologies, later editors can choose to accept and enlarge those existing canons or subvert them and create alternative canons.[3] Both attitudes, however, have provided a historical view and built a "heritage which [embraces both] the present and the past."[4] "Marketability" is also one of the deciding factors for editing anthologies.[5] Publishers are reluctant to invest too many pages in an anthology unless it can be used as a textbook at universities; if an anthology is to function as a textbook, it had better not contain too much material that may be considered offensive.[6] Anthologizing as rewriting is thus similar to refraction. It shows

[1] André Lefevere, "Anthologizing Africa," in *Translation, Rewriting, and the Manipulation of Literary Fame* (London: Routledge, 1992), 125.
[2] See Lefevere's discussion on different editions of African poetry anthologies in "Anthologizing Africa," 126–37.
[3] Lefevere, "Anthologizing Africa," 127.
[4] Lefevere, "Anthologizing Africa," 127.
[5] Lefevere, "Anthologizing Africa," 134.
[6] Lefevere, "Anthologizing Africa," 125.

a distinguished image of not only works but also writers of a specific genre, a period, or even a whole literature.

Investigating English anthologies of Taiwanese literature, one cannot ignore how works are intentionally selected to express the image of the culture, society, and people. Taiwanese literature has fared quite well in English translation. Readers who wish to understand Taiwanese literature can acquire this knowledge through English translation. However, even if they are smart and diligent in reading broadly and deeply in the large corpus of translated texts published since the 1970s, difficulties of knowing Taiwanese context always emerge and frustrate eager minds. One cannot avoid asking which determinants of selection are driven to manifest the literary landscape of Taiwan. In other words, anthologies of Taiwanese literature are formed at specific historical moments and require certain analyses. Inspired by Lefevere's discussion and theory of anthologizing as rewriting, this chapter reviews the translation of Taiwanese literature and its representation to the English-speaking world. Before martial law was lifted in 1987, ideological and political considerations often constrained editorial decisions. After 1987, writers, researchers, and translators had greater latitude to explore historical periods and facets of life that had previously been off-limits. The discussion, therefore, is divided into two parts, separated by this pivotal moment in modern Taiwanese history. The case studies include English translations of Taiwanese poetry, fiction, and essays, focusing primarily on anthologies, book series, and journals to trace the development of the representation of Taiwan in the English-speaking world through translation.

Foundation and Formation from the 1970s to the 1980s

The translation of Taiwanese literature into English only commenced in the 1970s. This period can be termed the age of the anthology. As David Wang points out, because of its inclusive format, the anthology has been considered one of the most efficient ways to promote Taiwanese literature abroad.[7] But the process of assembling an anthology necessarily implies certain editorial principles, including the notion of what constitutes Taiwanese literature, whether consciously articulated or not. It would be safe to say, then, that through the editorial policy behind it, an anthology is, to a certain extent, the representation of a culture or cultural identity. The pivotal question raised here will be: if we examine the available anthologies with this axiom in mind, what vision of Taiwan emerges for a foreign readership from this foundational period when the first steps toward forming a literary representation of the island were undertaken?

For fiction, the most significant anthologies during this period are Pang-yuan Chi's *An Anthology of Contemporary Chinese Literature: Taiwan: Short Stories, 1949–1974*

---

[7] David Der-wei Wang, "Translating Taiwan: A Study of Four English Anthologies of Taiwan Fiction," in *Translating Chinese Literature*, ed. Eugene Eoyang and Lin Yao-fu (Bloomington: Indiana University Press, 1995), 262.

(1975), Joseph Lau's *Chinese Stories from Taiwan: 1960–1970* (1976) and *The Unbroken Chain: An Anthology of Taiwan Fiction Since 1926* (1983), and Nancy Chang Ing's *Winter Plum: Contemporary Chinese Fiction* (1982). Poets, too, were fairly well represented in anthologies. Three of the most important poetry anthologies from the 1970s are Wai-lim Yip's *Modern Chinese Poetry: Twenty Poets from the Republic of China, 1855–1965* (1970), Angela C. Y. Jung Palandri's *Modern Verse from Taiwan* (1972), and Pang-yuan Chi's *An Anthology of Contemporary Chinese Literature: Taiwan: Poems, 1949–1974* (1975). Each of these anthologies offers the reader a distinct vision of Taiwanese literature.

Pang-yuan Chi's anthology attempts to present an image of Taiwan as "Free China" in opposition to Communist China.[8] It contains a broad selection of stories from 1949 to 1974 by three categories of writers: writers-in-exile, writers from the military, and younger writers who associated with *Literary Journal* (文學雜誌, published from 1956 to 1960) and *Modern Literature* (現代文學, published from 1960 to 1973), two very important literary journals from this early period. Chi's anthology contains twenty-three stories by seventeen writers. Among the older writers are Peng Ke (彭歌), Lin Hai-yin (林海音), Meng Yao (孟瑤), and Wang Shang-i (王尚義) and three retired military officers, including Chu Hsi-ning (朱西甯), Ssu-ma Chung-yuan (司馬中原), and Tuan Tsai-hua (段彩華). The younger writers in the anthology include Yu Li-hua (於梨華), Pai Hsien-yung (白先勇), Wang Wen-hsing (王文興), Huang Chun-ming (黃春明), Ou-yang Tzu (歐陽子), Shih Shu-ching (施叔青), Hsi Sung (奚淞), Lin Huai-min (林懷民), and Li Yung-ping (李永平). Chi's editorial selection constructs a literary continuity that starts with writers from the mainland who were active in the 1950s and then grows to encompass the island's younger writers. The implication is that Taiwan, as part of a larger unbroken chain, became the bastion of traditional Chinese culture that moved headlong into the modern world. The preface argues that the modern literature of Taiwan is the "outgrowth of a very long and rich tradition"[9] and that the younger writers, exposed to various forms of modernism, have been successful in amalgamating that tradition with modernity. Though it is not explicitly stated, Chi implies that the sociopolitical milieu of mainland China is not conducive to the development of modern literature that has been much destroyed by communist violence. For her, the situation in Taiwan is just the opposite.

Chi's memoir, *The Great Flowing River* (巨流河), provides insights into not only the editing process but also the rationale behind the anthology. She notes that although Taiwan as Free China was acknowledged internationally for creating an economic miracle, it was still perceived as a cultural desert. She believed that mainland China had not produced any literature since 1949, yet works from the mainland drew more attention than those from Taiwan. In contrast to mainland literature, in her view, the literature of Taiwan had "matured naturally owing to the diversity of the

---

[8] It is part of a two-volume set of poetry and fiction; I deal with the poetry volume below.
[9] Pang-yuan Chi, preface to *Short Stories*, vol. 2 of *An Anthology of Contemporary Chinese Literature: Taiwan: 1949–1974*, ed. Pang-yuan Chi et al. (Taipei: National Institute for Compilation and Translation, 1975), i.

subject matter and style; whether realism or art for art's sake, it reflected human life without taking a back seat to politics."[10] As for the selection process, she explains that "since the anthology was being published by the National Institute of Compilation and Translation, the selections had to be representative of all people and the selection process had to be fair, with no discrimination."[11] Within those parameters, she wanted to choose works that exhibited less Western influence and showed readers abroad the Taiwanese people as they really were. For her, this meant that overly pessimistic and decadent works were to be avoided. They did not represent what the many years of struggle in Taiwan had been about.[12]

Despite Chi's frankness, what she does not mention is that working for the KMT-ruled government agency or institute at that time entailed certain political restrictions. As the anthology was meant to depict Taiwan as *Free China*, the title focuses on *Chinese* literature rather than Taiwanese literature. This was a standard for all government publications throughout the 1960s and 1970s, as the KMT regime in Taiwan considered itself the sole legitimate representative of China. Chi's selections were also dependent on her governmental position. She could not include dissident writers such as Liu Ta-jen (劉大任) and Chang Hsi-kuo (張系國), who, after their involvement in the *Baodiao* Movement, had been blacklisted, or Chen Ying-chen (陳映真), who was in jail. The anthology, to some extent, reflects these official constraints.

Joseph S. M. Lau's two anthologies were the standard collections in English in the 1970s and 1980s. The first, *Chinese Stories from Taiwan: 1960–1970*, published in 1976, includes stories by eleven writers, all from the so-called second generation, many of whom were associated with the Modern Literature group, including Chen Jo-hsi (陳若曦), Wang Wen-hsing, Chen Ying-chen, Chi Teng-sheng (七等生), Wang Chen-ho (王禎和), Yu Li-hua, Chang Hsi-kuo, Lin Huai-min, Yang Ching-chu (楊青矗), and Pai Hsien-yung. In the preface to the anthology, Lau points out that, in making his selection, he was less concerned about the geographic origins of the writers than with reflecting a larger variety of Taiwanese experiences. The list of the authors in this collection shows Lau's strong identification with Taiwanese localness because they, unlike those in Chi's anthology, were all born or raised in Taiwan after the KMT withdrew from mainland China in the 1940s. Avowed modernists such as Wang Wen-hsing stand alongside writers such as Huang Chun-ming and Wang Chen-ho, who can deftly blend the local with modernist techniques, as well as more overtly ideological writers such as Chen Ying-chen and Yang Ching-chu. In making his selection, Lau benefited from working with American academic publishers, which freed him from the restrictions faced by Chi.

Lau's intention to include Taiwan-born writers does not mean that he promotes another sort of literary discrimination against China-born writers. Instead, he finds the distinction that Chi draws between Taiwanese writers and mainlander writers

---

[10] Pang-yuan Chi, *The Great Flowing River: A Memoir of China, from Manchuria to Taiwan*, ed. and trans. John Balcom (New York: Columbia University Press, 2018), 325.
[11] Chi, *The Great Flowing River*, 346.
[12] Chi, *The Great Flowing River*, 325.

no longer "viable."[13] For Lau, the decade covered in the anthology is of particular importance because it represented a distinct break from the writings of the Chinese émigrés who had more opportunities to acquire the spotlight in the 1950s. Lau's new literary aesthetic makes his selections outstanding. They correspond to Taiwan's social needs—the emergence of a strong identity after the UN recognized the PRC as the only representative of China in 1971 and the United States acknowledged the PRC in 1972. While these continuous diplomatic setbacks diminished the legitimacy of the KMT rule and reinforced local awareness, Lau's tendency to select new Taiwanese local writers seemed to convey his discontent with the KMT's outdated discrimination and diplomatic policies.

Lau's second anthology, *The Unbroken Chain: An Anthology of Taiwan Fiction Since 1926*, published in 1983, was the first collection to include writers from the Japanese colonial period. The works of four such writers, Lōa Hô (賴和), Wu Cho-liu (吳濁流), Chu Tien-jen (朱點人), and Yang Kuei (楊逵), are featured in this anthology alongside that of thirteen contemporary writers, many of whom, including Chung Li-he (鍾理和), Cheng Ching-wen (鄭清文), Li Chiao (李喬), Liu Ta-jen, Wang Chen-ho, Tung Nien (東年), and a very young Chang Ta-chun (張大春), are not represented in either his or Chi's earlier anthologies. *The Unbroken Chain* is a significant step forward in capturing the uniqueness of the Taiwanese experience and recovering a broader understanding of the island's diverse cultural milieu. The metaphor of the title conveys the anthology's key editorial principle: there is an abiding continuity from the writers of the Japanese colonial period to those of the postwar era. In the preface, Lau is careful to point out that the Japanese period had not been overlooked in earlier anthologies for political reasons but simply because so much of the material from the period had previously been unavailable to scholars and translators.[14] In 1979, however, the twelfth volume of *The Complete Pre-retrocession Taiwanese Literature* (光復前台灣文學全集), edited by Chung Chao-cheng (鍾肇政) and Yeh Shih-tao (葉石濤), had been published. The contents are mostly works originally written in Japanese, which complement the two-volume *Taiwanese New Literature during the Japanese Occupation Period* (日據下台灣新文學) edited by Li Nan-heng (李南衡),[15] which focuses on Chinese-language stories. This massive achievement transformed how Taiwanese literature was perceived, although the authors featured in this collection are mostly known for their anticolonial spirit. Those overly pro-Japan works were excluded to express the editors' "silent and tolerant criticism" of Japanese rule.[16] Influenced by the aesthetic tastes of Chung, Yeh, and Li represented in their anthologies, Lau's *The Unbroken Chain*, as is suggested by the

---

[13] Joseph S. M. Lau, introduction to *Chinese Stories from Taiwan: 1960–1970*, ed. Joseph S. M. Lau and Timothy Ross (New York: Columbia University Press, 1976), xxx.
[14] Joseph S. M. Lau, introduction to *The Unbroken Chain: An Anthology of Taiwan Fiction Since 1926*, ed. and trans. Joseph S. M. Lau (Bloomington: Indiana University Press, 1983), ix.
[15] Li Nan-heng, *Taiwanese New Literature during the Japanese Occupation Period* (Taipei: Mingtan, 1979).
[16] Chang Heng-hao (張恆豪) et al., editorial notes on *The Complete Pre-retrocession Taiwanese Literature*, ed. Chung Chao-cheng and Yeh Shih-tao (Taipei: Vista Publishing, 1979), 4.

book title, traces Taiwanese literature back to Japan-ruled Taiwan and demonstrates the rebellious spirit that has been inherited by contemporary Taiwanese people. This anthology—emerging after the rediscovery of Japanese-language works and, most importantly, after the Formosa Incident and the Lin Family Massacre—undoubtedly expresses Taiwan's ways of rebellion against the colonial power, not just the Japanese but also the KMT, to the English-speaking world.[17]

Lau's editorial choices represent a very different Taiwan from Chi's. Not only does he extend Taiwanese literary tradition back in an unbroken chain through Japanese occupation, but he fearlessly includes marginalized writers such as Liu Ta-jen and Chang Hsi-kuo, who had been blacklisted, and Chen Ying-chen, who had been jailed. He includes works about hardship and poverty, about the disintegration of rural society, about the loneliness and alienation that came with industrialization, and about political frustration. For example, Chung Li-ho is represented in the anthology by his postwar story, "Together through Thick and Thin," in which he writes realistically about rural poverty and hardship before Taiwan's economic miracle. Cheng Ching-wen's story "Betel Palm Village" is, as Lau says, a "period piece" that affirms traditional rural values over urban values resulting from industrialization. In a very surrealistic tale entitled "The Spheric Man," Li Chiao, a Hakka writer, moves away from realism to explore the absurdities of life through a Buddhist framework. Huang Chun-ming's "I Love Mary" is a story critical of America and of the way Chinese identity, in his view, is being undermined by Western materialism. In general, the stories in *The Unbroken Chain* represent a darker as well as a broader vision of Taiwanese society and culture. Lau's selections also encourage the Anglophone reader to see Taiwan as a unique entity, distinct from China and with its own problems.

Nancy Chang Ing's *Winter Plum: Contemporary Chinese Fiction*, which appeared in 1982, is an interesting anthology for a different reason. Unlike her predecessors, Ing does not seem to have any editorial purpose other than compiling a compelling anthology of well-written stories. This is in keeping with her approach to editing *The Chinese PEN*, where she similarly put less emphasis on what faction or school a writer was from as long as the writing was good.[18] *Winter Plum* features twenty-three translations of stories culled from *The Chinese PEN*. Ing selected not only old favorites but also work by several writers not included in previous anthologies. The anthology is organized alphabetically by author name, with no concern for historical perspective or other sequencing. The effect, as David Wang puts it, is to create "a space where

---

[17] The Formosa Incident was the KMT's crackdown on pro-democracy activists in December 1979. While several demonstrators, including Lin Yi-hsiung (林義雄), were still in detention in February 1980, an assassin broke into Lin's house and killed Lin's mother and his oldest daughter. The murder was possibly conducted by the KMT.
[18] The magazine *The Taipei Chinese PEN* or *The Chinese PEN* was founded by Nancy Ing in 1971 and has been in continuous publication since then. The title of the journal has changed a number of times, as have the editors, but the editorial policy has remained the same: the writing of any contemporary writer, regardless of ideological persuasion or ethnicity, is welcome as long as it is good writing. Incredibly, the journal has introduced the work of over two thousand Taiwanese writers to Anglophone readers.

'tradition' is manifest only in the simultaneous existence of the past and the present, the young and the old."[19]

Emergence of Nativist Voices in Poetry Anthologies of the 1970s

Three important poetry anthologies appeared in the 1970s. The first, Wai-lim Yip's *Modern Chinese Poetry: Twenty Poets from the Republic of China, 1955–1965*, published by the University of Iowa Press as part of a series of collections of poetry in translation, focuses on the second generation of Taiwanese poets, those who arrived in Taiwan with the KMT exodus from mainland China. In Yip's preface to the collection, he says that he was "driven [to compile the anthology] by an almost superstitious fear that much of the poetry […] would be obliterated by the avalanche of world crises."[20] Like Pang-yuan Chi, Yip's editorial choices are driven by a concern to legitimize Taiwan as the Republic of China, but the chief virtue of the anthology is its foregrounding, for the first time, of the high modernist verse of the 1960s. To this end, Yip includes a substantial selection of work by Shang Chin (商禽), Lo Fu (洛夫), Yang Mu (楊牧), Ya Hsien (瘂弦), Wai-lim Yip, Huang Yung (黃用), Chou Meng-tieh (周夢蝶), Yu Kuang-chung (余光中), Lo Men (羅門), Chin Tzu-hao (覃子豪), and Chi Hsien (紀弦). Of the twenty poets included in the anthology, only three (Yang Mu, Pai Chiu 白萩, and Hsiung Hung 夐虹) were born in Taiwan.[21]

An interesting side note to Yip's anthology is to be found in the animated critical response to the anthology, which culminated in a debate over the value in general of modern poetry in Taiwan. John Kwan-Terry, who was discontented with what he considered the overly westernized style of recent Taiwanese poetry, wrote a review attacking the highly individual styles of the poets in the anthology. This was followed by a critique from Tang Wen-piao (唐文標), an amateur man of letters, which condemned not only modern Chinese poetry but also modern Chinese literature as a whole. These criticisms aroused furious reactions from several other writers and scholars. The debate arguably changed the course of modern Chinese poetry by initiating a stronger critical awareness and unbiased critical standards in literary circles.[22]

---

[19] Wang, "Translating Taiwan," 265.
[20] Wai-lim Yip, preface to *Modern Chinese Poetry: Twenty Poets from the Republic of China, 1955–1965*, ed. and trans. Wai-lim Yip (Iowa City: University of Iowa Press, 1970), ix.
[21] In the 1930s, surrealism was introduced to Taiwan by Le Moulin Poetry Society. This movement was underestimated by its contemporaries, and due to the use of Japanese language, it was also quickly forgotten after the KMT's handover. In the 1960s, the use of surrealistic style by the mainland poets such as Ya Hsien, Lo Fu, and Shang Chin was a reintroduction of surrealism. The Japanese works of Le Moulin were rediscovered in 1995 when Yeh Ti (葉笛) translated them into Mandarin. A detailed discussion on Le Moulin can be seen in Chapter 4.
[22] Jing Wang, "Taiwan Hsiang-t'u Literature Perspectives in the Evolution of a Literary Movement," in *Chinese Fiction from Taiwan: Critical Perspectives*, ed. Jeanette L. Faurot (Bloomington: University of Indiana Press, 1980), 69.

Angela Jung Palandri's 1972 anthology, *Modern Verse from Taiwan*, is notable for being the first collection of either poetry or fiction to include the word "Taiwan" in its title, a highly significant move in and of itself. Her selections were explicitly based on the importance of the poets for *Taiwanese* poetry. As she states in the introduction, she chose poets whom she considered "to be significant in one phase or another of the new poetry of Taiwan. Most of the poets selected […] have published at least one volume of poetry and are well known in Taiwan's poetry circles."[23] Nevertheless, Palandri also makes a case for modern Taiwanese poetry as an expression of a broader *Chinese* literary tradition. Noting that, since 1949, Chinese poetry had begun to diverge in two directions, she argues that the greater and more dynamic of the two would be found where serious artists had the freedom both to exercise their originality and to lay claim to the rich legacy of native tradition, as in Taiwan. She asserts, therefore, that modern Taiwanese poetry is what mainland Chinese poetry is not. Though the poetry of Taiwan and the mainland stem from the same cultural roots, there is a deep "spiritual cleavage" between them.[24] Moreover, she observes that Taiwanese poetry has a greater affinity with poetry from elsewhere in the world, particularly the West, than with the poetry of mainland China.

However, her nearly exclusive focus on modernist poetics, particularly on émigré poets from the mainland, leads to some misrepresentation of Taiwan's poetry scene, a shortcoming common to all the poetry anthologies of the period. The two most significant issues are a lack of understanding of the island's previous literary history and a consequent lack of balance regarding the contemporary situation. For example, Palandri asserts that Taiwan had no poetry to speak of during the Japanese occupation and cultural domination of the island and that poetry was in a sense reintroduced to Taiwan with the arrival of Chinese émigrés from the mainland.[25] This erroneous assertion, owing to the limited information available about Taiwanese colonial literature, muddles the actual cultural continuity that Lau notes. The fact of the matter is that postwar Taiwanese poets drew from rich poetic traditions from both mainland China and the Japanese occupation. Taiwan, like mainland China, was influenced by the May Fourth Movement, but Taiwanese poets educated in Japanese also had access to the latest world literature in translation. Surrealism, as Yi-chen Liu discusses here in *Taiwanese Literature as World Literature*, was introduced to Taiwan in the 1930s by Taiwanese poets and reintroduced in the 1960s by émigré poets who had only then become aware of the movement.

As mentioned, Pang-yuan Chi's poetry anthology is part of a two-volume set of contemporary ROC literature in translation. The focus of the anthology is Taiwan's high modernist poets. The introduction traces the development of the various schools of modernist poetry on the island: the Modernist School, the Blue Stars Poetry Society, and the Epoch Poetry Society. The different positions of these schools focused on the

---

[23] Angela Jung Palandri, introduction to *Modern Verse from Taiwan*, ed. and trans. Angela Jung Palandri (Berkeley: University of California Press, 1972), 19.
[24] Palandri, introduction to *Modern Verse from Taiwan*, 4.
[25] Palandri, introduction to *Modern Verse from Taiwan*, 4.

issue of modernization, how much Westernization was necessary, and whether native tradition was an obstacle or, properly inherited, a great help. The introduction does mention the Bamboo Hat Poetry Society, which was founded by a group of Taiwan's local poets in reaction against the modernist program and sharing a different historical perspective from the émigré modernists in 1964. However, this poetry volume, as in the volume devoted to fiction, constructs a tradition of modern poetry stemming from China. For Chi, the modern poetry of the island shows "steady and firm development with the clearest successes."[26]

Seeing Taiwan as the legal successor of a rich Chinese tradition, Chi promotes the high modernists who write about the existential angst associated with exile from mainland China and, thereby, pays less attention to the nativist poets who have more to say about Taiwanese local society. As a result, she showcases the mainlanders, such as Chin Tzu-hao, Chi Hsien, Chou Meng-tieh, Lo Fu, Lo Men, Yu Kuang-chung, Shang Chin, Ya Hsien, Wai-lim Yip, Hsia Ching (夏菁), Lo Ching (羅青), and Fang Ssu (方思), and endorses few Taiwanese-born poets, such as Pai Chiu, Hsiung Hung, Yang Mu, Fang Chi (方旗), and Fang Hsin (方莘). The prejudice is not her fault because it truthfully represents how the literary history was perceived and how mainlanders enjoyed more literary capital and spotlight than islanders. It was not until 1979 that Taiwan rediscovered its colonial-era literature and acknowledged Japanese influence.

Beyond the Unitary Vision of Poetry since the 1990s

If the 1970s and 1980s were the age of the anthology, the 1990s saw an increase in multiple publications, including the translations of individual authors' novels,[27] poetry collections, anthologies of prose,[28] and the major new journal *Taiwan Literature: English Translation Series*, founded by Kuo-ch'ing Tu in 1996.[29] Born in the late stage of Taiwan's colonial era, Tu is a scholar-cum-poet involved with the editing of *Modern Literature* and the establishment of the nativist *Bamboo Hat Poetry Journal*. The journal is academic in nature and is important for its extensive translation of Japanese colonial literature, Hakka literature, and Indigenous writing, as well as issues

---

[26] Chi, *The Great Flowing River*, 325.
[27] Another feature of the period is the growth in the number of translations of single-author works. Many novels and short story collections by individual writers have been published by several publishers. The "Modern Literature from Taiwan" series, coordinated by Pang-yuan Chi, Göran Malmqvist, and David Der-wei Wang and published by the Columbia University Press, is worth noting. Jennifer Crewe, the chief editor at Columbia, commented that she was very interested in David Wang's suggestion that Columbia publish translations of Taiwanese writers because US publishers had shown an interest in publishing writers from mainland China, but very little attention was being paid to writers from Taiwan. Crewe had a good sense of the market. The series kicked off in 1998. Over twenty titles have been published to date.
[28] The literary essay has been far less popular in translation than fiction or poetry; this is hardly surprising since most readers prefer a good story or poem.
[29] It was published by the US–Taiwan Literature Foundation based at the University of California, Santa Barbara, later with the assistance of National Taiwan University.

devoted to single authors. Both Tu and his former coeditor Robert Backus understand Japanese, and thus the journal's translations of colonial-era works were rendered directly from the Japanese originals. Tu on several occasions stresses the autonomy of Taiwanese literature, although he places it in an inclusive multilingual and multiethnic framework of "world literatures in Chinese" (世華文學).³⁰ Anthologies are still produced but now are more frequently focused on a particular subject or theme rather than on making a grand gesture to represent the literary scene of the island as a whole. In short, the scope and depth of Taiwanese literature in translation increase. Indeed, there is an exponential growth in the translation of Taiwanese literature during this period and a continuous enlargement of the international literary representation of the island through translation that increasingly reclaims the past by translating writing that had been ignored: in particular, literature from the Japanese occupation and the White Terror.

The more narrowly focused anthologies of this period are well represented by two anthologies published by Columbia University Press as part of the "Modern Chinese Literature from Taiwan" series. *The Last of the Whampoa Breed: Stories of the Chinese Diaspora*, edited by Pang-yuan Chi and David Der-wei Wang in 2003, features stories of mainland exiles in Taiwan as told by their descendants, many of whom have become well-known writers. *Indigenous Writers from Taiwan: An Anthology of Stories, Essays, and Poems*, edited by John and Yingtsih Balcom and translated by John Balcom in 2005, was the first anthology of Taiwan's Indigenous literature to appear in English translation. The new "Taiwan Literature" series under Cambria Press published several other thematic anthologies recently, with contents covering women writers, queer literature, and stories of the White Terror and government atrocity, providing a diverse thematic representation of Taiwanese literature. Among them, *Queer Taiwanese Literature* (2021), edited by Howard Chiang, seems particularly timely, as Taiwan became the first country in Asia to legalize same-sex marriage in 2019. This collection is anticipated to help shape Taiwan's image as a relatively homosexuality-tolerant society to the Anglophone audience.

During the post–martial law period, approximately seven poetry anthologies appeared. Two worth noting are Michelle Yeh's *Anthology of Modern Chinese Poetry* (1992) and *Frontier Taiwan* (2001), coedited by Michelle Yeh and N. G. D. Malmqvist. Conceptually considered the most interesting anthologies of the period, they move beyond the unitary vision of the poetry scene of the previous period and strike out in new directions. Yeh's 1992 anthology is a fascinating reassessment and reconfiguration of modern Taiwanese poetry in twentieth-century Sinophone literature. On one level, she proposes a comprehensive introduction of modernist poetry that starts with the May Fourth period, which then diverges due to the historical cleavage between

---

30 To celebrate the journal's twenty-year anniversary, Tu gave a keynote lecture entitled "台灣文學的主體性和《英譯叢刊》回顧" [The Autonomy of Taiwanese Literature and a Retrospect of *Taiwan Literature: English Translation Series*] at National Taiwan University on July 1, 2017; Tu, 台灣文學與世華文學 [*Taiwanese Literature and World Literatures in Chinese*] (Taipei: National Taiwan University Press, 2015).

mainland China and Taiwan in 1949. Growing from the same roots, the poetries are distinct but do possess some similarities. In essence, the book—which compiles modernist poetry from the PRC starting from the May Fourth period and from the post–Cultural Revolution period and from Taiwan with the modernist poets of the 1960s and the island's subsequent decades of pluralism—demonstrates the continuity of Chinese modernist tradition across the Straits. The anthology achieves this sense of continuity and tradition but does so by erasing mainland China's "tractor poems" and Taiwan's poetry from the Japanese occupation period as well as much of the Indigenous verse. As a full-scale representation of modern Chinese poetry, the book has its limits; as a full-scale representation of modern Taiwan poetry, it has its limits, too. It is still an intriguing attempt to configure a tradition of Chinese modernist poetry. Of the sixty-six poets, only ten list their ancestral home as Taiwan.

Although Yeh's 1992 anthology provides a convincing and elegant testimonial to the idea of a modernist tradition in Chinese poetry, the critical introduction presents some problems, particularly with reference to Taiwan's place within that tradition. Instead of simply discussing the poetics and aesthetics of that tradition and how these unite that tradition despite divergences across the Straits, Yeh explains the tradition through a thesis on the marginalization of modern poetry. This becomes a theoretical straitjacket in which ideas are forced to fit. She argues that modernist poetry can be viewed collectively as an original and imaginative reaction to the marginalization of poetry in China during the twentieth century. This is a tantalizing notion that warrants consideration but ultimately comes across as reductive and at times contrived, at least in the sweeping fashion in which it is applied.

According to Yeh, "[Taiwan modernists'] works contrast sharply with the mainstream discourse promoted by the [KMT] government, particularly from the 1950s to the early 1970s, in challenging the anticommunist of the time and in engaging in the avant-garde."[31] However, since the anticommunist discourse promoted by the government could no longer be considered the dominant form of literary discourse from 1953,[32] Taiwan's modernists were less interested in critiquing government propaganda efforts than in filling the aesthetic void left by the government's proscriptions against a good part of China's modern literary heritage. The modernists did not believe that art needed to assume a socially consequential role, and social criticism was often limited to politically engaged statements and sometimes even followed the KMT's propagandistic discourse. Even though modernists like Shang Chin and Lo Fu have explored war trauma, escape, fear, and death, they seldom touched on larger issues of human rights, empowerment of the politically disenfranchised Taiwanese majority, democracy, and the rights of workers, women, and children.

The notion that modernism in Taiwan was somehow a marginalized form of discourse seems less than plausible. Neither the literary practice nor the place of

---

[31] Yeh, introduction to *Anthology of Modern Chinese Poetry* (New Haven: Yale University Press, 1992), xxxviii.
[32] Chi Hsien founded Taiwan's first postwar poetry group—the Modernist School—in February 1953.

modernist poets in society would likely warrant them being called marginal. Many studied in the best schools in Taiwan, some studied abroad and took prestigious academic positions, while others held high-ranking positions in the military or held editorial positions in the mainstream press. In fact, the so-called marginalized poets were published in the mainstream literary supplements. As such, perhaps the terms "elitist" or "alternative" might be more appropriate.[33] There was never much conflict between the modernists and the government, whereas a Taiwanese poet like Chao Tien-i (趙天儀) could lose a teaching job because of his political views or Li Chin-an (李勤岸) could lose an academic position simply for being a Taiwanese citizen with questionable political loyalties.[34]

If the modernists are deemed marginal, then what happens to genuinely marginalized Taiwanese poets? Again, the analysis of Taiwanese nativism is by theoretical necessity simplistic and misleading. While the modernists (largely those poets from the mainland) are praised for their marginalization and social consciousness, the same qualities among nativist poets are disparaged. Of course, the bottom line here is aesthetics: the modernists are aesthetically engaging, while the nativist poetry appears trite and cliched. What is missing here is a discussion of the nativist movement during this period and its historical roots, such as the increasingly polarized tension between the local population and the mainlanders. Many Taiwanese viewed the KMT government as a colonial power, not unlike the Japanese and in some cases worse, particularly after the February 28 Incident. Modernism was perceived by some nativists as a literature of the ruling elite from mainland China or as an extension of America's neocolonialism.[35]

Frontier Taiwan is the single most important anthology of modern Taiwanese poetry to date for both its introduction and content. The introduction is the most complete and balanced discussion of Taiwan's poetic tradition to be found in an anthology: it includes a sketch of the development of modern Taiwanese poetry from the end of the early years of the twentieth century through the late 1980s and ties together aesthetic concerns with economic and political changes over the same period. In addition, there is an extensive analysis of many poems. Yeh begins with a discussion of the colonial period and the dual tradition it inherited—the May Fourth Movement from China and the modernist tradition from Japan. In the early twentieth century, some Taiwanese poets wrote in Chinese, others in Japanese. Taiwan's Chinese-language writers were inspired by China's revolutionary May Fourth Movement, while Japanese-language writers were exposed to various forms of international modernism through Japanese

---

[33] Yvonne Chang regards Taiwan's postwar modernists as the "alternative" literary paradigm, whereas anticommunist writing is the "dominant" and the nativist "the oppositional." See her *Literary Culture in Taiwan: From Martial Law to Market Law* (New York: Columbia University Press, 2004), 5–7.

[34] Chao lost his job at the National Taiwan University in 1974 during the KMT's suppression of dissident academics, which is known as the National Taiwan University Philosophy Department Incident. Li's contract was terminated by National Sun Yat-sen University slightly before the lifting of martial law in 1987, as he was critical of the KMT regime.

[35] Chen Fang-ming, "我的後殖民立場" [My Postcolonial Stance], *United Daily News* supplementary, April 9, 2002.

translation. For example, in 1924 the Taiwanese writer Hsieh Chun-mu (謝春木), writing under the pen name Chui Feng (追風), published the first Japanese-language Taiwanese modern poems in the magazine *Taiwan* published in Tokyo, while Chang Wo-chun (張我軍), who studied at the Beijing Normal College, wrote and published *Lover in the Capital in a Time of Chaos* (亂都之戀), the first modern Chinese vernacular poetry collection in Taiwan in 1925. It was only in the later days of Japanese rule that Japanese became the nearly exclusive vehicle for poetic expression in Taiwan. This early development of poetry, for Yeh, has a late influence on the revival of local identity and the corresponding discussions about the use of the Taiwanese dialect in the 1970s.

With Retrocession, the poetry scene underwent tremendous changes. Japanese was largely prohibited and replaced by Chinese, and this silenced many local poets. The lacuna created was filled largely by poets from mainland China; some local poets were able to make the transition, becoming what is referred to as the "translingual generation." Yeh gives a clear and balanced description of this period, the anticommunist poetry promoted by the government and the subsequent rise of Taiwan modernism, driven largely by mainlanders, and most often the subject of earlier anthologies. In her discussion of modernism, Yeh again gives a fair description, offering pros and cons regarding the movement. On the one hand, she goes into some depth on the Bamboo Hat Society, which was composed almost exclusively of local poets and their attempts to carry on the modernist tradition. Quoting Lin Heng-tai (林亨泰), one of the early members of the Modernist Society, and a local Japanese-educated poet, she suggests that many of the modernists from mainland China lacked sufficient understanding of various forms of modernism, which the Japanese-educated poets had. This sort of consideration had not been seen in any previous anthology.

This is followed by a discussion of the critique of modern poetry elicited by Yip's anthology discussed above. Once again, this demonstrates the shortcomings of both sides of the debate on nativism. Yeh describes the social, economic, and political climate of the times and shows how they are tied to the rise of nativism on the one hand and neoclassicism among erstwhile mainland modernists on the other. At this point in the history of modern Taiwanese poetry, a shift occurred in which a Taiwanese consciousness, a Taiwanese identity, emerged and began to supplant the focus on Taiwan's relationship with Chinese tradition, a trend that grew stronger as the years went by. While tracing the weakening of mainlander-driven high modernism, Yeh demonstrates the continuity of the movement with later generations. A good example is the influence of the prose poetry of Shang Chin on younger poets, such as Tu Yeh (渡也) and Su Shao-lien (蘇紹連). The introduction leaves off with the island's poets focused more than ever on the Taiwanese experience and the general literary pluralism of the time.

Yeh's selection of texts was also the most comprehensive of any poetry anthology to date. Space limits always dictate the number of poets who can be included. For the first time, many local poets were introduced, including Japanese colonial period poets such as Yang Hua (楊華) and Yang Chih-chang (楊熾昌), poets of the translingual generation such as Cheng Chien-wu (陳千武) and Lin Heng-tai, and nativist poets such as Wu Sheng (吳晟) and Li Min-yung (李敏勇). While these elements of the poetic tradition are now represented, they remain just a tantalizing reminder of the diversity of the island's poetry. A greater number of poets born in the 1950s and 1960s also find space here, expanding the reader's view and understanding of these poetic generations and the continuities. Of the fifty poets included, thirty-two were born in Taiwan. Taiwan represented in this anthology is of poetic diversity as well as geographic, ethnic, and linguistic diversity. While the anthology represents an advance over its predecessors, there is still ample room for further work, particularly drawing from the Japanese occupation period.

Conclusion

For Lefevere, each anthology has its historical moment. They are intentionally edited by scholars who convey certain aesthetic views and political ideologies to foreign readers. They are usually considered textbooks for, in the case of Taiwanese literature, undergraduate students of Chinese or East Asian studies. This marketability decides the number of pages in which publishers are willing to invest. If an anthology is a place of negotiation between editors, publishers, and potential reviewers and readers, one can even argue that anthologizing Taiwan is synonymous with politicizing Taiwan, showing how Taiwan should be represented to the world. The 1970s and 1980s were a formative period in which anthologies played an important role in representing and defining Taiwanese literature and its traditions abroad. These anthologies of fiction offer distinct visions of Taiwanese literature. Chi's anthology makes the case for Taiwanese literature as a sort of culmination of a long tradition that originates in China, which, given the political situation and the threat posed by the mainland, seems quite natural; Lau's impulse, by contrast, offers two complementary visions, specifically that Taiwanese literature itself can be viewed as a unique tradition of its own, not necessarily related to mainland China, and that the modernist period from 1960 to 1970 is a unique phase within that tradition; last, Ing provides a happy hodgepodge of stories that perhaps better reflects the cultural diversity of the island.

There is considerable overlap among these three poetry anthologies; they all exhibit the same shortcomings. All try to construct modernist tradition that derives exclusively from mainland China, ignoring the dual legacies of China and Japan. A "Free China" tradition of poetry, more in tune with Western poetries, is constructed to represent the poetry scene of Taiwan. Second, the focus is generally on modernist poets and aesthetics. While the introduction to Chi's anthology of poetry does mention the Bamboo Hat Poetry Society as well as a few other societies, none of the work of these poets is included in Chi's, Yip's, or Palandri's anthologies, with the exception of Pai Chiu. Although the society, founded in 1964 as an alternative to various schools of modernism, is composed of local poets, it has largely been ignored.

Generally, the Bamboo Hat poets have been perceived as provincial, and their nativism has been rejected as realism and therefore of little interest. While many of Taiwan's modernists have proven to be among the exceptional poets of the twentieth century and are worthy of attention, the anthologies of poetry from Taiwan have often been one-sided. Regardless of the ignorance of Taiwanese nativism and the emphasis on Chinese inheritance, poetry represented in all three collections shows that modernism as developed in the 1950s and the 1960s of Taiwan was the heir to the poetic modernism of mainland China—a place where modernism was interrupted by the Second Sino-Japanese War, the Chinese Civil War, and the ascendency of the CCP. The emphasis on the modernist aesthetic achievement suggests that modernist discourse was more conducive to a common-ground dialogue with the West and, last, that the local nativist tradition was seen as provincial if it did not to some extent mirror what was happening in mainland China.

After the lifting of martial law, the second period—the 1990s to the present—was characterized by a relaxation of restrictions on research and writing and an increased number of translations. Funding possibilities became more varied. In terms of government funding, in addition to the "Chinese Books in Translation" (中書外譯) project that has been available since 1990,[36] there is an alternative channel offered by the "Books from Taiwan" scheme, which is orchestrated by the Taiwan Creative Content Agency (文策院), established in 2019. The former's partnership with Cambria Press has yielded seven volumes under its "Taiwan Literature" series, including Yeh Shih-tao's monumental *A History of Taiwan Literature*, known for its distinct Taiwan-centric literary perspective, whereas the latter also supports non-English translation projects. The image of Taiwan, as represented in the translation of literary works, has grown not only in complexity but also in nuance and subtlety. Taiwan is no longer a state-molded "Free China" but an island with its own rich and diverse multilingual and multiethnic literary tradition consisting of dialect literature, Hakka literature, and Indigenous literature. This chapter only discusses some anthologies, but Taiwanese fiction is gaining greater momentum recently, with some works being published by multinational conglomerate companies—such as Wu Ming-yi's *The Man with the Compound Eyes* published by Penguin Random House—instead of university presses, which usually attract a smaller academic audience. It also showcases the achievements of new-generation translators such as Darryl Sterk and Jeremy Tiang. All in all, Taiwanese works in translation are becoming increasingly accessible to the reading public, and the future for Taiwanese literature as world literature, at least in the Anglophone realm, continues to look promising.

---

[36] Previously under the charge of the Ministry of Culture, the project has been managed by the National Museum of Taiwan Literature since 2010.

8

Settling in the World Republic of Letters: Taiwanese Literature in French

Gwennaël Gaffric

Translation and the World Republic of Letters

In her insightful studies, French critic Pascale Casanova proposes the concept of the world republic of letters to examine how works seek literary and cultural capital to find a place in world literature. The path to literary consecration through translation is emphasized in her later article "Consecration and Accumulation of Literary Capital," in which she challenges the classic definition of translation as the movement of a text from one language to another within the framework of an "equal linguistic exchange." She also argues that the translation managed by institutions, sponsors, publishers, and translators is never linear, symmetrical, horizontal, and neutral.[1] For her, a vision of translation as a simple matter of conveying texts from one national literary field to another is not satisfactory[2] because this leads to a superficial analysis of the source text or investigation of the gap between the source text and the target culture.[3] The real relation between the two is thus underestimated or even ignored.

To understand the real stakes of the international circulation of tests, Casanova states that we should "depart from the national point of view, inverting the normal vision and placing the practice of translation in the universe of international literary exchanges, that is, in the world literary field."[4] The world literary field is structured between two forces: on the one hand, the "autonomous pole, the literary fields which are the most endowed with capital" and, on the other, the "most deprived national fields or emergent fields which are usually dependent on national political authorities."[5] The national fields are also structured based on the opposition between an "autonomous cosmopolitan pole" and a "heteronomous national and political pole."[6] The two

---

[1] Pascale Casanova, "Consecration and Accumulation of Literary Capital: Translation as Unequal Exchange," trans. Siobhan Brownlie, in *Critical Readings in Translation Studies*, ed. Mona Baker (London: Routledge, 2010), 287.
[2] Casanova, "Consecration and Accumulation of Literary Capital," 287.
[3] Casanova, "Consecration and Accumulation of Literary Capital," 287.
[4] Casanova, "Consecration and Accumulation of Literary Capital," 287.
[5] Casanova, "Consecration and Accumulation of Literary Capital," 288.
[6] Casanova, "Consecration and Accumulation of Literary Capital," 288.

opposing poles can be considered according to local/global or national/international dialectics. The position of each local/national space in the global/international structure depends on how the second pole recognizes and represents the first, and this recognition depends on what Casanova calls the "volume of capital."[7] The world republic of letters is thus made up of local/national literary poles that are located differentially (and hierarchically) in the world structure according to the place granted to them by the holders and distributors of literary capital, such as critics, editors, universities, and cultural and political institutions.

The object of this chapter is to comprehend the changes of "capital" distribution of Taiwanese literature in a specific pole of the world republic of letters: France.[8] Although the debates over the criteria for defining Taiwanese literature as world literature have raged for decades in Taiwan studies, the role of foreign translation as a process of *canonization* and *structuration* of national literary texts is often neglected. In the context of this contribution, I will focus on Taiwanese works that were originally published in Taiwan, regardless of the geographical origin of its author. Due to limited space, those authors who developed their careers or published works in Japan in the early twentieth century are not in the scope of my current research. The special cases of children's literature and comics from Taiwan will also not be discussed in this chapter, despite the recent dynamism of their translation into French.

This chapter is structured in two sections: first, a critical overview of the history of Taiwanese literature in French translation since the 1980s will be demonstrated, suggesting how the editors, translators, scholars, and institutions have contributed to the empowerment of a pole (Taiwanese literature) from a larger pole with which it was mainly associated (Chinese literature). This illustration of changing trends shows how Taiwanese literature uses its literary capital in different times to participate in the transversal pole, which is the pole of "world literature." The second section focuses on a comparative analysis between the three collections series of Taiwanese literature existing today in France, and how, among the sixty French translations of Taiwanese novels, poetry collections, and short story collections, the latest thirty-six publications from 2000 to 2021 can represent the image of Taiwan well. The strategies of visibility, and in particular the ways of making Taiwan visible within the French literary system, will be underlined by specifying my experiences with the series editors as well as my personal involvement as a translator and as director of the "Taiwan Fiction" collection series. This does not aim to defend my editorial predilection but to emphasize, to the most extent, the difference between my editing and translation strategies with other strategies implemented in other collections.

Rather than a study on the translations, I focus on the paratextual strategy mobilized for translated works that I mention in this chapter—a strategy of visibility and visuality, which allows more objective points of comparison than the heterogeneity assumed by

---

[7] Casanova, "Consecration and Accumulation of Literary Capital," 288.
[8] This chapter focuses more on the activities of translation, publication, and circulation in France, rather than on other Francophone areas such as Belgium, Switzerland, Canada, African countries, and Caribbean places because there are almost no Taiwanese publications in these regions.

texts and authors necessarily different, and for which a contextualization and a stylistic analysis would be needed.⁹ Gérard Genette introduces the term "paratext" for what appears in a literary work outside the text itself: the author's name, the title, the preface, the illustrations, and so on. As Genette points out:

> One does not always know if one should consider that they belong to the text or not, but in any case, they surround it and prolong it, precisely in order to present it, in the usual sense of this verb, but also in its strongest meaning: *to make it present, to assure its presence in the world*, its 'reception' and its consumption, in the form, nowadays at least, of a book.¹⁰

What interests us in the context of Taiwanese literature translations is precisely the different (paratextual) strategies that "offer" a text to its readers, and how these strategies reveal a particular way of assuring Taiwan's presence in the world.

Historicizing Taiwanese Literature in French

An overview of Taiwanese literature in French translation enables us to grasp the image of Taiwan.¹¹ The first Taiwanese work in French may be Huang Chun-ming's (黃春明) short story "Sayonara, Goodbye" (in French title, "Sayonara, au revoir," translated directly from the Chinese title "莎喲娜啦·再見," a work first seen in *China Times* in 1973), published in 1979.¹² However, the confidentiality of the literary magazine in which it was published did not make it a very meaningful marker of the editorial representation of Taiwanese literature in France. In the following year, Chen Jo-hsi (陳若曦), a Taiwanese islander who moved to China in 1966 and witnessed the Cultural Revolution, received an opportunity to publish the French version of the realistic novel *The Execution of Mayor Yin* (*Le préfet Yin et autres histoires de la Révolution Culturelle*, 尹縣長), which is the first Taiwanese collection of short stories in French. Although it was originally published in Taiwan in 1976, this work was not directly linked to local Taiwanese culture but described what had happened on the mainland—a primary reason why the French publishing houses desired to know China rather than Taiwan.

---

⁹ To my knowledge, very few Taiwanese works have changes to be retranslated, except *Taipei People* (台北人) by Pai Hsien-yung (白先勇) and *The Butcher's Wife* (殺夫) by Li Ang (李昂).

¹⁰ Gérard Genette, "Introduction to Paratext," trans. Marie Maclean, *New Literary History* 22, no. 2 (1991): 261.

¹¹ The history of French translation can be seen in my article "台灣文學在法國的現狀" [The Status of Taiwanese Literature in France], *Journal of Taiwanese Literature and History Studies*, no. 3 (2011): 131–63. This article appears outdated today because dozens of other Taiwanese works have been introduced into French.

¹² Angel Pino, "台灣文學在德、美、法三國:歷史及現狀一瞥" [An Overview on the History of Taiwanese Literature in Germany, the US, and France], *Chung-Wai Literary Monthly* 34, no. 10 (2006): 158.

The translator was Simon Leys (a pseudonym of Pierre Ryckmans), from Belgian, one of the European sinologists who publicly denounced the violence of the Cultural Revolution at that time, particularly in his work *The Chairman's New Clothes: Mao and the Cultural Revolution* (*Les Habits neufs du président Mao*), published in 1971. The translator's interest, his academic capital, the publisher's predilection, and the French readers' curious eyes on China all contributed to the translation and circulation of the work.

In the Cold War era, the logic of anticommunism overshadowed Taiwan, a "Chinese region" that played the part of the defense against Communist China. The work *Fool in the Reeds* (*L'Innocent du Village-aux-roseaux*, 荻村傳, originally serialized in 1950 in *Free China Journal*), composed by the KMT official Chen Chi-ying (陳紀瀅), was translated in 1983 to inform the French readers of the inevitability of social upheavals in mainland China after the handover of the CCP. The French translator was the sinologist Jacques Reclus, a grandnephew of the acclaimed thinker Élisée Reclus as well as a zealot who participated in the dissemination of theories of anarchism in China. Although the literary value is now debatable for its ideological orientation, its political value enabled it to be translated. The anticommunist discourse corresponded to the KMT's national narrative that the real China, the ROC, had moved to Taiwan. For the KMT and the world, Taiwan was part of the ROC and was representative of China. Thus, works from Taiwan should express what "China" could mean to the world. What was at play was a will to introduce not Taiwanese but Chinese content. A similar phenomenon is discovered by Pei-yin Lin in the two cases of anthologies in English translation, which are *Twentieth-Century Chinese Stories* edited by Chih-tsing Hsia in 1971 and *An Anthology of Contemporary Chinese Literature* by Pang-yuan Chi in 1975, respectively. Both anthologies, according to Lin, considered "modern Taiwanese literature an extension of Chinese literary tradition *outside* the communist 'bamboo curtain.'"[13] Taiwanese literature in the France of the 1980s or in the United States of the 1970s served as an observation platform to represent Chineseness and denounce Chinese communism. Taiwan did not exist but made itself present as a supplement or an appendix to China.

Another example was Pai Hsien-yung's novella *Childhood in Guilin* (*Enfance à Guilin*, 玉卿嫂, originally published in 1960 in *Modern Literature Magazine*), translated in 1987 by Francis Marche and Kong Rao-yu. On the back cover, the book described itself as a "short Chinese novel," without any further reference to Taiwan as the place where it was originally written and published. The original title, *Nanny Yu-ching*, was replaced with the reference to the Chinese city Guilin, which expressed a misunderstanding that the work was Chinese-produced.

Very few Taiwanese literary works were still available in the French language in the 1990s, despite translations from a few mainland writers, such as Pai Hsien-yung, Wang Wen-hsing (王文興), and Chen Jo-hsi. As Pei-yin Lin has also shown, the works in translation give an impression that the Chinese literary tradition is best preserved

---

[13] Pei-yin Lin, "Positioning 'Taiwanese Literature' to the World: Taiwan as Represented and Perceived in English Translation," in *Positioning Taiwan in a Global Context: Being and Becoming*, ed. Bi-yu Chang and Pei-yin Lin (London: Routledge, 2019), 13–29.

not in China but in Taiwan. This is probably true and can be seen even in the 2004 anthology edited by the French scholar Chantal Chen-Andro. She sees modernism transplanted from the mainland to Taiwan by Chi Hsien (紀弦), Shang Chin (商禽), and Lo Fu (洛夫) in her anthology *Fugitive Sky: Anthology of New Chinese Poetry* (*Le Ciel en fuite, Anthologie de la nouvelle poésie chinoise*, 2004). Although the literary achievement of those Chinese mainland poets should be acknowledged, Chen-Andro's editing strategy implied that Taiwan was not worthy of notice before the handover of the ROC in 1945.

In the 1990s, the progressive democratization of the island, the easier accessibility to literary works by pre-martial law Taiwanese writers, and the interest of a new generation of French researchers in Taiwan all contributed to a reevaluation of the Taiwanese literary experience. In the preface to Wang Wen-hsing's novel *Family Catastrophe* (*Processus familial*, 家變, originally published in 1973, translated into French in 1999), the translator Sandrine Marchand expresses the tension between seeing Taiwan as the best preservation of Chinese literary culture and tradition and appreciating Taiwan's uniqueness and local modernity:

> Paradoxically, Taiwan, which is in search of cultural identity, has managed better than fifty-year-old [Chinese Communist Party] in preserving and flourishing traditional Chinese culture and its art of writing. [...] These differences are particularly important regarding the choice of a subject and the freedom of writing. [...] Maybe it is a political consequence [...] but Taiwanese literature has [now] its own characteristics, a relationship with the external world imbued with subjectivity, a consideration of the literary style. All these [are impossibly] confused with those of the writers of the PRC.[14]

The editorial context was composed at the end of the twentieth century when very few writers were published in French and the image of Taiwan, largely associated with the idea of an alternative "free" or "nationalist" China, was overwhelmingly absent from media discourse. The relation to the Chinese culture is embodied in the author Wang Wen-hsing, who has well illustrated the ambiguity of perceiving Chinese writing and tradition. Wang creates multiple Chinese phrases and his own rhythms of texts to problematize the Chinese language. For Marchand, this seemingly assumes Chinese legacy in Taiwan but simultaneously bids farewell to Chinese tradition and indicates that only Taiwan, as a marginal place far away from China, enjoyed the privilege of the avant-garde movement while China experienced Cultural Revolution and destroyed its Chinese heritage.

Strongly disagreeing with the meridian of French-dominant criteria that Taiwan is a free and traditional version of China or an inseparable part of China—either the ROC or the PRC—Marchand desires to amend the outdated Chinese discourse and acknowledge the existence of Taiwanese literature and its studies. This attempt to make Taiwanese literature more acknowledged is sometimes denied by the ignorance of

---

[14] Sandrine Marchand, introduction to *Processus Familial*, by Wang Wen-hsing, trans. Sandrine Marchand (Paris: Actes Sud, 1999), 1.

publishers. This can be seen in Marchand's translation of Wang Wen-hsing's *Backed against the Sea* (*Un homme dos à la mer*, 背海的人). She recalls:

> [W]e sometimes confront publishers' resistance to [French alienation that is made purposefully to follow the strangeness of] Chinese language. I had this experience when I translated *Backed against the Sea*, a work stylistically much more complex than [the author's previous work] *Family Catastrophe*. The publisher whom I initially cooperated with, for example, asked me to "clean" all the [author's intentional] repetitions and all the [author's deliberately] typographical error, and to write in "good French."[15]

From 2000 onward, Taiwanese literature in French appears more diverse, with texts written by female, indigenous, and native writers. This exponential growth can be explained by two major factors: first, the development of Taiwan studies conducted by local French scholars, and second, the pivotal roles of Taiwanese cultural and political institutions.

For the first dimension, France had no influential scholars like Pang-yuan Chi, Chih-tsing Hsia, and Joseph Shiu-ming Lau in the United States to introduce Taiwanese literature to French readers in the twentieth century. Taiwanese literature in French largely depended on the enthusiasm of single French sinologists and translators, such as Pierre Ryckmans, Jacques Reclus, and André Lévy, who translated many Chinese classics and rarely explored Taiwanese works in the 1980s and 1990s. Recently, the studies were fostered by the French translator-scholars such as Marie Laureillard, Isabelle Rabut, Angel Pino, Sandrine Marchand, Coraline Jortay, Matthieu Kolatte, and me. The acknowledgment and construction of Taiwan as a legitimate academic object of studies since the 2000s have contributed to the establishment of Taiwan as "an ontological space" and enabled Taiwan to speak by and for itself, without constantly being reduced to another sample of China or being understood through China.

In addition to the involvement of individual French scholars, Taiwanese political and cultural institutions largely contribute to the legitimization and dissemination of Taiwanese literature, mainly through translation and publication grant programs. Since 1990, about forty Taiwanese books in French have benefited from the grants proffered by the Council for Cultural Affairs (文建會), the Ministry of Culture (文化部), the National Museum of Taiwan Literature (國立台灣文學館), and the Taiwan Cultural Center in Paris (巴黎台灣文化中心). The latter is the cultural office of the Taipei Representative Office in France.[16]

The grant programs show, as Pascale Casanova writes, that

---

[15] The book will be published in another publishing house in 2022. See Sandrine Marchand, "Sandrine Marchand: 'Croiser d'autres langues dans le métissage des syllabes,'" interview by Fabienne Durand-Bogaert, *Genesis*, no. 38 (2014): 139–44.

[16] For a study on publication grants over the period 1990–2011, see Liao Shih-wen, "政府公部門的翻譯贊助與台灣文學的外譯：以《台灣文學外譯書目提要 (1990–2011) 為例" [Governmental Patronage on the Translation of Taiwanese Literature into Foreign Languages: A Case of *Bibliographical Synopses of Translated Taiwan Literature (1990–2011)*], *Bulletin of Taiwanese Literature*, no. 18 (2014): 305–26.

in the world literary universe, translation is both one of the main weapons in the struggle for literary legitimacy and the great authority of specific acts of consecration. For a dominated writer, struggling for access to translation is in fact a matter of struggling for his or her existence as a legitimate member of the world republic of letters, for access to the literary centers (to the critical and consecrating authorities).[17]

In the case of Taiwan, this struggle through translation is also a struggle for the constitution of an autonomous pole beyond a place dominated by Chinese literature.[18] The process of differing and empowering Taiwanese image can be observed in the paratexts of the translated works. In the past, book covers were often labeled "translated from Chinese" (without mentioning Taiwan), and now, the new label "translated from Chinese (Taiwan)" is welcome. Most of the book covers today clarify without ambiguity the Taiwanese origin of the authors and the texts, while prefaces, forewords, postscripts, and footnotes now offer information specific to the languages, history, culture, and environmental context of Taiwan. A comparative exemplar is that the anthology, translated from Pang-yuan Chi's English volumes entitled *An Anthology of Contemporary Chinese Literature* (1975) into French in 1989, was still introduced as modern Chinese literature,[19] whereas the recent anthologies conspicuously mention the geographical and political identity illustrated by the authors.[20]

The worlding of Taiwanese literature in French is noticeable these years. This process is deliberately conducted by Taiwanese institutions, French publishing houses and universities, and individual agents such as translators and series editors. Additionally, literary festivals and literary awards play pivotal roles in promoting Taiwanese literature to a larger stage of world literature. This can be observed in the participation of Taiwanese writers in French literary festivals, such as Wu Ming-yi (吳明益), Shu Kuo-chih (舒國治), and Chou Tan-ying (周丹穎) at the Amazing Travelers Festival (Festival des Etonnants voyageurs) in Saint-Malo; Wu Ming-yi and Walis Nokan at the Atlantides Festival (Festival Atlantides) in Nantes; Sabrina Huang (黃麗群) at the Book

---

[17] Casanova, "Consecration and Accumulation of Literary Capital," 295.
[18] From Ng Kim Chew's perspective, Casanova's world republic of letters sees "Europe literature" as a legitimate and referential center to Latin American and African literatures who use those European colonial languages such as French, English, German, Spanish, and Portuguese. The use of European languages enables those postcolonial writers to be seen in Europe, and thus receive more literary capital, in comparison with Mandarin and Arabic writers. In the case of the "Sinophone" world republic of letters, Chinese literature occupies the position of Europe, discriminating against the periphery of Taiwanese literature, Hong Kong literature, and Malaysian Chinese literature. See Ng Kim Chew, "南方華文文學共和國：一個芻議" [The Sinophone World Republic of Southern Letters], *Sun Yat-sen Journal of Humanities*, no. 45 (2018): 1–20.
[19] *Anthologie de la littérature chinoise contemporaine*, trans. André Nougé, ed. Pang-yuan Chi et al. (Taipei: National Institute for Compilation and Translation, 1989). The English anthology is *An Anthology of Contemporary Chinese Literature: Taiwan: 1949–1974*, ed. Pan-yuan Chi et al. (Taipei: National Institute for Compilation and Translation, 1975).
[20] The volumes are *Anthologie historique de la prose romanesque taïwanaise modern*, ed. Angel Pino and Isabelle Rabut (Paris: Youfeng, 2016–2018) and *Formosana: histoires de démocratie à Taiwan*, ed. Gwennaël Gaffric (Paris: L'Asiathèque, 2021).

Fair (Salon du Livre) in Paris, Chi Ta-wei (紀大偉) and Kao Yi-feng (高翊峰) at the Utopiales Festival (Festival des Utopiales) in Nantes. Taiwanese writers are often the only Asian or Chinese-speaking representatives of these literary festivals. Participation in these events helps to acknowledge Taiwan's soft powers: the voice, identity, and autonomy of the country. The co-presence of Chinese and Taiwanese writers is also an opportunity to engage in equal discussions between China and Taiwan, as at the Utopiales Festival in 2017 when Taiwanese writer Kao Yi-feng and Chinese writer Hao Jingfang (郝景芳) were in the same roundtable panel.

It sometimes happens that certain works are the subject of an unexpected "canonization." This is particularly the case of nominations or literary prizes, such as the award for the Best Island Novel (all languages combined) obtained by Wu Ming-yi's novel *The Man with Compound Eyes* (*L'homme aux yeux à facettes*, translated in 2014 from the 2011 work 複眼人), at the Island Book Fair (Salon du Livre insulaire) in Ouessant, or the nominations for Chi Ta-wei's novel *The Membranes* (translated in 2015 from the 1996 work 膜) or his 2021 collection of short stories *Pearls* (*Perles*, 珍珠), which has been shortlisted for the Fantasy and Science Fiction Award (Grand Prix de l'Imaginaire) and the Guimet Museum Asian Literary Award (Prix du Musée Guimet).[21] As a symbol of legitimacy and critical aesthetics, festivals and literary awards are the passports to getting access to the international/transcultural territory still largely unexplored by Taiwan.

The Series of Taiwanese Literature in French

Knowing the operation of the book series helps to understand how Taiwanese works are promoted in France.[22] The translation project "Lettres de Taïwan," directed by Isabelle Rabut, Angel Pino, and Chan Hing-ho, was established in the end of the 1990s on the model of the "Bibliothèque asiatique," in which Pino had participated. Lettres de Taïwan is *nomadic*, meaning that it does not belong to a specific publishing house. It instead helps to find suitable publishers for each book proposal. In total, fourteen books, including poems, short stories, anthologies, and novels, have been published by four different publishing houses—Actes Sud, Bleu de Chine, Christian Bourgois, and You Feng. Another book series, "Taiwan Fiction," directed by me, was founded in 2015 in cooperation with the Asiathèque publishing house, which specializes in Asian literatures, philosophies, and languages. Eight books have been published to date. "Poésie de Taïwan," directed by Marie Laureillard, was founded within the

---

[21] The case of the novel *The Membranes* by Chi Ta-wei is significant because this novel, which was originally published in the "Taiwan Fiction" collection series, has been re-edited in the prestigious collection of Livre de Poche and is now regularly cited as a world masterpiece of queer science fiction.

[22] The strategies of publication and translation illustrated in this chapter are based on two interviews with Isabelle Rabut, one of the series editors of the "Lettres de Taïwan," and Marie Laureillard, the series editor of the "Poésie de Taïwan," in autumn 2020.

Circé publishing house, which mainly publishes poetry from all over the world. Fourteen books have already been published to date. The three series have witnessed the flourishment of French translation since Taiwan considerably promoted its local identity and cast away the authoritarian experiences in the fully democratic era of the 1990s.

Translation is a form of transferring cultural/literary capital, the value of a text, and its degree of legitimacy. The criteria of getting translated depend not only on the marketable and aesthetic value of the text in French but also on the canonical potential mostly emphasized by the well-versed editors who specialize in Taiwan studies, share certain cultural capital, and foresee the circulation of translations in France. The mode of process and operation is similar for the three series. The directors are scholars who have already produced Taiwanese literary translations with other publishers before being involved in the collection series. The series editors sometimes play the roles of translators for various reasons, such as a good knowledge of the author, personal taste, limited financial resources or short translation deadlines, or replacement of an unavailable translator. In some cases, translators propose books to the series editors, who examine the proposals and choose whether to accept them. This is particularly important for "Poésie de Taïwan" because several projects are initiated by translators themselves. Other prerogatives are generally granted to the directors, including those to discuss and determine the Chinese/Taiwanese transcription standards, and the format of paratexts, such as prefaces, postfaces, footnotes, and sometimes even book covers. This happens particularly to my "Taiwan Fiction" series. Generally, the series editors are responsible for applying for grants from various organizations, be they French or Taiwanese, monitoring the translation rights contracts. Since these editors know about Taiwan, they are required to do copy editing, proofreading, and revising the translations produced by their colleagues to affirm the best quality of texts. This process includes a time-consuming discussion with translators on different translation options and recommendations, which is a rare experience for translating works from other European languages. Some proposals fail to attract the publishers' eyes, mostly for technical or commercial reasons such as lengthy texts, too unusual or experimental literary format, or problems with the relevance of the text in the catalog. These limitations are why the "Lettres de Taïwan" collection series was formed to be *nomadic*, to assign texts of different periods, genres, and styles to suitable publishers. In principle, the mission of the series editors is no different from that of a publisher: he or she must ensure the success of the books and consider how they can be circulated globally for potential readership. This whole process is carried out each time, in consultation with the editors, sometimes with translators, or even with the institutions who subsidize the projects. The choice of which books should get translated is always a negotiation between different forces. As Pei-yin Lin notices in the English translation of Taiwanese works, there continues to be a "compromise in which the editor's preferences, the contents, and the targeted audience's tastes all come into play."[23]

---

[23] Pei-yin Lin, "Positioning 'Taiwanese Literature' to the World," 25.

The three series have their own features that are not shared with each other. The historical period is broader for the project of the "Lettres de Taïwan" collection series, as it spans from the period of Japanese colonization to the early 2000s. Since the project cooperates with multiple publishers, the genres can be more diverse: poems, short stories, novels, and anthologies. As Isabelle Rabut indicates:

> We constantly seek texts which have the best literary quality and play a pivotal role in the literary history [...] without falling into a sociological vision of literature by, to illustrate, publishing texts merely written by women or specific communities: even if this approach appears in our anthology of short stories that cover a long period, from the Japanese period to the end of the 1990s, the factors of historical and aesthetic values are still important and always appliable to the rest of our collections.[24]

The "Poésie de Taïwan" collection series highlights three poetry proposals per year. Marie Laureillard states:

> We try to find a balance for a variety of the three books by choosing at least one living contemporary poet—women are sometimes preferable. We also want to introduce poets in the earlier era of Taiwan, such as Yu Kuang-chung (余光中), Lo Fu (洛夫) or Chou Meng-tieh (周夢蝶), to avoid overemphasizing the contemporary or emerging young authors and ignoring the sense of history. We are looking for "solid values" rather than fleeting successes. [...] Our series showcases the modernist movement of the 1950s and the 1960s—a time that was influenced by the West but did not reject Chinese heritage. We also emphasize the emergence of the local culture embodied in the ensuing nativist movement of the 1970–1980 period, and the period of democratic pluralism since the lifting of martial law in 1987. Political, ecological, indigenous, postmodern poetic works, both in Taiwanese dialects and Mandarin, all should not be forgotten.[25]

Among the three series, "Taiwan Fiction" intends to give more voice to contemporary Taiwanese authors who have published works after 1987 or exclusively after 2000, without concern for their literary canonization. This explains why some very recent texts not (yet) consecrated by literary criticism in Taiwan have already been published in the collection. The lower emphasis on whether the works are canonized in Taiwan explains why some texts that are not (yet) consecrated by Taiwanese scholars and readers have already been translated into French, such as works by Huang Chong-kai (黃崇凱), Chou Tan-ying, Lay Chih-ying (賴志穎), and so on. Except for the canonized screenplay of Hou Hsiao-hsien's (侯孝賢) *The City of Sadness* (*La Cité des douleurs*, 悲情城市, 1989, written by Chu T'ien-wen 朱天文 and Wu Nien-chen 吳念真), most

---

[24] Isabelle Rabut, interview by author via email, November 7, 2020.
[25] Marie Laureillard, interview by author via email, November 11, 2020.

of the latest publications are fiction, aiming to introduce emerging authors whose works present urgent issues in France and the rest of the world, such as environmental, indigenous, queer, and democratic issues.

While investigating the publications of the three series, one can notice a certain degree of differences. Rabut's "Lettres de Taïwan" showcases a view of Taiwanese literary history by including as many works as possible in a compressed form. Instead of sociopolitical significance, the aesthetic and historical importance is the key factor to decide if the works are worthy of translation. "Poésie de Taïwan" accepts historical perspectives and highlights female poetry, and my "Taiwan Fiction" can be politically and socially oriented, underlining the thickness of history, particularly the White Terror, which is hardly known by French readers. Since the three series are well defined in their own interest and field, there is almost no competition between them or overlapping of texts and authors. The exceptions are always acclaimed and multi-genre works. One such author is Chu T'ien-wen, with her short stories in the "Lettres de Taïwan" and the above-mentioned screenplay in "Taiwan Fiction." Another is Walis Nokan (瓦歷斯·諾幹), especially with his poetry collection *The Mountain Is Dreaming* (*La Montagne rêve*, 山也有夢, translated in 2015) in "Poésie de Taïwan" and his short story collection *The Path of Dreams* (*Le Sentier des rêves*, 瓦歷斯微小說, originally published in 2014, translated in 2018) in "Taiwan Fiction."

The three collections differ in their strategies of making paratexts. In the "Poésie de Taïwan" collection series, Marie Laureillard invites the translator to write a preface of around twenty pages about the author's biography and poetics. Laureillard finds it "essential to identify the author and locate the main traces of his/her creation."[26] The use of footnotes is decided by a translator, who may avoid overinterpretation and believe that the text should be expressed by itself or may adopt multiple references to clarify the text and some cultural backgrounds for French readers. In the "Lettres de Taïwan," the series editors take the responsibility of writing criticism for each book. Isabelle Rabut specifies, "We write forewords or postfaces only where they are essential to enlighten the reader. As for footnotes, we do not limit the quantities." In "Taiwan Fiction," the series editor writes a foreword or postface to contextualize the author's achievement in his or her own literary career and Taiwanese literary history, as well as to provide some perspectives and interpretations. The addendum, written by the author, a specialist, or a French writer, can cover the story of how the book comes into being, how the idea for the book is developed, and what the book means for French readers. The use of footnotes is decided by the series editor or translators if validated by the series editor.

Transcribing Taiwanese proper names and toponyms is always an issue for translators and editors. As Marie Laureillard says:

> The transcription of each author's name is a predicament. Usually, we ask the author if he or she prefers the pinyin transcription adopted in the PRC or the

---

[26] Marie Laureillard, interview by author via email, November 11, 2020.

Wade-Giles used in Taiwan. We also value the opinion of the translator. The rule is quite flexible. [...] As for the toponyms mentioned in the poems, if they relate to Taiwan, we adopt the transcription used in Taiwan, but if they are to China, we opt for pinyin instead.[27]

Although the Wade-Giles system is the norm for the "Taiwan Fiction" series, the transcription for the Taiwanese Hokkien regularly uses the Tâi-lô system—an official romanization system, particularly for this Taiwanese language. The Tâi-lô system is applied in the translation of Wu Ming-yi's *The Illusionist on the Skywalk* (*Le Magicien sur la passerelle*, translated in 2017 from the 2011 work 天橋上的魔術師) and Chu T'ien-wen and Wu Nien-chen's screenplay *The City of Sadness*. The works published in the "Lettres de Taïwan" seldom use the Tâi-lô system to transcribe the proper names of Taiwanese Hokkien, except in Huang Chun-ming's translated work of "The Gong" ("Le Gong," translated in 2001 by Emmanuelle Péchenart, from the 1969 work 鑼), in which the nickname of the main character, "Stupid Child" (憨欽仔),[28] is transcribed into Gam Khim-a, rather than Han Qinzai in the pinyin system or Han Chin-tzu in the Wade-Giles system. Since the pinyin system, mainly used in China, is considered a gesture of assimilation for the marginal Sinophone communities that struggle to preserve the diversity of spelling, the adoptions of the Wade-Giles system and the Tâi-lô system imply not merely the complexity of the linguistic situation in Taiwan but also the awakening of local identity.

Apart from these divergences in transcription and paratextual strategies, the three collection directors nevertheless agree on an indisputable fact: the published translations are put at the service of the recognition and legitimation of the literary value of Taiwanese literature in general, which explains particularly the diversity of authors (and sometimes of genres and formats) translated.

Conclusion: Translation and Performativity

The display of translating Taiwanese literature to French suggests the correlation between the political and academic representation of Taiwan and the diversity of Taiwanese literary texts in translation. The examples illustrated above show the fact that translation is not a singular poietic (*poïétique*), a term coined by Paul Valéry, but plural dimensions of poietics, namely, a sort of multiple ideological participation in accepting book proposals, finding grants, deciding the content and style, choosing languages, writing criticism, designing book covers, packaging all loose information, and marketing books. Translation is analogous to the notion of performativity described by Jacques Derrida, for every act of writing and every related experience consists of Translation is analogous to the notion of performativity described by

---

[27] Isabelle Rabut, interview by author via email, November 7, 2020.
[28] Perhaps a more accurate transcription can be "Gong-gin-a" for "stupid child" (戇囝仔).

Jacques Derrida, for every act of writing and every related experience consists of "giving space for singular events, and inventing something new in the form of acts of writing which [...] give[s] oneself to a [poetic]-literary *performativity* at least analogous to that of promises, orders, or acts of constitution or legislation which do not only change language, or which, in changing language, change more than language."[29]

As an "act of language" that "changes more than language," translation participates in this performative function, not only by disrupting those normative representations—the wrong image of Taiwan under the umbrella of Chineseness, the minor position of Taiwan in the world, and the grant discourse of the PRC—but also by providing a platform for French readers to know Taiwanese heterogeneity within its literature, to escape from the PRC's political encroachment, to recognize minority discourses, to enjoy the values of freedom and democracy, and to let the imagination run wild. An illustration of translation as an "act" can be seen in the anthology *Formosa: Stories of Democracy in Taiwan* (*Formosana: histoires de démocratie à Taïwan*), which I had the honor of editing and was published in 2021. The nine short stories were all written after 1987, the date I have chosen to mark "contemporary" Taiwanese literature. This project was intended to be a response to the ignorance of the French media about the Taiwanese democratization process—its successes, failures, hopes, and attempts—as well as the diversity of historical experiences of its different inhabitants. It was not meant to substitute a literary view for a historical perspective but to showcase how literature provides deep thoughts for historical events, how fiction can shift the scales of time and space, how writers can use individual trajectories as their navigation for historical events, and how their works can represent a noninstitutional, more complex, and ambiguous history. The choice of the texts for this anthology was aimed to contextualize literary productions and historical events but not to simplify these texts into a plain representation of the social context—that is, not to make them a simple sociological illustration of a Taiwanese experience or spirit but rather to show how Taiwanese literature can not only illustrate the hopes for democracy and reflect on the imperfectness of the political system but also move any individual beyond Taiwan and, hence, arouse a possible political practice in France.

If the practice of French translation is a practice of promoting the unseen groups, such as Taiwan, one can remember the concept of minor literature, developed by Gilles Deleuze and Félix Guattari, and use it to explain the situation of Taiwanese literature and comprehend how fiction can be linked with the value of democracy.[30] Minor literature attempts to dislocate the major languages—both Chinese source texts and French target language—and make them alienated to themselves. Like any text rendered in minor literature, translation is an act of deterritorialization, namely, breaking the borders of Taiwanese literature as well as China's grand narrative. The

---

[29] Jacques Derrida, "This Strange Institution Called Literature: An Interview with Jacques Derrida," interview by Derek Attridge, in *Acts of Literature*, ed. Derek Attridge (London: Routledge, 1992), 55. Emphasis mine.

[30] Gwennaël Gaffric, "Démocratie Made in Formose," in *Formosana: histoires de démocratie à Taïwan*, ed. Gwennaël Gaffric (Paris: L'Asiathèque, 2021), 286–8.

question of how to "become the nomad, the immigrant, the gypsy of his own language," provoked by Deleuze and Guattari,[31] can be effortlessly answered: by translating. Through the act of translating Taiwanese literature, translators extricate Taiwan from a set of predetermined literary, political, and linguistic signifiers, reject the identity that is fixed and squeezed by Chineseness, confer it with a nomadic, liberal, and democratic characteristic, and encourage readers to hear a diversity of voices.

---

[31] Gilles Deleuze and Félix Guattari, "What Is a Minor Literature?," trans. Robert Brinkley, *Mississippi Review* 11, no. 3 (1983): 19.

9

Voices from Alternative Literary Fields: Translating Taiwanese Literature into Italian

Federica Passi

Do twenty translations suffice to deem Taiwanese literature important to an Italian readership? If we consider only the raw data, the answer might be no. Twenty literary works (including novels and short stories) are the total of translations into Italian from Taiwanese works since 1997.[1] This number seems to indicate that the Italian literary field lags behind those of French- and English-speaking countries. Comparisons with the Japanese literary field are even more uneven: due to its colonial history, Japan has a particularly close and long-standing relationship with Taiwan and, consequently, profound knowledge of the country.

For a deeper understanding of the entry of Taiwanese literature into Italian, however, raw numbers of publications may be insufficient. When approaching literary exchange between two countries in the international arena and the meanings these can take on, publication data requires interpretation and may be just one of many elements worthy of consideration. In this chapter, I delineate how Taiwanese literature has adopted certain modes to enter academia and the cultural field in Italy, with a special focus on translation. I first demonstrate useful methodologies in relation to the concept of world literature. Next, I analyze the main translations of Taiwanese works published in Italy during the past twenty-four years, seeking to identify the significance of these publication projects and what role they have played. The study of the key factors that contribute to cultural exchange between Italy and Taiwan leads to some final considerations, in which I attempt to read Taiwanese literature in Italy not only as a field of study but also as a field of action.

Worlding a Minor Literature

To assess the place of Taiwanese literature in Italy, it is necessary to first position the two literary fields in relation to one another in the context of world literature. As Franco

---

[1] This number does not include children's literature, which adds about seventeen more titles.

Moretti insightfully notes, "World Literature is not an object, it's a problem."[2] The complicated relationship between world literature and a single literature, or between two literatures interacting with one another, can be viewed from multiple perspectives.

To illustrate, one of the most debated and frequently cited models for studying literary exchange in today's world is that proposed by Pascale Casanova in her *World Republic of Letters*. In her provocative description of international exchange in the literary field, Casanova stresses the importance of accumulated literary capital and discloses the hidden rules for literary interactions between dominating and dominated languages, whose exchange is inevitably unequal. In the "world republic of letters," the West (and the city of Paris, particularly) is the "literary Greenwich meridian," able to define the criteria and hold the power of consecration.[3] In Casanova's reading, the Chinese language, despite its "large number of speakers" and "great literary tradition," is "little known or recognized in the international literary market" because the linguistic and literary capital of a language is determined "not by the number of writers and readers of the language, but by the number of literary polyglots who use it and by the number of literary translators who are instrumental in the circulation of texts from or toward the literary language."[4] Her description of the struggle for legitimacy of literatures written in dominated languages, such as Chinese, within the world republic of letters has been groundbreaking and enlightening in many respects and has exerted a powerful influence in the field of translation. Translation, Casanova argues, can be viewed from two perspectives. First, it can be a means of "accumulation of capital," which occurs "when, through a collective strategy, the dominated national literary field attempts to import literary capital" by translating "great universal texts." Second, it can enact "literary consecration," which happens "when the dominating consecrators import a text from a dominated literary field"; this is the "only specific means of being perceived, becoming visible, of existing" in the international literary field.[5] Translation is thus an experience of unequal exchange at different levels—including linguistic, social, and political levels—and puts into play multiple dynamics, including struggle, domination, legitimation, and hierarchy.

Casanova's paradigm aptly describes the fundamental dynamics operating at the core of the literary flux between areas with different linguistic and cultural capital. The dominating position of some European languages, such as English, is indeed self-evident—the dramatic discrepancy between the number of English texts translated into Chinese and the number of Chinese texts translated into English can stand as clear evidence of this. However, Casanova's model, which is based on the case of francophone literature, has an intrinsically Eurocentric perspective that might limit its applicability in other milieus and its capacity to fully account for the case of East Asian literatures in

---

[2] Franco Moretti, *Distant Reading* (London: Verso, 2013), 46.
[3] Pascale Casanova, "Consecration and Accumulation of Literary Capital: Translation as Unequal Exchange," trans. Siobhan Brownlie, in *Critical Readings in Translation Studies*, ed. Mona Baker (London: Routledge, 2010), 295.
[4] Casanova, "Consecration and Accumulation of Literary Capital," 289–90.
[5] Casanova, "Consecration and Accumulation of Literary Capital," 290–91 & 296.

relation to the world. As Yingjin Zhang remarks on the possibility of mapping Chinese literature onto, and as part of, world literature, "every view is local and hence partial in a global perspective," and "mapping China in world literature cannot succeed if one is confined to a single viewing position, no matter how global it claims to be."[6] If a Eurocentric aspect is always considered and equivalent to a global perspective, Zhang's statement encourages readers to challenge this dated myth and embrace a new Weltanschauung: the exchange of two local, minor literatures can also be seen as global and part of world literature. Such importance of *equality* is unfortunately ignored by Casanova, who focuses too much on *unequal* relations with the European center. East Asian literatures constantly interact with one another, and this international level should also be taken into consideration, as their readership, markets, and literary fields are not only economically impactful but also very lively.

Tackling this issue in his "A World Republic of Southern [Sinophone] Letters," Carlos Rojas describes three possible responses to Casanova's model. First, we can reject the model outright based on its "ethnocentric and deeply provincial worldview" in favor of "a more inclusive category of world literature."[7] Second, we can affirm Casanova's model on the basis of its descriptive capacity, as there is clear evidence of "obsession with Western recognition" occurring in dominated literary fields—China's Nobel Prize complex can function as an apt example.[8] Instead, Rojas concentrates on a third potential response: to rethink the underlying assumptions of Casanova's model, challenge its perspective, and illustrate the possibility of imagining multiple world literatures. The assumption that China is not outstanding in the "international market," as shown in Casanova's model, is true only if we identify "international" with the West. There are other markets and other literary fields, such as East Asian fields, where Chinese-language literature occupies a much more preeminent position and operates "independently of what Casanova rather parochially calls 'the international market'" and with "mechanisms for assessing literary value that also are mostly independent of the Eurocentric institutions."[9]

Rojas thus emphasizes the existence of international literary fields beyond Europe (or Paris in Casanova's term). One of the autonomous entities without centripetal forces is named the republic of southern letters. What is particularly interesting in Rojas's discussion is his emphasis on marginalized literary works of Sinophone communities, for they offer an alternative response to some centripetal logic (such as Sinocentrism). These marginalized works can be interpreted as, in the words of Gilles Deleuze and Félix Guattari, "minor literatures" because these authors do not identify with many of the values and ideals associated with the tradition of the language they use. The way they exhibit suggests, instead, a different, centrifugal logic, and these authors see this

---

[6] Yingjin Zhang, "Mapping Chinese Literature as World Literature," *CLCWeb: Comparative Literature and Culture* 17, no. 1 (2015): 8.
[7] Carlos Rojas, "A World Republic of Southern [Sinophone] Letters," *Modern Chinese Literature and Culture* 30, no. 1 (2018): 44.
[8] Rojas, "A World Republic of Southern [Sinophone] Letters," 45.
[9] Rojas, "A World Republic of Southern [Sinophone] Letters," 47–48.

logic to be of primary importance "to assert their distance or independence" from any hegemonic literary center.[10] This position is realized in the works of Ng Kim Chew (as the main object in Rojas's argument), who valiantly envisions a "republic of southern Sinophone letters." In addressing Chinese-language literature from the "South Seas" (*Nanyang*) regions, which include Hong Kong, Taiwan, Singapore, and Malaysia, Ng identifies two contrasting intentions behind the actions of authors and movements of literary works: First, there is a need for some authors to connect to a Chinese-language literary field centered on mainland China, because of ancestral affinity or economic development. There is, however, a second intention, expressed by other authors, who recognize this hegemonic center but, instead of striving for recognition and consecration by it, attempt to maintain their own peripheral and independent position. In Rojas's reading, Ng's model can be strongly linked to "archipelagic thinking," which substitutes Casanova's relations to a hegemonic center with a new model that simultaneously acknowledges the isolation of islands within archipelagoes and affirms equal connections among islands.

These considerations can help us analyze Italian translation of Taiwanese literature by assessing the possibility of more nuanced relationships between these two literary fields. If Taiwanese literature can be easily labeled as a system of texts written in a "dominated" language, under-recognized in the international literary market, and struggling to export its literary production, we should not forget that its "dominated" position is only partial. As I have pointed out elsewhere, Taiwan's peripheral position, if compared to the literature of China, has also, at times, been of *potentiality*.[11] Taiwan not only plays an active and central role in relation to the literatures of Southeast Asia but also overcomes the label of dominated literature in relation to China. This happens, for instance, when sensitive works by Chinese authors find their way to print in Taiwan. Chinese and Taiwanese literary fields dynamically influence world literature.

If Taiwanese language, literature, and culture cannot be "dominating," Italian language, literature, and culture cannot be defined as "dominating" either. Although Italian humanities have a long and outstanding tradition and stand among the major European literary fields, there are a limited number of contemporary authors whose works are translated and circulate globally if compared with, for instance, Anglophone writers.[12] Thus, while the Italian market can be considered a literary center from Casanova's perspective, we should not forget that it is also a field partially dominated by other bigger and more influential literary fields.

The necessity of shifting our perspectives, from Casanova's unequal relations between dominated and dominating countries to Ng's and Rojas's new republic of letters that celebrates equality and centripetal force, is particularly important to

---

[10] Rojas, "A World Republic of Southern [Sinophone] Letters," 49.
[11] Federica Passi, "The Literary Island: Isolation and Integration as Key Elements in Reading Taiwan Literature," in *Connecting Taiwan: Participation, Integration, Impacts*, ed. Carsten Storm (London: Routledge, 2018), 191–2.
[12] The global resonance of Italo Calvino and Umberto Eco or of recent cases, such as the books by Elena Ferrante and Andrea Camilleri, can serve as an example for Italian literature as world literature here.

comprehend the cultural exchange between Taiwan and Italy. Italian translation of Taiwanese literature is significant because, first, Italian is another language (and one from the dominating European literary field) that can act as a vehicle for Taiwanese literature to enter the world,[13] and second, because this translation activity can be seen as an alternative cultural exchange that involves a higher degree of freedom and opens up the possibility of a more nuanced understanding of dominated and dominating languages and a less stereotypical assessment of the importation and reception of literature.

Positioning Taiwanese Literature in Italy

The introduction of Taiwanese literature to Italy is a rather recent phenomenon. The first translations date back to 1997, and it was during this decade that Taiwanese literature started to attract attention in Italian academia, with pioneering MA and PhD dissertations being written on the subject and researchers tackling it in their work.

An important characteristic in this period was the positioning of Taiwanese literature (which was—and is still—the main area of Taiwan studies developed in Italy): it first grew as a research topic within the well-established category of sinology.[14] On the one hand, this was helpful because this niche research area could grow and gain visibility within the bigger category without coming into competition with it; on the other hand, the emerging studies were easily overshadowed by the concept of Chinese studies (or sinology), placing Taiwanese literature in a peripheral position that was not easy to overcome.

Another aspect relates to the nationality of researchers who have a strong influence on the degrees of importation of Taiwanese culture. Since Italy has not experienced a significant influx of Taiwanese immigrants, researchers of Taiwanese literature are purely Italians, all of whom have trained to be sinologists.[15] This situation is dramatically different than that in English-speaking countries (notably the United States), where, on the contrary, the active presence of literary researchers from Taiwan triggers the development of the field. This is the case with literary scholars such as Joseph Lau, Leo Ou-fan Lee, David Der-wei Wang, and Yvonne Chang, all of whom have connections

---

[13] For Kuei-fen Chiu, the number of languages into which a writer's work is translated is one of international recognition indicators of how global a writer can be. Other indicators include international awards, international book reviews or reports, and anthologies by international publishers. See "'Worlding' World Literature from the Literary Periphery: Four Taiwanese Models," *Modern Chinese Literature and Culture* 30, no. 1 (2018): 15.

[14] It should be noted that in Italy "sinologia" is used with a wider meaning compared to the English term "sinology": originally used to describe the study of Chinese literary, philosophical, and historical classics, it is now intended to include the study of modern and contemporary China and global Chinese culture and thus incorporates the meaning of the term "Chinese studies" as commonly used in the English-speaking world.

[15] This happens in France too. For the circulation of Taiwanese literature in France, see Gwennaël Gaffric's chapter in this volume.

with Taiwan, and whose contributions to Taiwan studies are prominent within and even beyond American academia.

As noted above, the introduction of Taiwanese literature to Italy happened under the banner of "Chinese literature" and, specifically, thanks to a set of research titles published in the United States starting at the end of the 1980s, among which the following should be mentioned: *Modern Chinese Women Writers: Critical Appraisals*, by M. Duke in 1989; *Worlds Apart: Recent Chinese Writing and Its Audiences*, edited by H. Goldblatt in 1990; *Modern Chinese Writers Self-Portrayals*, edited by H. Martin in 1992; *The Columbia Anthology of Modern Chinese Literature*, edited by J. Lau and H. Goldblatt in 1995; *Chinese Literature in the Second Half of a Modern Century: A Critical Survey*, edited by Pang-yuan Chi and David Der-wei Wang in 2000; and *The Columbia Companion to Modern East Asian Literature*, edited by J. Mostow in 2003. All these books contributed, at different times, to broadening the meaning of the label "Chinese literature" that includes significant works by authors from Taiwan, placing them exactly at the same level as Chinese authors. Moreover, the prestige enjoyed by these international scholars surely added value to this new research area. As will be made evident later in the chapter, this trend also left its mark on the way Taiwanese literature was introduced to Italy, contributing to its early visibility, but preventing it, later, from expressing a definite identity.

The attention Taiwanese literature attracted among Italian academics can be reasoned from two different perspectives: on the one hand, it explains the relatively limited visibility this literature still enjoys among common readers, but on the other hand, it also speaks to the local interest in promoting it. It is a fact that Taiwanese literature found its way into the Italian book market not as a result of direct promotion by Taiwanese institutions but due to the interest of individual Italian researchers. One could argue, however, that this entry can sometimes be supported, whether actively or passively, by institutions of Taiwan. To illustrate, the Center for Chinese Studies at the National Central Library has hosted various Italian scholars with opportunities to conduct their China-related research and come into contact with Taiwanese literature and culture in Taipei, thereby arousing their interest in Taiwan studies in their future careers. Academia also plays an active role in the field of translation: university-based scholars, acting as institutional consecrators, have made the most important contribution to the practical availability of Taiwanese literary works in Italian.

Taiwanese Literature in Italian

The first fictional works from Taiwan introduced to Italian were Pai Hsien-yung's (白先勇) short story "Wandering in the Garden, Waking from a Dream" ("Vagando nel giardino, risveglio dal sogno," 遊園驚夢) and Chen Jo-hsi's (陳若曦) "The Crossroads" ("Il bivio," 路口), both of which were translated by noted sinologist Mario Sabattini and included in the 1997 coedited volume *The Lacquer Brush: An Anthology of Chinese Fiction from the Ming Dynasty to the Present Time* (*Il pennello di lacca. La narrativa cinese dalla dinastia Ming ai giorni nostri*). Published by Editori Laterza, an eminent

Italian publishing house with a vast catalog of critical, political, and philosophical texts, the book was supplemented with a comprehensive historical introduction, detailed authors' biographies, and critical analyses of the translated works. The choice to include these two short stories in such a collection of Chinese literature gave Taiwanese works their first shot at visibility in academia, as the book enjoyed a broad distribution and later appeared in syllabi of most university courses of Chinese literature. Taiwanese literary works were thus framed within (and not in competition with) the discipline of Chinese literature. In hindsight, this was a common starting point for the introduction of Taiwanese works abroad. At that time, the process of identity building for Taiwanese literature was still in the initial stages, and the literary image of the island (mostly unknown to laymen) was inevitably associated, by scholars in and outside Taiwan, with Chinese literature through contrasting claims for its inclusion or independence, or for proposals that it belongs to a wider definition of Chinese literature.

New fictional works from Taiwan began to appear in Italian in the mid-2000s. In 2005, Einaudi published sinologist Maria Rita Masci's translation of Pai Hsien-yung's *Crystal Boys* (孽子, *Il maestro della notte*, literally, the master of the night). The cooperation between the translator and the publishing house is understandable because Masci constantly played an influential role in introducing Chinese writers, such as Mo Yan (莫言), Yu Hua (余華), Su Tong (蘇童), Wang Anyi (王安憶), and others, and Einaudi, one of Italy's major houses, had already published outstanding Chinese authors, including Yu Hua and Mo Yan. The novel's back-cover copy presented the book as a queer work by one of the foremost writers with both Chinese and Taiwanese backgrounds, thereby suggesting a Taiwanese story situated in the broader context of Chinese culture. Except for *Crystal Boys*—a work composed by a Chinese mainlander—Einaudi seems uninterested in Taiwan itself and has published no other works related to Taiwan to date.[16]

Anna Maria Paoluzzi, an independent researcher of Taiwanese literature, published three books with the small press Pisani: Wang Chen-ho's (王禎和) short story collection *Men in Taiwan* (*Uomini a Taiwan*, 2006), Li Ang's (李昂) sexually controversial work *The Butcher's Wife* (*La moglie del macellaio*, 殺夫, 2007), and Po Yang's (柏楊) politically disputed *Ugly Chinamen* (*Brutti cinesi*, 醜陋的中國人, 2007). In the introductions and notes, the translator provides her readers with the literary and social context of the original works. Wang's, Po's, and particularly Li's works are examples of controversial writings that use universal problems such as gendered crime and human weakness to gain the advantage of selection, translation, and publication abroad: as Kuei-fen Chiu aptly remarks, Li Ang can be considered a "global multicultural model" whose feminist discourse resonates in (and is thus recognized by) Western literary circles.[17]

---

[16] Einaudi actually published a booklet in 2006 by Liang Shih-chiu (梁實秋), *The Noble Art of Insulting* (*La nobile arte dell'insulto*), which marked its first appearance in a European language. However, this book of practical Chinese thought, while written by an author who resided in Taiwan for many years, lies outside the scope of this article's focus on Taiwanese literature.

[17] Chiu, "'Worlding' World Literature from the Literary Periphery," 19–23.

In 2008, Chu T'ien-wen's (朱天文) "Fin de Siècle Splendors" ("Splendori *fin de siècle*," 世紀末的華麗) and Chang Hsi-kuo's (張系國) "One Hundred and Eight Ways to Kill One's Wife" ("Centootto modi per uccidere la moglie," 殺妻), translated by Francesca Tarocco and Giorgio Meloni, respectively, were included in a collection of Chinese fiction entitled *Made in China: New Chinese Writers* (*Made in China: Nuovi scrittori cinesi*). Timely published by Mondadori on the eve of the Beijing Olympics, this intended to show China as it appeared in literary texts. Ironically, it introduced an array of writings of the recent thirty years not only from the PRC (from Yu Hua and Wang Anyi to Ding Liying and Zhu Wen) but also from Hong Kong (Liu Yichang and Xi Xi) before the takeover and from Taiwan.

In 2013, Luca Pisano's translations of the short stories "Remains" (殘留) and "Flow" (流), by Liu Na-ou (劉吶鷗), with the Italian titles "Scarti" and "Scorrere" respectively, were included in a collection of stories by authors living in and writing about Shanghai of the 1930s, including Bao Tianxiao, Mu Shiying, Shi Zhecun, and others. The publishing house Atmosphere Libri, which published not only this anthology but also other China-related works, generously gives space to literature written in Chinese and promotes both acclaimed authors (such as Su Tong, Liu Heng, Ye Zhaoyan, and Yan Lianke) and authors who are new to Italian readers (such as Lu Nei, Shuang Xuetao, and Wei Wei). Like Mondadori and Einaudi, Atmosphere Libri is less concerned about Taiwan as a whole, well-developed country and has not published any books specifically dedicated to its literary achievement.

In 2014 a new book by Wang Chen-ho appeared, this time published by Orientalia. This small publishing house, founded by two sinologists, has brought readers books by authors from Asia (such as the Chinese writer Su Tong) and university textbooks related to Asian culture and other works, including a recent collection of short stories by Chinese-Italian writers. Among the books from Taiwan available in Italy, Wang Chen-ho's novel, *Rose, Rose, I Love You* (玫瑰玫瑰我愛你), translated by sinologist Anna Di Toro with the Italian title *Rosa rosa amore mio*, is probably the translation that has attracted the most attention for its experimental approach to translation. Di Toro rendered the multilingualism of the original text (where standard Chinese, local dialect, Japanese, and English intermingle) with a mix of Italian, Sicilian dialect, and English, adapting not only the language of the novel but its whole setting and all the historical and cultural elements to the Sicilian context. The adaptation, far from the "arbitrariness, prejudices, [and] ethnocentrism [...] of mediators and translators" highlighted by Casanova,[18] developed out of a toilsome but respectful process. As a matter of fact, feeling it necessary to justify the difficult (and, I would add, courageous) choice, the translator explained her reasons in the book introduction, clearly out of fear that "readers [when reading a novel from Taiwan] might feel disappointed in their legitimate expectations to immerse themselves in an exotic world."[19] This translation,

---

[18] Casanova, "Consecration and Accumulation of Literary Capital," 297. In the passage, Casanova refers to supposed mediators and translators who feel themselves to be in competitions with authors and thus resort to adopting arbitrary, ethnocentric, and ignorant strategies to cancel out the author. The case of Anna Di Toro and Wang Chen-ho is rather the opposite.

[19] Anna Di Toro, introduction to *Rose, Rose, I Love You*, by Wang Chen-ho (Rome: Libreria Editrice Orientalia, 2014), 5.

or rather adaptation, was indeed a milestone in the introduction of Taiwanese literature to Italy: after using, for years, the vehicle of Chinese literature (as in the case of the first translated fictional works) or, alternatively, introducing readers to the cultural reality of Taiwan through literature (as in the case of books published by Taiwan-friendly Pisani), for the first time, a literary work was translated only as such, not focusing on the expectations of readers but rather on the needs of the original text. The case of Wang Chen-ho's novel also recalls Damrosch's insight into world literature, which, he argues, is made up of books that circulate and "gain in translation."[20] The novel would have suffered major loss if translated literally, and the arduous process of adaptation to the Italian local context was intended to give it new life, carving out a new space for it in the category of world literature.

Kuei-fen Chiu's aforementioned comment on Li Ang's *The Butcher's Wife* can also be applied to Chiu Miao-chin's (邱妙津) *Last Words from Montmartre* (蒙馬特遺書), a lesbian semi-autobiography translated by Silvia Pozzi and published by Jaca Book in 2016 with the Italian title *Ultime lettere da Montmartre*.[21] It is true that publishers likely pay particular attention to controversial topics, such as queer themes, especially when coming from authors on the periphery. Chiu Miao-chin's novel, however, attracted attention not merely for its queer exposure but also for its aesthetic value and successful translation. The only book from Taiwan to reach the pages of this publication, it received a very positive review by Chinese literature and film scholar Paola Iovene in the review magazine *The Index of the Month's Books* (*L'indice dei libri del mese*). Defined as a "compelling work," this Taiwanese novel is appreciated for its insightful analysis of queer psyche with a disturbing and straightforward literary style.

In the same year, the short story "A Daughter: A Sad Story" ("Una figlia. Una storia triste," 女兒) by Lo I-chun (駱以軍), translated by Anna Di Toro, made its way to Italian readers through the translation magazine *Characters* (*Caratteri*). The presence of a Taiwanese short story in the pages of *Characters* is an exception, as the magazine is the creation of the Chinese magazine *People's Literature* (人民文学) in cooperation with two Italian translators and the Beijing's Foreign Language Press to introduce writers and poets from contemporary China to an Italian readership.

Sinologist Rosa Lombardi translated and edited the only two Taiwanese collections of poems available in Italy: Hsi Mu-jong's (席慕蓉) *The River of Time: A Poetry Anthology 1959–2009* (*Il fiume del tempo. Antologia poetica 1959–2009*) in 2016 and Yang Mu's (楊牧) *I Came from the Sea: Poems 1958–2012* (*Sono venuto dal mare. Poesie 1958–2012*). Both published by Castelvecchi and carried on the tradition of facing-page translation with introduction and notes by the translator.[22] In the introductory pages, entitled "Taiwanese Modern Poetry and Yang Mu," Lombardi describes the historical and cultural environment in which Taiwanese poetry developed. She also

---

[20] See David Damrosch, *What Is World Literature?* (Princeton: Princeton University Press, 2003), 289.
[21] Pozzi is one of the most active translators of Chinese literature in Italy, who has also rendered Yu Hua, Han Han, and Lu Nei, among others.
[22] Facing-page translation has been quite common in foreign poetry translation since the nineteenth century as a form of publication that addresses both academic specialists and common readers.

rigorously takes Yang Mu's poems as examples to challenge the common but dated discourse of Taiwanese literature as a mere component of Chinese literature. In situating Yang Mu's poetry in the Taiwanese context, she underlines how the colonial past, the heritage of Japanese and Chinese culture, and European influences have shaped the island's culture, which can be called "a peculiar hybridization."[23] For this reason, "Taiwan shows characteristics which are very different from mainland China, despite geographic proximity and strong linguistic and cultural affinities between the two countries."[24]

In 2018, two Taiwanese novels were published in Italy: Wang Ting-kuo's (王定國) *My Enemy's Cherry Tree* (*Il ciliegio del mio nemico*, 敵人的櫻花) and Chi Wei-jan's (紀蔚然) *Private Eyes* (私家偵探). Maria Gottardo and Monica Morzenti, well known for their renditions of Chinese literature (from Eileen Chang to Su Tong, from Zhu Wen to Zhang Jie), translated Wang Ting-kuo's *My Enemy's Cherry Tree* as their first Taiwan-related project. Published by Neri Pozza, the novel received some complimentary reviews but was perceived as a book of Chinese literature for lack of sufficient information about Taiwan on the book jacket. The confusion over nationality did not happen in Chi Wei-jan's *Private Eyes* with the Italian title *L'ombra nel pozzo* (literally "the shadow in the well") translated by Riccardo Moratto as part of publishing house Marsilio's crime fiction series. In a recent article on the translation of the book, Moratto explains that the value of this detective story lies in its capacity to depict a typical set of Taiwanese characters and environment while expressing universal human feelings, frailties, and aspirations. His translation intends to respectfully "safeguard the Taiwanese cultural component" in order to guide the Italian reader to "get an idea of the sociocultural reality of Taiwan."[25] He also makes clear his firm intention to avoid using "a flat linguistic register that eliminates individual and cultural identity and leads to a standardization of very different voices" while maintaining a respectful attitude toward Italian readers and resorting to cuts to streamline the story and make it more effective, where necessary. Readers' online reviews show that a translator's intention to highlight Taiwanese characters and cultural environment can be effortlessly noticed and much appreciated.

In 2021, Wu Ming-yi's (吳明益) acclaimed novel *The Man with the Compound Eyes* (複眼人) was translated by Silvia Pozzi with the title *Montagne e nuvole negli occhi* (literally "mountains and clouds in the eyes"), thus significantly altering the original title to sound more exotic and, apparently, reader-friendly. The publishing house Edizioni E/O included the novel in the "From the World" series (Dal mondo), along with three hundred books from around the world. Significantly, the book is presented as a novel from Taiwan, and the author as Taiwanese, with no reference to Chinese

---

[23] Rosa Lombardi, "La poesia moderna taiwanese e Yang Mu" [Modern Taiwanese Poetry and Yang Mu], in *Sono venuto dal mare. Poesie 1958–2012* [*I Came from the Sea: Poems 1958–2012*], by Yang Mu, ed. and trans. Rosa Lombardi (Rome: Castelvecchi, 2017), 15.

[24] Lombardi, "Modern Taiwanese Poetry and Yang Mu," 15.

[25] Riccardo Moratto, "Translating Taiwanese Literature into Italian: A Short Case Study of *L'ombra nel pozzo* by Chi Wei-Jan," *Academia Letters* (May 2021): 3.

literature either on the book cover or on the publisher's website. The translation of Wu Ming-yi into foreign languages has been a major literary event that surpasses the typical parameters of translation and "[goes] off the page" to include several promotion activities, as his English translator Darryl Sterk describes in an article about his translation experience.[26] Discussing the "worlding" of Taiwanese literature, Kuei-fen Chiu refers to Wu Ming-yi as a model of globalization: not only does the theme of the novel (an ecological catastrophe) have clearly global resonance but the book's wide promotion by the Taiwanese government speaks of a "successful integration of national and global interests."[27] Although the book has not yet received such active promotion in Italy by the Taiwanese government, the very current topics of nature and environment speak to Italian readers (as is evident from online reviews), and the book also contributes to a more definite and independent position for Taiwanese literature in Italy: while the borders of this literature are not yet clear to common readers, a new step has been made toward recognition of this literature as a corpus that is irreducible to literature from China.

Finally, we must add Taiwanese comic books and children's literature to this list: in 2018, Martina Renata Prosperi, a PhD student, translated Sean Chuang's (小莊) graphic novel *'80s Diary in Taiwan* (*I miei anni '80 a Taiwan*, 80 年代事件簿). The publishing house Add Editore, which had introduced Li Kunwu's (李昆武) trilogy to Italy, released this book as part of the same series dedicated to Asia. In 2018, two picture books, Crystal Kung's (水晶孔) *The Little Drifter* (*Il piccolo vagabondo*, 流浪小孩) and Chen Wen-sheng's (陳穩升) *The Baker's Journey* (*Baker. Il viaggio del fornaio*, 麵包師之旅), were published by Bao Publishing and Tunué, respectively. The publishers' websites explicitly categorize these works as Taiwanese and underline their excellent capacity to express universal sentiments, as has been widely commented on in blogs and online reviews. In addition to comic books, children's literature such as Chen Chih-yuan's (陳致元) *Gu-ji Gu-ji* and Jimmy Liao's (幾米) several works attract Italian readers.

Key Players in Translating Taiwanese Literature

As Casanova emphasizes, translation plays an extremely important role in the exchange that takes place in the world literary field. It becomes a particularly delicate issue when it is the vehicle for introducing, to other areas, literary works from dominated languages and fields: without translation, they would likely remain invisible. Such a decisive process not only involves an author and a translator but also many agents, such as institutional agents who promote a country's literature abroad, and foreign agents who are independent from the country of the source text. If the export agents

---

[26] Darryl Sterk, "Taiwanese Literature off the Page," *Books from Taiwan*, December 12, 2014. https://booksfromtaiwan.tw/latest_info.php?id=18.

[27] Chiu, "'Worlding' World Literature from the Literary Periphery," 24.

(the Taiwanese in this case) emphasize the need to acquire foreign recognition and represent a better image of their own culture, the import agents, generally speaking, tend to emphasize the cultural and economic expectations of the target literary field.

This divergent approach is evident in the case of Taiwan and Italy. On the one hand, Taiwan is using its soft power to break through the siege of China and reclaim Taiwan's autonomy in the world. The example of Taiwanese agents can be seen in the administration of Taiwan's Ministry of Culture (MoC). As one of the leading exponents to commit itself to the *worlding* of Taiwanese literature, it selects literary texts based on Taiwan's needs, makes them easily accessible, and promotes them through translation funding and promotion activities abroad. The literary works promoted by the MoC are not classics but rather contemporary works and especially works that appear to be more in tune with the tastes of foreign readers and the demands of current global literature. However, the MoC's role is less evident and active in Italy compared with other countries. According to the list of recipients of MoC translation funding in the last seven years, as published on the ministry's website for the publication project Books from Taiwan, only three projects submitted by Italian publishers have received funding (namely Sean Chuang's *'80s Diary in Taiwan*, Wu Ming-Yi's *The Man with the Compound Eyes*, and Chu T'ien-hsin's *In Remembrance of My Buddies from the Military Compound*, which has not yet been published). Whether due to scarce applications from Italy or harsh competition for funds, this figure indirectly suggests the high self-reliance and autonomy of Italian agents in selecting and translating Taiwanese works.

On the other hand, Italian agents, such as literary agents, publishing houses, editors, and translators, contribute to the growth of Taiwanese literature in translation; if we analyze the multiple choices and strategies of translating specific works made by the above-mentioned agents, the situations appear quite diversified. To illustrate, the publishing houses can be very small—such as Pisani, Orientalia, and Atmosphere Libri—with limited distribution but more reputation among academics than common readers or independent but widely known among readers—as in the case of E/O and Add Editore. Other publishing houses, such as Mondadori, Einaudi, and to a lesser extent Neri Pozza, are major and well established. This partly differs from the publication of English translations of Taiwanese literature; over the past five decades, these have been published not only by small commercial publishing houses but also by major university presses with considerable visibility worldwide.[28]

Italian translators are either academics or in some way connected with academia, as is the case in other European countries. They can thus be considered part of the group of "institutional consecrators" of this foreign literature, in Casanova's terms, even though their consecrating capital varies according to their different positions (from full professors to adjunct professors and PhD students). Much associated with Italian universities, translators should not only completely comprehend the cultural and economic conditions of the Italian literary field but also meet the needs of imported

---

[28] See Kenneth S. H. Liu, "Publishing Taiwan: A Survey of Publications of Taiwanese Literature in English Translation," in *The Global Literary Field*, ed. Anna Guttman, Michel Hockx, and George Paizis (Newcastle: Cambridge Scholar Press, 2006), 213.

literature. Half of these translators are also researchers of Taiwanese literature and motivated by the intention to introduce it to Italy. The result is that the choice of works usually comes from negotiations between the translator's concept of Taiwanese literature, her or his interests, and the editorial and commercial requirements of Italian publishers.

This sort of negotiation can be perceived from how the literary works are represented in Italy: most works are contemporary and have not been systematically introduced. Therefore, common readers—after reading available translations—will hardly capture a clear idea of the historical evolution of the island's literature and culture. It is also apparent that no all-encompassing, coherent plans, strategies, and principles lie behind the translation of Taiwanese literature. Although a well-planned introduction can be achieved through the creation of a book series, as Gwennaël Gaffric has illustrated in his chapter,[29] the Italian translation of Taiwanese literature instead depends on individual actions taken by different agents. This general situation recalls that of Chinese literature, whose introduction to Italy—although much more diversified compared with Taiwanese literature—remains, to date, unsatisfactory for lack of a systematic approach to the importation of Chinese works.[30]

The case of Taiwanese literature in Italy serves as evidence that a minor literature can be used for *alternative* cultural exchange and slowly build its own reputation, even though it has no preestablished identity and capital and can be easily marginalized by other dominating literatures. By alternative, I refer to two main levels of meaning. The first is that Taiwanese literature, as a minor literature that was assimilated into Chinese dominating literature, is now gradually making its way in the Italian literary field. It finds out its position as an alternative voice. Many sinologists see in Taiwanese literature the *potentiality* of emancipating Chinese-language works from China and its literature. This can be seen in a different approach to translations. While the book covers of Chinese novels in translation often show cultural and historical exoticism, expressing limited imagination concerning the oriental world, translations of Taiwanese literature usually touch the sociohistorical ground. Although the island's history and culture are almost unknown, or at least quite nebulous to foreign readers, Taiwan is often perceived today as "different" from China. Marginality and isolation are not necessarily negative and can be a passport to enter another country.

On a second level, *alternative* can also refer to the role currently being played by the translation of Taiwanese works. For Italy, the translation of Taiwanese literature does not imply the importation of literary capital as it is conceived by Casanova (unfortunately, Taiwanese works are rarely recognized worldwide as great universal texts). Alternatively, it can be considered an accumulation of alternative capital: importing Taiwanese literature suggests an alternative way to see the Chinese-speaking

---

[29] See Gaffric's chapter in this volume for a presentation of the three series dedicated to Taiwanese literature in France.
[30] See Paolo Magagnin, "Dieci anni di letteratura cinese in Italia. Situazione, ostacoli, prospettive" [A Decade of Chinese Literature in Italy: Challenges and Prospects], *Tradurre* [*Translate*], no. 16 (2019). https://rivistatradurre.it/dieci-anni-di-letteratura-cinese-in-italia/.

world, recognize its complexity, and even transcend the totality of China and embrace other Sinophone regions like Taiwan, Hong Kong, and Malaysia. For an export country like Taiwan, the exportation of its literary texts to Italy (even though still quantitatively unsatisfactory) means visibility and, ultimately, acknowledgment of its existence in the international literary field. It expresses its *potentiality* in providing fresh and unexpected views for the world.

While investigating the position of translated literature in the literary polysystem, Even-Zohar summarizes the role of translated literature as follows: it can be "primary," meaning active in promoting innovation and change in the new system it enters and introducing new elements that were unknown before translation, or it can be "secondary" when it is modeled according to widely accepted norms and conventions. In the second case, translated literature is not a vehicle for innovation but paradoxically becomes a conservative factor.[31] When it comes to the translation process and practice, producing a primary literature in translation might mean violating the conventions of one's own literary field and challenging rigid and homogenized literature.[32] To improve the position of Taiwanese literature in Italy, vitalize Italian literature, and increase Italian literary capital, import agents should not underestimate the active and innovative roles they can play within Italian culture.

The Italian literary field can be deemed partially peripheric and dominated within the central and dominating group of the major European literatures, as it partly modeled itself on external dominating literatures such as American, English, or French literature. When encountering other minor and dominated literatures, it can probably be considered less threatening and haughty. This provides a platform for two sides of agents—be they publishers or scholar-translators—to equally exchange their minor literatures and, particularly for Italian agents, take responsibility to identify Taiwanese literature as national literature and rethink the literature written in Chinese, of which Taiwanese literature is a considerable and active part.

---

[31] See Itamar Even-Zohar, "The Position of Translated Literature within the Literary Polysystem," in *Papers in Historical Poetics* (Tel Aviv: Tel Aviv University, 1978), 21–27.

[32] I deliberately use "global" here instead of "world," meaning a literature that conforms to the universal market, whereas world literature thrives on intra- and intercultural alterity. See Martin Kern, "Ends and Beginnings of World Literature," *Poetica* 49, no. 1/2 (2018): 1–31.

10

From Taiwan's Literature to Taiwanese Literature: A Paradigm Shift in Japanese Translation

Ying-che Huang (translated by Sherlon Chi-yin Ip)

"Modern Chinese literature" used to be regarded in Japanese academia as encompassing literature from Taiwan and Hong Kong as well as from the mainland. Writings from Taiwan and Hong Kong were studied merely as subsidiaries of mainstream Chinese culture, language, and traditions. However, with the democratization of Taiwan that began in the second half of the 1980s, the uniqueness of Taiwanese literature has caught the attention of Japanese researchers and made it a popular field of study. The reasons behind this development of "literature of Taiwan" into the distinct research field of "Taiwanese literature" lie not just in Taiwan's democratization but also in efforts initiated in the 1990s by Taiwan's Council for Cultural Affairs (CCA)—since 2012, the Ministry of Culture—to promote "Chinese books in translation" (中書外譯), in part by subsidizing overseas publishers. Supported by such translations, "Taiwanese literature" gained recognition as an independent research field in Japan. This chapter surveys the Japanese discourse on Taiwanese literature and its translation over the past four decades. In discussing the reception of Taiwanese literature in Japanese literary and scholarly circles, I explore some of the main issues that arise from Japanese translations of Taiwanese literature in relation to the paradigm shift in Japan.

Taiwanese Literature in Japan in the 1970s and 1980s

Taiwanese literature began to gain attention in Japan in the 1970s in the context of immensely polarized views of "Nationalist Taiwan" and "Communist China." Left-wing, "progressive intellectuals," who were the majority in Japan, had long regarded KMT-ruled Taiwan as a reactionary, counterrevolutionary entity and had little time for literature from the island. However, the establishment of diplomatic ties between China and Japan in 1972 prompted them to revisit the Taiwan issue. At the same time, movements for the rights of ethnic minorities were gaining momentum in the West. Leftist Japanese intellectuals were also influenced by these movements and began to pay more attention to the Korean and Chinese expatriate communities in Japan, the *Burakumin* and *Ainu* minorities, and the Okinawa issue. Moreover, various

Southeast Asian countries were condemning postwar Japan's "neocolonial" economic aggression and its patronage of prostitution in the region. These concerns forced Japanese intellectuals to confront the country's colonial past, including its occupation of Taiwan.[1] The enthusiastic reception of the Japanese translation of Huang Chun-ming's (黃春明) *Sayonara, Goodbye* (さよなら・再見, published by Mekon in 1979) in Japan can be largely attributed to this discussion on decolonization.[2] The novel, a thinly veiled attack on Japanese economic aggression and patronage of prostitution in East Asia, echoed the growing concern with Japanese "neocolonialism" in progressive cultural circles.

Another key champion of Taiwanese literature in Japan at this time was Kokuki Tai (戴國煇), an active Japan-based historian promoting Taiwan's autonomy since the 1970s. He was behind the reissue of Taiwanese Hakka novelist Wu Cho-liu's (吳濁流) important Japanese-language novels *Taiwan before the Dawn* (夜明け前の台湾, 1972), *Struggling in the Mud* (泥濘に生きる, 1972), and *Orphan of Asia* (アジアの孤児, 1973),[3] which called on the Japanese to reflect on their colonial past in Taiwan. Tai founded the "Association for Modern and Contemporary History of Taiwan" (AMCHT, 台湾近現代史研究会) in Tokyo in 1978 and its influential academic journal *Historical Studies of Taiwan in Modern Times* (台湾近現代史研究). The pioneering scholars of Taiwanese literature in postwar Japan, such as Wakabayashi Masahiro (若林正丈), Haruyama Meitetsu (春山明哲), Kurihara Jun (栗原純), Matsunaga Masayoshi (松永正義), Kawahara Isao (河原功), Okazaki Ikuko (岡崎郁子), and Chin Seidai (陳正醍), were all members of this association.

The debates on nativist literature that emerged in Taiwan with democratization also caught the attention of Japanese scholars and influenced their view of Taiwanese literature in the 1980s. Kokuki Tai's AMCHT made a concerted effort to encourage its members to translate the works of Hung Hsing-fu (洪醒夫), Sung Tse-lai (宋澤萊), Tseng Hsin-yi (曾心儀), José Lee (李雙澤), Lee Chiao (李喬), Chen Ying-chen (陳映真), and Cheng Ching-wen (鄭清文) and produced three collections of short stories, *Caifeng's Dream: Selections of Modern Taiwanese Fiction, I* (彩鳳の夢：台湾現代小說選 I, 1984), *The End-of-War Reparations: Selections of Modern Taiwanese Fiction, II* (終戦の賠償：台湾現代小說選 II, 1984), and *Three-Legged Horse: Selections of Modern Taiwanese Fiction, III* (三本足の馬：台湾現代小說選 III, 1985). These titles had an immense impact in Japan. Matsunaga Masayoshi's brilliant long essay, "The History and Characteristics of Taiwanese Literature," included in

---

[1] Simomura Sakujirō (下村作次郎), "台湾文学在日本" [Taiwanese Literature in Japan], 中国文化研究 [*Chinese Cultural Research*], no. 18 (2001): 1–22. This journal is published by Tenri University.

[2] Huang Ying-che (黃英哲), "翻譯台灣：黃春明與日本" [Translating Taiwan: Huang Chun-ming and Japan], 文訊 [*Wenhsun*], no. 360 (October 2015); collected in Huang's 櫻花・流水：我的東瀛筆記 [*Cherry Blossoms and Flowing Water: Notes on Japan*] (Taipei: Yunchen, 2017), 60–8.

[3] The first two works were published in 1972 by Shakai Shisosha (literally "social thought company"), a Tokyo publishing company that can be traced back to the "Social Thought Study Group" established by the disciples of Kawai Eijirō, a controversial Japanese interwar-era social thinker, in 1947. *Orphan of Asia* was published in 1973 by Tokyo's Sinjinbutsu Ōraisha, a publisher specializing in historical books.

Caifeng's Dream, can be regarded as representative of the discourse on Taiwanese literature in Japan in the 1980s.

In this essay, Matsunaga concedes that "Taiwanese literature is a part of Chinese literature" but argues that "it is not easy to define in what sense that is the case [...] [since] Taiwan's course of development is, by and large, separated from that of mainland China in modern times."⁴ Mainstream Japanese opinion at this time rarely questioned the idea that Taiwanese literature was essentially just a branch of Chinese literature or, at best, was "Chinese literature in Taiwan." Nevertheless, Japanese scholars had to take into account the fact, as Matsunaga notes, that the social, political, and economic situations of Taiwan and mainland China were growing farther and farther apart. Matsunaga's argument, for example, does not exclude the possibility that Taiwan's ambiguous political status may, at least someday, justify its literature being treated as a separate area of study from Chinese literature. As he points out:

> Literary works written in the Chinese language by ethnic Chinese in Singapore and Malaysia cannot be termed as Chinese literature, nor can English writings in Canada and Australia be called English literature, despite the influence from the English literary tradition.⁵

Matsunaga observes that a good number of literary works had been produced by both local Taiwanese poets and Qing officials in Taiwan over the two hundred years of Koxinga and Qing rule from the seventieth to nineteenth centuries but that these works had not managed to establish an identity of their own beyond a certain regional or local flavor.

After Taiwan became a Japanese colony in 1895, large-scale local military resistance against colonial rule continued until the defeat of the Tapani Uprising in 1915. Taiwan was then confronted with the concurrent tides of the May Fourth Movement in mainland China, the Taishō Democracy in Japan, and the growing postwar advocacy of national self-determination in the world at large. Many Taiwanese responded by advocating for a vernacular Chinese revival along the lines of the mainland's May Fourth Movement, while others argued for a "vernacular Taiwanese" literature based on the Minnan and Hakka dialects in order to achieve a "unification of the written and spoken language" (言文一致) in Taiwan. Opinions on the traditional literature of Taiwan also diverged. Some preferred a more inclusive approach and a gradual transition to modern literature, while others contended that the traditional literature, having fallen out with the times, should be regarded as obsolete and left behind once

---

⁴ Matsunaga Masayoshi, "台湾文学の歴史と個性" [The History and Characteristics of Taiwanese Literature], in 彩鳳の夢: 台湾現代小説選I [*Caifeng's Dream: Selections of Modern Taiwanese Fiction, I*] (Tokyo: Kenbun, 1984), 176–216; later included in Matsunaga Masayoshi, 台湾文学のおもしろさ [*The Fun of Taiwanese Literature*] (Tokyo: Kenbun, 2006). The quotation is cited in *The Fun of Taiwan Literature*, 30. All translations of quoted Japanese texts in this chapter are made by me, with the generous help of Sherlon C. Y. Ip.

⁵ Matsunaga, "The History and Characteristics of Taiwanese Literature," 31.

and for all. Masayoshi argues that the development of modern Taiwanese literature has been so heavily influenced by the new literature movement in mainland China that it could be said to have been formed on the same basis and to have developed in the same essential direction. After giving an overview of the trajectory and character of Taiwanese literature from the age of the Tungning Kingdom in the Ming dynasty to the 1970s, Masayoshi expressed a view that was commonly agreed upon by Japanese scholars at that time:

> The problematic point of modern Taiwanese literature lies in the multilayered structure of nationalism between "China" and "Taiwan." Despite their differences, the literature of Taiwan and mainland China share the same issues. Therefore, the literature of Taiwan and mainland China both constitute a part of Chinese literature, and Taiwanese literature can be treated as another branch of Chinese literature.[6]

Taiwanese Literature in Japan in the 1990s

After the lifting of martial law in 1987 and the abolition of the National Mobilization for Suppression of the Communist Rebellion in 1991, many long-standing social and cultural "taboos" and restrictions were relaxed in Taiwan. With more room for freedom of expression, new voices and ideas began to be heard, and many previously obscure literary records also came to light. In Japan, a more diverse perspective on Taiwanese literature began to emerge. Yamaguchi Mamoru's (山口守) preface to his 1991 anthology of Taiwanese literature, *Banana Boat: Heading toward Taiwanese Literature*, for instance, contends, rather pointedly, that "to understand Taiwanese literature, one must first understand the history of Taiwan, not just the history of the language in which it is written."[7] The reason, he argues, lies in the separate historical development of the island:

> Taiwan has a largely different historical background from that of the other lands of Chinese culture. This special context offers it a distinctive identity that defies the simple label as a part of Chinese literature.[8]

As Yamaguchi points out, originally Taiwan had been inhabited by Austronesian peoples untouched by Chinese culture. It was not until the seventeenth century, when large numbers of Han people migrated to the island from the Fujian and Guangdong regions during the Ming Koxinga and Qing periods, that Taiwan became "sinicized."[9]

---

[6] Matsunaga, "The History and Characteristics of Taiwanese Literature," 31–32.
[7] Yamaguchi Mamoru, "バナナボートの乗船券: 序にかえて" [A Ticket to the Banana Boat: A Preface], in バナナボート: 台湾文学への招待 [*Banana Boat: Heading toward Taiwanese Literature*] (Tokyo: JICC, 1991), 2.
[8] Yamaguchi, "A Ticket to the Banana Boat: A Preface," 2.
[9] Yamaguchi, "A Ticket to the Banana Boat: A Preface," 3.

In 1895, following China's defeat in the First Sino-Japanese War, Taiwan was ceded to Japan, which effectively severed its ties with China. However, although Japanese rule modernized the island, its purpose was simply to exploit Taiwanese resources. Japan was just a plunderer on a national scale. Its actions, justified by the colonial state apparatus as a "great national policy,"[10] would have been treated as a crime if carried out by an individual. Although Japanese rule was not completely authoritarian, it did force the Taiwanese people to live under harsh conditions, and any resistance was put down fiercely. Meanwhile, the Taiwanese people could only look on across the Taiwan Strait as the major historical events of China's modernization, such as the 1911 revolution and the May Fourth Movement, unfolded. Reunification after the Second World War was prevented by the KMT's retreat to Taiwan after the communist revolution, and Taiwan and mainland China have been separated politically for the best part of a century since then. Numerous literary works from Taiwan have portrayed this tragic history while envisioning a hopeful future. Postwar Taiwanese literature can be seen as simultaneously embodying both traditional Chinese values and modern Western ones, both Chinese consciousness and Taiwanese consciousness, both realism and idealism, as well as other dichotomies of human life.[11]

In the 1990s, Japanese scholars came to realize the distinctive autonomy of Taiwanese literature and no longer regard it as a branch of Chinese literature. At this time, the CCA began to actively promote the "Chinese Books Translation and Publishing" project, which included a vigorous program of Japanese translations of Taiwanese literature, and to sponsor international conferences on Taiwanese literature. In 1992, the CCA organized a symposium specifically on Chinese-to-Japanese translation and invited Japanese scholars of modern Chinese literature as well as publishers to encourage and subsidize the circulation of contemporary Taiwanese literature in Japanese translation. This symposium ultimately led to Japanese versions of Cheng Ching-wen's *Alishan Sacred Trees* (阿里山の神木, translated by Okazaki Ikuko, 1993) and Li Ang's *The Butcher's Wife* (夫殺し, translated by Fujii Shōzō 藤井省三, 1993). The latter, in particular, won high acclaim in Japan and came to be regarded as the pinnacle of Taiwanese feminist writing. In 1994, the international academic conference Lōa Hô and Writers of His Contemporary Age: Taiwanese Literature during the Japanese Occupation (賴和及其同時代的作家 : 日據時期台灣文學國際學術會議) took place at the National Tsing Hua University in Taiwan with the support of the CCA. The first conference to have "Taiwanese literature" in its title, this conference was attended by almost the entire Japanese scholarly community in the field of Taiwanese studies. It signaled the beginning of active involvement by Japanese researchers in the translation of contemporary Taiwanese literature.

In 1997, the CCA attempted for the first time to collaborate with the Japanese commercial publisher, Kokusho Kankoukai, which specialized in world literature titles. Together, they released several important translations in a contemporary Taiwan

---

[10] Yamaguchi, "A Ticket to the Banana Boat: A Preface," 3–5.
[11] Yamaguchi, "A Ticket to the Banana Boat: A Preface," 3–5.

literature series, which was met with immense success. Starting with Li Ang's *The Lost Garden* (迷いの園, translated by Fujii), a ten-volume series of "Modern Taiwanese Literature" (edited by Fujii Shōzō, Yamaguchi Mamoru, and Ying-che Huang) was launched by Kokusho Kankoukai in early 1999. Almost at once, *The Lost Garden* received high praise from Ueno Chizuko (上野千鶴子), the renowned Japanese feminist scholar, in a review entitled "A Portrayal of Taiwanese History and Female Sexuality from a Woman's Perspective," published in *Nikkei*, one of the three leading newspapers in Japan. Ueno's review included this forthright acknowledgment of Taiwan's distinctive identity:

> [*The Lost Garden*] can be regarded as a manifesto of the "national literature" of Taiwan. It successfully portrays the territory's complex "postcolonial" state and offers a subtle narrative of the multilayered domination and oppression that Taiwan has experienced from China, Japan, and the US.[12]

Later the same year, the series published Yamaguchi Mamoru's translation of *The Taipei Story* (台北ストーリー), an ingenious chain story made up of contributions by Pai Hsien-yung (白先勇), Chang Hsi-kuo (張系國), Huang Fan (黃凡), Ping Lu (平路), Chu T'ien-wen (朱天文), Chu T'ien-hsin (朱天心), and Chang Ta-chun (張大春). Again, this title was warmly received by Japanese critics. For instance, the review published in the *Tokyo Shimbun*'s supplement commented that "each writer, from his/her own standpoint, showcases the diversity of Taipei as an enormous consumer city, as well as the complicated, harsh, dark histories it has built."[13]

In summer 2000, Chu T'ien-hsin's *The Old Capital* (古都, translated by Shimizu Kenichirō 清水賢一郎) completed the series. This collection of linked stories exploring issues of memory and identity in contemporary Taipei immediately caught the attention of Japanese readers and became the talk of the time, as it had been in Taiwan, especially among elite readers of high literature. In August 2000, it was named by *Asahi Shimbun* (朝日新聞) as one of the top five fiction titles of the first half of the year and included in the newspaper's recommendation list. Critics uniformly hailed *The Old Capital* as a work of intellect and depth open to many different interpretations. Its success confirmed that Taiwanese literature had established its place in the Japanese literary marketplace and that the "Modern Taiwanese Literature" series had succeeded in firmly establishing the new and distinctive "Taiwanese literary paradigm" in Japan.

---

[12] Ueno Chizuko, "女性の目で描く台湾の歴史と性" [A Portrayal of Taiwanese History and Female Sexuality from a Woman's Perspective], 日本経済新聞 [*Nikkei*], April 18, 1999.

[13] See "*The Taipei Story*, authored by Pai Hsien-yung et al., edited by Yamaguchi Mamoru, published by Kokusho Kankoukai: Showcasing the Diversity in a Large Consumer City" [「台北ストーリー」山口守編 (国書刊行会): 一大消費都市の多様性を現出], *Tokyo Shimbun* [東京新聞], July 25, 1999.

Taiwanese Literature in Translation in the Twenty-First Century

In 2000, Yeh Shih-tao's (葉石濤) *A History of Taiwan Literature* (translated into Japanese as 台湾文学史 by Nakajima Toshio 中島利郎 and Sawai Noriyuki 澤井律之), which was the first book comprehensively introducing Taiwanese literature in 1987, was published in Japan. For postwar Japan, this was also the first book written by a Taiwanese scholar. Using a location-based conception of history, it can be seen as an important theoretical export of the "Taiwanese literary paradigm," as its publication prompted Japan to review the nature and characteristics of Taiwanese literature.

Yeh penned his own Japanese preface to the collection, in which he points out that the historical memory and new literature of postwar Taiwan were completely sidelined during the long period of martial law and White Terror that followed the February 28 Incident. He also notes that the martial law was still in force when he was writing *A History of Taiwanese Literature*, so he could not fully express his own ideas in that book, including his conviction that Taiwanese literature, built upon the land and its people, was not something subservient to either Chinese or Japanese literature. The Chinese and Japanese literary traditions were both part of the literary language of Taiwan, but the reverse was not the case; the literature of Taiwan was not a part of the literary language of China or Japan. Once again, Yeh stresses his long-held view of the distinctiveness and fundamental independence of Taiwanese literature.[14] As Nakajima, one of the Japanese translators of *A History of Taiwanese Literature*, points out clearly in his notes to that book, its main contribution was to free the idea of "Taiwanese literature" from the framework of "Chinese literature."[15]

Sakaguchi Naoki's (阪口直樹) subsequent review, "An Outlook of the Starting Point of Taiwanese Literature: A Review of Yeh Shih-tao's *A History of Taiwanese Literature*," usefully summarizes the views of Japanese scholars of modern Chinese literature on the subject.[16] According to Sakaguchi, Yeh's history presents a strong case for the uniqueness of Taiwan and its literature by clearly revealing the island's distinct historical development and showcasing the complexity and diversity of Taiwanese culture and literature. Sakaguchi argues that *A History of Taiwanese Literature* book offers Japanese readers, first, an understanding of the separate historical trajectory of Taiwan and the ways in which the literature of the island, in responding to that history, has established Taiwan's separate identity through the search for the origins of that identity and the expression of its individual characteristics and, second, an

---

[14] Yeh Shih-tao, "日本語版序文" [Preface to the Japanese Edition], in 台湾文学史 [*A History of Taiwanese Literature*], trans. Nakajima Toshio and Sawai Noriyuki (Tokyo: Kenbun, 2000), 1.

[15] Nakajima Toshio, "「台湾文学史」解説" [Notes to *A History of Taiwanese Literature*], in *A History of Taiwanese Literature*, 287–303.

[16] See Sakaguchi Naoki, "台湾文学を展望するための原点: 葉石濤《台湾文学史》を書評して" [An Outlook of the Starting Point of Taiwanese Literature: A Review of Yeh Shih-tao's *A History of Taiwanese Literature*]. The article was first published in 中国文芸研究会会報 [*Japanese Association for Chinese Literature and Art Studies Bulletin*], no. 240 (October 28, 2001), reprinted in Sakaguchi, 中国現代文学の系譜: 革命と通俗をめぐって [*The Genealogy of Chinese Modern Literature: Issues of Revolution and the Popular*] (Tokyo: Tōhō Shoten, 2004), 424–26.

appreciation of the "multinational characteristics" of Taiwanese literature. In this regard, he asserts that, in line with the concept of "marginal literature," the issue of "national language" in Taiwan arose from its unique marginality. Historically, there had been two "national languages" in Taiwan, both colonial in nature, but the modern island is still searching for a third "national language." Taiwanese literature can thus be seen as a dynamic experiment in creating a modern national mode of expressing Taiwan's distinctive national identity.[17] For Sakaguchi, these insights nevertheless leave two important questions unanswered. First, since the characteristic features of Taiwanese literature lie in its multilingual and multicultural background, should it then be regarded as a distinct literature or as a hybrid but provincial literature? Second, how can one construct a firm theoretical basis for a Taiwanese literature that is distinct from the many local literatures of China?

At about the same time, Fujii Shōzō published his important paper "The Hybridity of Taiwanese Culture: From the Dutch Rule to the Haruki Phenomenon,"[18] which describes how the island has been a recipient of different regional cultures ever since the Dutch Formosan era and has integrated them into a unique "Taiwanese culture." Fujii makes use of the concept of "weeds" in the well-known essay "What Is Literature?" by British literary critic Terry Eagleton, arguing that a common feature of the terms "literature" and "weeds" is that they do not refer to any concrete object and their definitions differ from person to person. Just as weeds are not a particular kind of plant but rather a judgment that can be subjectively applied to any plant according to how it is valued, the notion of literature is also grounded in value judgments. Eagleton points out that such value judgments are "historically variable" and closely linked with "ideologies," which refer not to personal preferences and tastes but to the assumptions by which certain social groups exercise and maintain power over others.[19] Thus, the value judgments that determine for various readers what constitutes "Taiwanese literature" are determined in turn by ideologies. For instance, Taiwan's literature has always operated on the cusp of disunity between the spoken and written language, with the literary language changing from classical Chinese during the Qing dynasty and the early years of Japanese colonial rule to Japanese during the mid- and late colonial era, and finally to Beijing Mandarin in the postwar years. The resulting literary products, therefore, bear ideological influences from the Qing dynasty, the Japanese Empire, and the Republic of China, yet—whether written in Japanese or classical or vernacular Chinese—can still be regarded as "Taiwanese literature" as long as they embody the common consciousness of Taiwan and Taiwan's national values.

Fujii notes that while he uses "weeds" (雜草) as a metaphor for Taiwanese literature, Yeh Shih-tao compares Taiwanese writers to "wild grass" (野草). Both metaphors offer a

---

[17] Sakaguchi, "An Outlook of the Starting Point of Taiwanese Literature," 424–26.

[18] Fujii Shōzō, "台湾文化のクレオール性： オランダ統治から「村上春樹現象」まで" [The Hybridity of Taiwanese Culture: From the Dutch Rule to the Haruki Murakami Phenomenon], in 講座: 台湾文学 [Lectures: Taiwan Literature], ed. Yamaguchi Mamoru (Tokyo: Kokusho Kankoukai, 2003), 10–12.

[19] Qtd. in Fujii, "The Hybridity of Taiwanese Culture," 12.

concise picture of how Taiwan, until recently, had always been under the rule of foreign powers. Marginalized as a colony and dominated by a succession of different hegemonic regimes, the island necessarily developed a multinational, "hybrid" culture and literature in response to the various forces of resistance, competition, and integration that were generated in a polyethnic society.[20] Within this historical trajectory of "hybridity," as Fujii is one of the scholars to observe, a distinctive "Japanophilia" (哈日) has persisted in Taiwan, as evidenced by the popularity of contemporary Japanese writers such as Haruki Murakami (村上春樹). Granted that this phenomenon is mostly seen in popular culture, which, from a traditional perspective, might be considered "inferior" to more refined tastes, Japanese genre fiction does engage with a broad range of social, cultural, and historical issues. Arguably, popular literature's exploration of such issues, even if simplistic, is a key part of the recent revival of interest in the so-called "novel for the masses" (大眾小說) and in "popular literature" (通俗文學) in general in Taiwan. In any case, Taiwan's "Japanophilia" remains unarguably an important component of the heterogeneous umbrella of Taiwanese culture.[21]

Since 2000, *Wintry Night* (寒夜), *Crystal Boys* (孽子), and *Notes of a Desolate Man* (荒人手記) have been some of the most exciting titles under Kokusho Kankoukai's "Modern Taiwanese Literature" series. In her review of Li Chiao's *Wintry Night* (translated by Miki Naotake 三木直大 and Okazaki Ikuko) in 2006, the journalist Saisho Hazuki (最相葉月) praises the novel for its depiction of the tension between the dominating and dominated ethnicities in Taiwan under Japanese colonial rule and for its juxtaposition of the same sentiments felt by both sides.[22] Pai Hsien-yung's *Crystal Boys* (translated by Chin Seidai) and Chu T'ien-wen's *Notes of a Desolate Man* (translated by Ikegami Sadako 池上貞子) were also published in 2000 and gained a great deal of attention and a favorable, intelligent reception. The insightful review of *Crystal Boys* by Yomoda Inuhiko (四方田犬彦) in the well-known literary magazine *Shinchō*, headlined "The Lotus Utopia," notes, for example, that *Crystal Boys* is an excellent illustration of one of the most valuable features of creative writing in all times and ages, in both East and West: its ability to offer a glimpse into the social and psychological realities of lives lived on the margins.[23]

Crystal Boys is set in Taiwan in the 1970s, a time when homosexuality was neither understood nor accepted by mainstream society, and showcases the conflicts, compromises, anxieties, and escapism that plagued the lives of Taiwanese homosexuals. The tiny New Park in central Taipei was the cruising ground for lives that had to be lived in the dark. As night descended, they gathered there, paying no heed to backgrounds, class, or wealth, focusing only on the imperatives of sensual pleasure and a fellowship of equality as impoverished, lonely teenage boys came under the wing of wealthy elders. Yomoda argues not only that the New Park of the story represents the emergence and

---

[20] Fujii, "The Hybridity of Taiwanese Culture," 13–14.
[21] Fujii, "The Hybridity of Taiwanese Culture," 31–37.
[22] Saisho Hazuki, "台湾の客家人の苦難の半世紀刻む" [Depicting Half-a-Century of Suffering by the Taiwan Hakka People], *Asahi Shimbun*, February 19, 2006.
[23] Yomoda Inuhiko, "蓮花のユートピア" [The Lotus Utopia], 新潮 [*Shinchō*], July 2006, 256–57.

realization of a utopia that was otherwise denied by society at large but that the quest for such utopias is a sort of allegory for resistance to tyranny in Taiwan. The feeling of abjection can also be an allegory for Taiwan as an orphan in international affairs after it has been expelled from the United Nations in 1971.

By the early 2000s, with the support of the Ministry of Culture, Japanese translations of Taiwanese literature were being introduced to the Japanese public almost as soon as the originals came out in Taiwan. In 2008, the four volumes of the "Taiwan Sexual Minority Literature" series (台湾セクシュアル・マイノリティ文学, edited by Sirouzu Noriko 白水紀子, Tarumi Chie 垂水千惠, and Ying-che Huang) were released by the Sakuhinsya publishing house with the support of the CCA. The first three volumes comprised, respectively, translations of Chiu Miao-chin's (邱妙津) full-length novel *Notes of a Crocodile* (ある鰐の手記), Chi Ta-wei's (紀大偉) short story collection *Membrane* (膜), and a collection of short stories entitled *Groom, New "Husband"* (新郎新"夫") featuring works by Hsu Yu-sheng (許佑生), Wu Chi-wen (吳繼文), Juan Ching-yueh (阮慶岳), and others—all works were composed from the early 1990s to 2008. The series concluded with a volume of queer criticism, *Father China, Queer Taiwan* (父なる中国、母（クイア）なる台湾?). Collectively, the series was hailed by Japanese writers and scholars for being in pace with the latest writing on sexual minorities from the Euro-American world, and more advanced than what was available from other Asian countries. In Japan itself, virtually no comprehensive sexual minority literature was to be found prior to the publication of this series. Indeed, these translations of Taiwanese writing provided Japanese researchers with a textual basis for the study of LGBTQ literature in Japan and quickly became adopted as basic reference texts at several gender research centers and in gender studies seminars at Japanese universities.

LGBTQ discourse had begun to emerge in academia in Europe and North America in the 1990s. It spread to Japan quickly, but its impact was limited to the small number of scholars of Anglo-American literature there. Among scholars of Japanese literature, it received little attention. Even by the early 2000s, key terms such as "LGBTQ" and "queer" were still not in wide circulation in Japanese academia. The pivotal moment came only in 2008 with the newly established "Taiwan Sexual Minority Literature" series, which deeply impressed Japanese literary scholars with works that could be placed on par with the most advanced European and North American queer writing. Since the series represented voices from a nearby and culturally similar people, these Taiwanese texts served as a more natural reference point for Japanese queer theory. The full impact of the series was acknowledged in 2018 when Japan's Association for Showa Literary Studies (昭和文学会), a renowned and long-established academic organization dedicated to research in Japanese literature, convened a forum entitled "What Is Queer Reading: To Read, to Fight, and to Change" (クイア・リーディングとは何か：読む・戦う・変革する) to reflect on the relative paucity of queer works in the Japanese literary arena. The invited participants included some of the most important scholars of Japanese literature, such as Iida Yuko (飯田祐子), Takeuchi Kayo (武内佳代), and Nakagawa Shigemi (中川成美), and of Anglo-American literature, such as Shimizu Akiko (清水晶子), as well as one of the "Taiwan Sexual Minority Literature" series editors—Tarumi Chie. During the meeting, Tarumi Chie pointed out that Chi Ta-wei's work "The Ceremony" (儀式) had been inspired by Ōshima Nagisa's (大島渚) eponymous 1971 film *The Ceremony* and that the influence from Haruki Murakami's (村上春樹) 1987 novel *Norwegian Woods* (ノルウェイの森) is equally clear in Chiu Miao-chin's in the lesbian-themed *Notes of a Crocodile*.[24] In short, the release of the "Taiwan Sexual Minority Literature" series in Japan officially had driven much of the LGBTQ research in Japanese academia. By then, the impact of Taiwanese queer writing was no longer limited to the small circle of Japan's Anglo-American literary scholars. Japanese scholars had also noticed that most of the queer literary masterpieces in Chinese came from Taiwan rather than China. This was testimony to the fact that Taiwanese literature was no longer subordinate to mainland Chinese literature but had become an independent pioneer of new subjects and directions in the development of Chinese-language writing.

Between 2010 and 2011, the well-known Japanese publisher Jinbun Shoin (人文書院) published a four-volume series called "Taiwan Tropical Literature" (台湾熱帯文学シリーズ). Subsidized once again by the CCA, this series featured translated works by Taiwanese-Malaysian and Sinophone Malaysian writers based mainly in Taiwan. It includes Li Yung-ping's (李永平) *The Jiling Chronicles* (吉陵鎮ものがたり, translated by Ikegami Sadako and Oikawa Akane 及川茜), Chang Kuei-hsing's (張貴興) *Elephant Herd* (象の群れ, translated by Matuura Tuneo 松浦恆雄), Ng Kim Chew's (黃錦樹) *Dream and Swine and Aurora: Collected Works of Ng Kim Chew* (夢と豚と黎明: 黃錦樹作品集, translated by Ohigashi Kazushige 大東和重, Haneda Asako 羽田朝子, et al.), as well as a collection of short stories by Li Zishu (黎紫書), Shang Wanyun (商晚筠), and others entitled *Termite Incubus* (白蟻の夢魔: 短編小説集, translated by Arai Shigeo 荒井茂夫, Nishimura Masao 西村正男, et al.). The series has perhaps impressed Japanese scholars and readers more than any other translations of contemporary Taiwanese literature and arguably done more than any other publication to make Taiwanese literature a firm presence in Japanese academia as an independent field of study. Unoki Yō (宇野木洋) points out that the very existence of Sinophone Malaysian literature, not to mention its creativity and dynamism, has prompted scholars everywhere to reconsider the meaning and scope of "China" in relation to the field of modern "Chinese" literature.[25] Native-speaking Chinese researchers overseas now also have to take into account various notions of Chinese identity, as reflected in categorizations such as "Chinese-language literature" (with a broader but dated scope), "world literatures in Chinese" (exemplified, for example, by scholars such as Kuo-ch'ing Tu and Liu Denghan), and "Sinophone literature" (e.g., David Der-wei Wang, Shu-mei Shih).[26] Japanese scholars in particular

---

[24] See the minutes of the forum published in 昭和文学研究 [*Showa Literary Studies*], no. 77 (September 2018): 2–30.

[25] Unoki Yō, "対象.方法の拡散的多様化に直面する中国現代文学研究領域: 戦後日本の研究営為を踏まえつつ現在的課題を探る" [The Diversified Target Readers and Methodologies in the Field of Modern Chinese Literature: A Review of Studies in Postwar Japan as a Search for the Contemporary], 現代中国 [*Modern China*], no. 90 (2016): 36.

[26] Unoki, "The Diversified Target Readers and Methodologies in the Field of Modern Chinese Literature," 36.

now recognize that "Taiwanese literature" no longer belongs unproblematically within the scope of "China" in the field of modern Chinese literature. "Taiwanese literature" has finally confirmed its independence and uniqueness, and it can be said that Taiwanese literature from Taiwan has completed its paradigm shift in Japan.

Conclusion

In recent years, discussions of the relationship between "Taiwanese literature" and "Sinophone literature" have begun to emerge in Japanese academia as Japanese translations of Taiwanese literature continue to stimulate a rethinking of what constitutes "modern Chinese literature" as well as concepts such as "Sinophone literature," "marginality," and "indigenization." "Sinophone," like "Anglophone" and "Francophone," can be regarded as essentially a postcolonial concept, if we consider it, in terms of historical periodization, as referring to the deterritorialization and reterritorialization of prior literary and cultural contexts. "Sinophone" thus inherits its significance from national literatures of the Global South or from the development of postcolonial or decolonizing literary theory. The question of how it corresponds to the global context of late capitalism and neoliberalism, however, deserves further study. Since the 1990s, the translation into Japanese of Taiwanese literature, with support from the CCA and later the Ministry of Culture, has contributed to a transformation in Japanese understanding of modern "Chinese" literature. This translation project, buoyed by official support, publication subsidies, and academic exchanges, needs to continue. Taiwanese literature can grow and flourish even more from this ongoing cultural dialogue.

It is worth noting that, since the 1990s, the publication of Japanese translations of Taiwanese literature subsidized by the CCA and Ministry of Culture has not been limited to genre fiction but has included some of Taiwan's most challenging modern prose and poetry as well as a growing body of Taiwanese Indigenous literature published in its own separate series. Works by new, younger writers such as Wu Ming-yi (吳明益), Egoyan Zheng (伊格言), Hu Shu-wen (胡淑雯), Wang Tsung-wei (王聰威), Kuo Chiang-sheng (郭強生), Hsu Chia-tse (徐嘉澤), and Huang Chong-kai (黃崇凱) have also been successfully translated into Japanese and well received by Japanese lovers of serious literature. Moreover, a new generation of Japanese translators of Taiwanese literature has emerged in the twenty-first century. Several forward-looking young translators and scholars such as Amano Kentarō (天野健太郎), Misu Yusuke (三須祐介), Tumori Aki (津守陽), Aketagawa Satoshi (明田川聰士), Yagi Haruna (八木はるな), Oikawa Akane, and the Taiwan-based Kuramoto Tomoaki (倉本知明) are now actively involved in the translation of Taiwanese literature. This is a very promising development. Meanwhile, more senior translators and scholars, including Fujii Shōzō, Miki Naotake, Sirouzu Noriko, Ikegami Sadako, Simomura Sakujirō, and Sawai Noriyuki, are no less diligent in carrying on the task of translating Taiwanese literature. The Japanese translation and reception of contemporary Taiwanese literature continue to grow.

To date, nearly all the translators of Taiwanese literature in Japan have been university professors, including the younger translators mentioned above. A notable exception is Amano Kentarō. In 2012, this professional translator, together with his wife Huang Pi-chun (黃碧君), set up the copyright agency Bunbundo (聞文堂) and, with subsidies from Taiwan's Ministry of Culture, began to energetically promote Taiwanese literature in Japan's publishing industry. In the six short years before his untimely death in 2018, Amano published twelve book-length translations of Taiwanese literature. His translation of Lung Ying-tai's (龍應台) *Big River, Big Sea: Untold Stories of 1949* (台灣海峽: 一九四九), published by Hakusuisya (白水社) in 2012, sold very well and has been reprinted several times. His translation of Wu Ming-yi's *The Magician on the Skywalk* (步道橋の魔術師), published by Hakusuisya in 2015, has also been in great demand. It was shortlisted for the 2016 Best Translation Award (日本翻訳大賞) and selected as the third-prize winner of the 2016 Bookstore Award "Translated Novel Category" (本屋大賞「翻訳小説部門」).[27] These successes show clearly that Japanese readers respond enthusiastically to new literature from Taiwan. They also signal that serious Taiwanese literature is no longer a mere academic specialty in Japan but has grown into a subject of general interest. The twenty-first century has thus witnessed the paradigm shift in the reception of Taiwanese literature in Japan. This highly encouraging development makes it clear that Taiwanese literature in Japanese translation will continue to stimulate and inspire Japanese scholars and readers and promote the acceptance of Taiwanese writing as a distinct national tradition within the larger world of Sinophone literature.

---

[27] The award was voted on by the employees of Japan's bookstores with the aim of identifying the most popular novels from the previous year. See Lin Ke-hung (林克鴻), "二〇一六日本書店大獎，東山彰良、吳明益雙雙入榜!" [The 2016 Japan's Bookstore Prize: Both Hagashiyama Akira and Wu Ming-yi on the List!], *Readmoo News*, April 13, 2016.

11

Made in Taiwan: Reading Chiu Miao-chin's Lesbian Tales as World Literature

Wen-chi Li

In the 1987 Hollywood film *Fatal Attraction*, the protagonist Dan Gallagher, played by Michael Douglas, is a successful, wealthy Manhattan lawyer with an attractive wife and a daughter he dotes on. At the beginning of the film, he could not be more satisfied with his happy, conventional life. This all changes after an encounter with Alex Forrest, a seductive female played by Glenn Close. They meet at a business party and have a brief but memorable conversation. Not knowing if they will ever meet again, they are surprised—and delighted—to encounter one another at a business meeting the following day, but Dan restrains his urge to flirt with her. After the meeting, he rushes outside on the way to his next appointment. Rain is bucketing down, but his umbrella refuses to unfurl. Emerging from the building at that moment, Alex comes up to him and jokingly asks, "Made in Taiwan?" This breaks the ice and gives Dan a chance to invite her to a restaurant. This is the beginning of the "fatal" affair that unravels Dan's comfortable life.

The umbrella scene, though brief and trivial in content, is possibly one of the best-known images of Taiwan in twentieth-century Western culture. It succinctly captures Taiwan's reputation at the time as little more than an exporter of cheap, shoddy consumer goods. By the 1980s, as a result of land reform, liberalization of market controls, massive foreign investment, and substantial US aid for the development of infrastructure, communication networks, and education, Taiwan had become a thriving source in the rapidly globalizing marketplace of commonplace items such as textiles, toys, bicycles, various gadgets, and, as the film playfully notes, umbrellas. To consumers in the West, however, the label "made in Taiwan" identified not merely the origin of an item, but also suggested something cheap and unreliable.

In Taiwan, on the other hand, the booming export sector meant improved standards of living, health care, and education, an embrace of Western modernity, and greater personal freedom, leading eventually to the lifting of martial law in the same year, coincidentally, that *Fatal Attraction* was released. Since the late 1980s, however, Taiwan's increasing economic power, wealth, technological know-how, and civil awareness have transformed the image of "made in Taiwan." Taiwanese consumer brands such as Giant and Merida for bicycles, Maxxis for bicycle tires, Evergreen for container transportation, and Asus, Acer, Transcend, and TSMC for electronics have come to be associated with quality and reliability, while Taiwan itself is now widely identified with the progressive social norms and democratic political values shared with the industrialized West.

The end of the White Terror, the robustness of the economy, the improvement of the social welfare system, and, most importantly, the awakening of a strong sense of Taiwanese identity have also made the people proud of what is "made in Taiwan." Taiwan's national "brand" is no longer that of "free" China in exile, but one of Taiwan itself. The revival of its real name, Taiwan, long suppressed under the KMT, only intensified the Taiwanese people's desire, once they had the opportunity, to assert the island's distinctive identity and build its international prestige in diplomatic, sport, and cultural domains as well as in manufacturing and business, during the post-martial-law years. Thus, it is no surprise that in the field of literature successive Taiwanese governments, especially since the 1990s, have supported the export of Taiwanese soft power through projects of translation and publishing in English, French, German, Korean, and Japanese.

Among all the translations of Taiwanese literature, whether subsidized by the government or not, works highlighting gender issues, such as the feminist writer Li Ang's (李昂) *The Butcher's Wife* (殺夫, 1983, translated into English in 1986) and gay issues, such as Pai Hsien-yung's (白先勇) *Crystal Boys* (孽子, 1983, translated in 1989) and Chu T'ien-wen's (朱天文) *Notes of a Desolate Man* (荒人手記, 1994, translated in 1999), have been among the most widely circulated worldwide and the most popular with foreign readers. Their translation and publication in the 1980s and 1990s coincided with a burgeoning global interest in gender and sexuality marked by English translations of Michel Foucault's *The History of Sexuality* (three English volumes published in 1978, 1985, and 1986), Luce Irigaray's *This Sex Which Is Not One* (1977, translated in 1985), and Julia Kristeva's *The Black Sun* (1987, translated in 1989) and equally influential original works in English such as Eve Kosofsky Sedgwick's *Epistemology of the Closet* (1990), Judith Butler's *Gender Trouble* (1990), and *Bodies That Matter* (1993). At the same time, militant activist groups such as ACT UP (the initialism for AIDS Coalition to Unleash Power, 1987), Queer Nation (1990), and the Lesbian Avengers (1992) drew increasing public attention to the practical politics of sexuality and gender.

Translated Taiwanese texts on similar themes intrigued Western readers with models of gender and sexual resistance in a distant place that was nevertheless recognizable and relatable. When Sedgwick in *Tendencies* (1994) told readers they were living in the "moment of Queer,"[1] she referred to the American culture or Western culture in general. From my perspective, this can also be applied to the robust gender rebellions taking place in distant cultures like that of Taiwan from the 1980s onward.

Among all those "made in Taiwan" queer novelists, Chiu Miao-chin (pinyin: Qiu Miaojin, 邱妙津) is an author whose works are translated into English, French,

---

[1] Eve Kosofsky Sedgwick, *Tendencies* (London: Routledge, 1994), vii.

German, Spanish, Italian, and Turkish, receive international circulation and fame, and create more resonance than Pai Hsien-yung and Chu T'ien-wen among foreign readers with gender troubles experience. Chiu was born in Changhua County, Taiwan, in 1969. After studying psychology at National Taiwan University, she moved to Paris in 1994 to pursue studies in clinical psychology and feminism at the University of Paris, VIII, where she took courses with Hélène Cixous. In Paris in 1995, shortly after completing her final literary work, she committed suicide by stabbing herself in the heart. She was twenty-six. The stigma of homosexual desire, the failure of relationships, the melancholy, and the fear of coming out, all these are intertwined with other emotions such as angst, self-doubt, and self-abhorrence in her semi-autobiographical works *Notes of a Crocodile* (鱷魚手記, 1994; hereafter *Notes*) and the text that serves as her suicide note *Last Words from Montmartre* (蒙馬特遺書, posthumously published in 1996; hereafter *Last Words*).[2] The global popularity of her works is evidenced by over five hundred English reviews on the Goodreads and Amazon websites. Chiu's reputation, which has only grown since her death, appears to confirm the potential of translated literature to operate as a form of national soft power in the world arena.

However, like the complex supply chains of globalized manufacturing that make the "made in Taiwan" label difficult to take literally, the complex transnational cultural influences in a globalized world mean that no national literature can be the product of only that nation. Scholars of comparative literature have long accepted the necessarily hybrid nature of "local" texts, and the contributors to this book *Taiwanese Literature as World Literature*, as the title itself suggests, are keenly aware of how deeply Chinese, Japanese, American, and European cultures—and literary movements as varied as the May Fourth Movement, Japanese and French surrealism, modernism, and postmodernism—have influenced Taiwanese literary representations. When applied to queer literature, this recognition of the importance of creolization and hybridization raises several questions: To what extent are these queer Taiwanese works composed of genuinely Taiwanese elements? What does "made in Taiwan" mean in relation to queer writing? Should, or can, a local movement and queer identity be "protected" from global influences? And in relation to queer world literature, how can queer Taiwanese writers write back? Why, in particular, have Chiu's works circulated more widely as "global" texts than those of other queer Taiwanese writers such as Pai Hsien-yung and Chu T'ien-wen?

To make an initial attempt to answer these questions, this chapter explores approaches to, and practices of, translation to show how multiple influences have contributed to the construction of Taiwanese queer identity in Chiu Miao-chin's two major works. In the process, I discuss how these works have circulated beyond Taiwan and why they have attracted such a large readership. My starting point is Lawrence Venuti's discovery of how translation can change the perception of a text and the identities of people. I then consider the mix of Chinese and Western influences

---

[2] Her translations are *Notes of a Crocodile* trans. Bonnie Huie (New York: New York Review Books, 2017) and *Last Words from Montmartre* trans. Ari Larissa Heinrich (New York: New York Review Books, 2014).

that contributed to Chiu's sense of identity. Finally, I explore the reviews of English translations of Chiu's works on Goodreads and relate the readers' comments to the "made in Taiwan" global brand. By historicizing Chiu in the Taiwanese queer context and scrutinizing some popular global feedback on her works, I wish to demonstrate how the hybridity of Taiwanese queer texts enables them to participate in the global debates around gender and sexuality while, at the same time, refreshing the "made in Taiwan" brand.

Translation and Identities

In "Translation and the Formation of Cultural Identities," Venuti argues that translation wields enormous power in the construction of local cultures.[3] Foreign texts, once translated and introduced to the target country, are always "dehistoricized."[4] They are "removed from the foreign literary traditions where they draw their significance" and "rewritten to conform to styles and themes that currently prevail in domestic literatures." The translations thereby "establish peculiarly domestic canons for foreign literatures [...] that conform to domestic aesthetic values and therefore reveal exclusions and admissions, centers and peripheries that deviate from those current in the foreign language."[5] Venuti calls this a process of "domestication" in which foreign texts are "inscribed with linguistic and cultural values that are intelligible to specific domestic constituencies."[6] Thus, translation can be an instrument to shape domestic attitudes toward foreign countries, specific ethnicities, races, and nationalities or foster admiration or hatred based on ethnocentrism, racism, or patriotism.[7]

If, as Venuti argues, translation constructs a domesticated representation of a foreign text, and therefore of the culture and identities the text expresses, it also influences a domestic subject and shapes the interests and agendas of particular social groups in the target culture.[8] Every translation is in conjunction with paratexts, that is, discourses beyond the translation itself such as the book cover art, the advertising copy, and the opinions of reviewers, both those quoted on the dust jacket or in the front matter as well as amateur and professional reviews online or in print. A book's paratexts also include how it is read and taught in schools, universities, and other institutions.[9] The wide circulation of translated foreign texts in churches, state agencies, bureaucracies, health-care facilities, businesses, and places of learning can change or consolidate "literary canons, conceptual paradigms, research methodologies, clinical techniques,

---

[3] Lawrence Venuti, "Translation and the Formation of Cultural Identities," in *Cultural Functions of Translation*, ed. Christina Schäffner and Helen Kelly-Holmes (Bristol, PA: Multilingual Matters, 1995), 10.
[4] Venuti, "Translation and the Formation of Cultural Identities," 10.
[5] Venuti, "Translation and the Formation of Cultural Identities," 10.
[6] Venuti, "Translation and the Formation of Cultural Identities," 9.
[7] Venuti, "Translation and the Formation of Cultural Identities," 10.
[8] Venuti, "Translation and the Formation of Cultural Identities," 10.
[9] Venuti, "Translation and the Formation of Cultural Identities," 10.

and commercial practices" in the demotic culture.[10] These cultural agencies, both individuals and institutions, frame and shape the reception of foreign texts by domestic readers. Invariably, they privilege certain values and features of the foreign text and obscure others. Moreover, since the translated texts are selected and imported by agents with particular interests and ideologies in different times, the representations that the translations construct can never be consistent. They will have the gaps and contradictions of any discourse "assembled from heterogeneous cultural materials, domestic and foreign, past and present."[11]

The inconsistencies, in turn, enable new agencies to precipitate disciplinary revisions and construct new identities because identity is never fixed but, as Stuart Hall observes, undergoes "constant transformation."[12] Two examples proposed by Venuti attest to how translation can form a new discourse that promotes cultural resistance, innovation, change, and heterogeneity. The first example includes the modern perspectives on reading and translating Aristotle in Anglophone academia propelled by the philosophies of Heidegger and Sartre, which began as radical challenges to the traditional approaches but have now become orthodox in classical scholarship.[13] The second example is the fourth-century translation of the Bible known as the *Vulgate*, translated directly from the Hebrew for the first time by Jerome of Stridon. Earlier Christians had understood their faith based on "institutionally validated translation that was 'familiar' and 'ingrained' in their memories."[14] Their identities were deeply rooted in the Greek Old Testament—the Septuagint—and other credible Greek and Latin sources.[15] Jerome's version provoked a furor at the time because the church depended on a "stable process of identity formation enacted not simply by a particular translation, but by the repeated use of it 'read by so many generations.'"[16] His translation, revealing the diversity of Roman, Greek, and Jewish cultures, was accepted only slowly, eventually replacing the Septuagint and becoming the standard Latin version of the Bible. Both examples show the potential of translation to be "highly subversive of domestic ideologies and institutions."[17]

Making Chiu Miao-chin

Venuti's theory of translation can be extended to include ideologies, perspectives, speeches, and sentiments that originate in foreign lands, travel to another country, and shape identity. This broad sense of translation can illustrate how understandings of, and attitudes toward, homosexuality have changed during the twentieth century and

---

[10] Venuti, "Translation and the Formation of Cultural Identities," 10.
[11] Venuti, "Translation and the Formation of Cultural Identities," 12.
[12] Stuart Hall, "Cultural Identity and Diaspora," in *Identity: Community, Culture, Difference*, ed. Jonathan Rutherford (London: Lawrence & Wishart, 1990), 225.
[13] Venuti, "Translation and the Formation of Cultural Identities," 11–13.
[14] Venuti, "Translation and the Formation of Cultural Identities," 20.
[15] Venuti, "Translation and the Formation of Cultural Identities," 20.
[16] Venuti, "Translation and the Formation of Cultural Identities," 20.
[17] Venuti, "Translation and the Formation of Cultural Identities," 23.

how these changes have accumulated to form a distinctive queer identity in Taiwan. To comprehend the making of Taiwanese queer identity and better understand the making of Chiu's queer identity, it is necessary to read the ingredient list, that is, the historical sediments that weigh down the Taiwanese queer identity and have produced shame, melancholy, angst, frustration, self-doubt, and in Chiu's case and that of many others, even self-destruction.

The pressures that formed Chiu's queer identity can be elucidated by considering how female homosexuality particularly has been constructed historically in Sinophone communities. In premodern China, female-to-female eroticism did not receive the same attention as its male-to-male counterpart. Romantic feelings between women fell under the broad rubric of "sisterhood, friendship, and emotion."[18] If women's same-sex attraction was mentioned at all in writing by men, it was categorized with "the insignificant, the laughable, the naughty, and on rare occasions, the anomalous."[19] Since their intimate bonding was camouflaged under the concept of sisterhood, their behavior did not either provoke the fictional community's suspicions or challenge heteronormative marital values centered around the concept of the patrilineal family.

Undisguised depictions of same-sex romantic love became more acceptable in modernist Chinese literature, especially in the works of female writers such as Lu Yin (廬隱), in whose *Old Acquaintances by the Seaside* (海濱故人, 1923) two schoolgirls express their love for one another. They do not, however, totally renounce heteronormativity. Both are courted by men and get married after graduation. Across the Taiwan Strait, the camaraderie of school days can also be seen in the story "Seasons of Bloom" (花開時節, 1942) by Yang Chien-he (楊千鶴), written during the Japanese colonial period. In this story, graduation and marriage would terminate the best-friend-forever school-days alliance, hinder self-realization, and erase female autonomy. Lu's modern bosom friends and Yang's Taiwanese schoolgirls create, even if temporarily, a female world that can be accepted because it is assumed by others to be innocent. Eventually, however, they must all negotiate with heteronormative or patriarchal values, particularly through the norms of marriage and reproduction. Beyond this, the female-to-female carnal desire remained a taboo even into the modern period. Even though the May Fourth Movement's sexual-enlightenment discourse began to acknowledge love between women, it maintained the taboo on female-female orgasmic sex, which it continued to regard as ignominious.[20]

Discourse around homosexuality cannot be indispensable from foreign influence, which includes translation of terminology, sexology, literature, and film. Although there is a long tradition of same-sex relations being accepted or at least tolerated in

---

[18] Tze-lan D. Sang, *The Emerging Lesbian: Female Same-Sex Desire in Modern China* (Chicago: The University of Chicago Press, 2003), 17.
[19] Sang, *The Emerging Lesbian*, 21.
[20] Sang, *The Emerging Lesbian*, 132.

Sinophone communities, traditional Chinese terminology for sexual practices focused on "actions, tendencies, and preference" rather than any concept of an "innate sexual essence."²¹ Instead of saying what someone "is," Chinese people usually say who (or what) the person "resembles" or "does,"²² hence the ancient images of "cutting sleeves" (斷袖) for male-to-male eroticism and "eating in pairs" (對食) or "polishing mirrors" (磨鏡) for female-to-female sex. Thus, traditional Chinese discourse did not express discrimination or stigma but merely described specific behaviors, including those considered unusual and rare.

This discourse began to be reshaped at the beginning of the twentieth century, however, when Chinese intellectuals coined the term *tongxing'ai* (同性愛, literally "same-sex love") from the Japanese *dōseiai*, which had been in use in Japan since the early twelfth century. In early twentieth-century Japan, this term was adapted to comprehend emerging modern European sexology and was later adopted in China as *tongxing'ai*. Based on the loanword, variants such as *tongxinglian* (同性戀) or *tongxinglian'ai* (同性戀愛) were invented to describe attractions that could not be included in "love between man and woman" (男女之戀愛).²³ Since republican China was keen to absorb the latest European psychosexual theories of Richard von Krafft-Ebing, Havelock Ellis, and Sigmund Freud, *tongxinglian* was soon augmented by less neutral terms such as *xingbiantai* (性變態) and *xingnizhuan* (性逆轉), which were coined to translate European concepts of "perversion" and "inversion."²⁴ The traditional nonjudgmental view of same-sex eroticism held by Chinese people underwent a dramatic transformation.

In 1952, when the American Psychiatric Association published the first edition of the *Diagnostic and Statistical Manual of Mental Disorders* (*DSM*), it listed "homosexuality" as a "sociopathic personality disturbance." In the second edition, published in 1968, homosexuality was reclassified, only somewhat less pejoratively, as a "sexual deviation." It was not until 1973 that the *DSM*'s publisher, the American Psychiatric Association (APA), removed the diagnosis of "homosexuality" as a mental disorder from the *DSM*.²⁵ Framed in the aftermath of the APA's decision, Taiwanese gay writer Kuang Tai's (光泰) 1976 novel *The Man Who Escapes Marriage* (逃避婚姻的人) was a plea for social acceptance of homosexuals and an end to the stigmatization caused by Western psychiatric discourse. The novel provoked heated discussions, and not surprisingly, attracted harsh criticism. In one typical response, a doctor, Hu Wei-heng (胡維恆), repeated the theories of childhood causation that had been advanced by orthodox Western psychology before 1973: hatred of the mother, a homosexual or absent father, feminist ideas that undermine traditional male roles, and so on.

---

[21] Bret Hinsch, *Passions of the Cut Sleeves: The Male Homosexual Tradition in China* (Berkeley: University of California Press, 1990), 7.
[22] Hinsch, *Passions of the Cut Sleeves*, 7.
[23] Sang, *The Emerging Lesbian*, 102–3.
[24] Sang, *The Emerging Lesbian*, 100.
[25] Jack Drescher, "Out of DSM: Depathologizing Homosexuality," *Behavioral Sciences* 5, no. 4 (2015): 569.

Predictably, Hu ignores the APA's recent conclusion that homosexuality is a normal variation of human sexuality and recommends treatment as early as possible when homosexual inclinations are observed or suspected.[26]

This discrimination in the name of psychology continued in Taiwan during the 1980s. In *Homosexuality, Suicide, and Psychosis* (同性戀，自殺，精神病, 1983), for example, the sociologist Peng Huai-chen (彭懷真) condemned homosexuals as a "sick part" of society.[27] He classified homosexuality with disorders of "child development," "sexual perversions and abnormalities," "suicidality," "pill addiction and alcoholism," and "pedophilia."[28] He also saw female homosexuality as an unpleasant consequence of psychological stresses such as lack of interaction between mother and father, an experience of rape, feelings of inferiority to men, and parents' disappointment with having a daughter rather than a son.[29] Despite more recent changes in thinking in the West, local experts in psychoanalysis, urology, and other branches of medicine continued to rely on the pre-1973 Western "science" of homosexuality. Taiwan thus moved away from a Chinese tradition that had been tolerant of homosexuality and embraced a westernized, homophobic mentality of contempt, hatred, antipathy, and aversion to LGBTQ identities that, ironically, was already obsolete—at least among progressive thinkers—in its place of origin.[30]

Was it this historical background that formed Chiu Miao-chin's interest in studying psychology? Did she study the subject to analyze her own queer psyche? In *Notes*, she explores the character of the protagonist Lazi entirely through psychological motivation and personality traits, without giving even the slightest indication of Lazi's physical appearance. Around the time of the book's first publication in 1994, two girls who attended the same high school where Chiu had once studied died by double suicide, which led to media speculation that the girls had been in a lesbian relationship. Medical experts and psychologists were called on to comment and analyze the two girls' motives. Chiu may have been thinking of this when, in *Notes*, she satirizes the reaction to the discovery of "the Crocodiles" in human society. For example, she observes that, following the discovery, "various crocodile experts had begun to crop up,"[31] all of them spouting contradictory pseudoscientific nonsense:

---

[26] Hu Wei-heng, "漫談同性戀：由逃避婚姻的人談起" [On Homosexuality: Reading *The Man Who Escapes Marriage*], *Health World*, no. 7 (1976): 44–45.

[27] Peng Huai-chen, 同性戀，自殺，精神病 [*Homosexuality, Suicide, and Psychosis*], (Taipei: Olive Foundation, 1983), 5. See also Jens Damm, "From Psychoanalysis to AIDS: The Early Contradictory Approaches to Gender and Sexuality and the Recourse to American Discourses during Taiwan's Societal Transformation in the Early 1980s," in *Perverse Taiwan*, ed. Howard Chiang and Yin Wang (London: Routledge, 2017), 65.

[28] Damm, "From Psychoanalysis to AIDS," 66.

[29] Peng, *Homosexuality, Suicide, and Psychosis*, 47. Qtd. in Damm, "From Psychoanalysis to AIDS," 68.

[30] This does not mean that tolerance in old China was ahead of the West and Western-following Taiwan. In Western culture, same-sex eroticism was not always discriminated against. This can be perceived in Shakespeare's sonnets or Sappho's poetry. It was the emergence of psychosexual theories at the end of the nineteenth century that started to change the discourse and incite homophobic sentiments in Europe, China, and Taiwan.

[31] Chiu, *Notes*, 205.

From the standpoint of the development psychologist, [the Crocodiles] were aberrant species. In accordance with their discipline's understanding of crocodile families, their research indicated distinct differences from humans at every stage of development from birth to puberty as well as in maturity.[32]

She adds that these "scholars" cited psychology to explain the necessity of preventing any increase in cases of crocodile mutation in society, which would ultimately contribute to a "broader trend toward a full-fledged crocodile ecology and generic mutation."[33]

At the same time that Taiwanese "experts" were adopting out-of-date Western theories of abnormal psychology to account for homosexuality, fear of AIDS was at its height. The epidemic was officially documented in the United States in 1981, and initially named "GRID," or "gay-related immune deficiency," in 1982. Although this news, along with the pejorative term "gay cancer," was reported in a Taiwanese magazine in the same year, it is not until the first native case in 1984 and the death of the American actor Rock Hudson in 1985 that what had until then been seen as a "Western problem" began to worry Taiwanese people and trigger widespread discussion of the morality—and supposed dangers—of homosexuality.[34] The term *AIDS* was initially translated as *aisibing* (愛死病, literally "love-death disease"), suggesting a fatal illness caused by "making love." A later translation that gained wide currency, *aizibing* (愛滋病, literally "love-infestation disease"), perhaps imported from Hong Kong,[35] was no better, implying as it did that the places or people were "infected" because of "making love," in other words, sexual promiscuity.[36] Both translations associated same-sex sexual relations with disease and implied that gay men in particular were inherently promiscuous and addicted to casual, anonymous sex.[37] A 1985 article by the urologist Chiang Han-sheng is a typical example of how such translations, and the discussions they encouraged, quickly led to gay male sex being linked simultaneously to disease and immorality. Chiang explains virtually all common STIs, including hepatitis, chlamydia, syphilis, gonorrhea, genital warts, and HIV, as divine punishment for sexual debauchery, warning that "the more complicated the sexual activities are, the more diseases they produce and the harder they are to cure."[38] Homosexuals, he advises, must avoid getting "stained" by staying "vigilant" and "simple" in their sexual relationships. AIDS thus generated a new view of globalization, one that suggested that Taiwan could not be saved from the pandemic and the moral and social corruption that supposedly fueled it.

---

[32] Chiu, *Notes*, 205–6.
[33] Chiu, *Notes*, 205–6
[34] Damm, "From Psychoanalysis to AIDS," 74–75.
[35] Damm, "From Psychoanalysis to AIDS," 76.
[36] Hans Tao-Ming Huang, *Queer Politics and Sexual Modernity in Taiwan* (Hong Kong: Hong Kong University Press, 2011), 79.
[37] Damm, "From Psychoanalysis to AIDS," 76; Huang, *Queer Politics and Sexual Modernity in Taiwan*, 77.
[38] Chiang Han-sheng, "玻璃圈裡的污垢：談同性戀男子的傳染病" [The Stain in the Glass Circle: On Infectious Disease of Homosexuals], *Health World*, no. 118 (1985): 8.

In addition to Western theories of abnormal psychology and the effect of the AIDS pandemic, one cannot ignore how, since the 1950s, certain foreign literary works and films conditioned the Taiwanese people's perceptions of modernity, helping to fill the moral and intellectual void caused by the KMT's political repression and strict social engineering. Foreign works that expressed homosexual eroticism such as Thomas Mann's *Death in Venice*, Yukio Mishima's *Confessions of a Mask*, and André Gide's *If It Die…*, and gay writers such as Oscar Wilde, Tennessee Williams, and Walt Whitman began to be known by Taiwanese readers. André Gide was especially popular through *If It Die…* and *Madeleine* (*Et nunc manet in te*). *Madeleine* was translated by Nieh Hua-ling (聶華苓) and serialized in *United Daily News* in 1960 with a new, more "poetic" Chinese title that can be translated as *The Sorrow of My Heart* (遣悲懷), and was inspired by the ancient Chinese poet Yuan Chen's (元稹) identically titled work. The appropriated title seems to have been intended to link Gide's reflections on his difficult, complex relationship with his wife Madeleine with Yuan's similar thoughts on the frustrations of marriage. Although *Madeleine* does not highlight Gide's homosexuality, Nieh Hua-ling in a footnote in her translation used the phrase "homosexual defect" (同性戀的毛病) to describe Gide's sexual orientation.[39] The translation, in combination with the editor's introduction and the appropriated title, has the effect, to use Venuti's term, of "domesticating" Gide and his homosexual history.[40] It is no surprise that in *Last Words*, the protagonist, Zoë, falls back on Gide's work to express her regret for the breakup with her girlfriend:

> I [have had] my copy [of Gide's *The Sorrow of My Heart*] for five years and I [have] often turned to it while writing this fiction of human nature, for Gide's sincere account is filled with the power of love and resentment—it consoled me during this painful process of writing. Only a spirit of artistic sincerity can console the souls of humankind.[41]

Chiu's allusion to Gide suggests not merely how the translation of *Madeleine* has helped to form her queer identity but also how she has localized the foreign text. Gide's remorse for his wife's suffering is appropriated by Chiu to express her regret for the end of her relationship with her girlfriend as well as her struggle to fit into a normalizing society.[42]

The evidence of how these foreign works have shaped the queer identity of Chiu Miao-chin can be seen in both *Notes* and *Last Words*. In *Notes*, Lazi uses Pär Lagerkvist's *The Dwarf* to describe how she is like a "hideously deformed dwarf stuffed into a jar, pressed up against the layer of glass cutting off [her] senses."[43] She goes on to compare the social pressures she endures because of her queerness to the distortion of

---

[39] Qtd. in Chi Ta-wei, *A Queer Invention in Taiwan: A History of Tongzhi Literature* [in Chinese] (Taipei: Linking, 2017), 123.
[40] Chi, *A Queer Invention in Taiwan*, 123.
[41] Chiu, *Last Words*, 141.
[42] Chi, *A Queer Invention in Taiwan*, 124.
[43] Chiu, *Notes*, 70.

the dwarf's body when a fire is lit under the jar and "the dwarf's body contorts violently as the flames heat the glass."[44] In *Notes*, the allegorical figure of Crocodile has secret crushes on human beings of all kinds and gives all its love interests the alias Kōbō Abe after reading that author's *The Face of Another*.[45] Chiu Miao-chin (or the Crocodile) has read Abe's hero in a queer way, if that hero's disfigured and horrific face as well as his self-abasement, sadness, and loneliness can be read, again, as a metaphor for issues of self-esteem regarding queer body image and identity. She internalizes the image of the dwarf, the man with a distorted face, and the crocodile to express a psyche that is troubled by heteronormative discourse.

A careful reader will notice that the motif of suicide appears not only at the end of Chiu's two novels but comes constantly into view through references to translations of foreign works. In *Last Words*, the protagonist Zoë refers to the French lesbian writer Marguerite Yourcenar's *Memoirs of Hadrian*, in which Antinous, a beautiful youth, commits suicide, sacrificing himself to remind the emperor Hadrian of the nature of his eternal love.[46] In addition to the French lesbian writer, Japanese novelists are incorporated into Chiu's literary tapestry to highlight her protagonists' suicide thoughts. In *Notes*, Lazi, after ending the relationship, juxtaposes the loss of her lover with the death of Naoko in Haruki Murakami's *Norwegian Wood*: "I've lost Naoko! Her beautiful flesh has vanished from this world!"[47] In *Last Words*, while Zoë's favorite author, Yukio Mishima, who committed ritual suicide by *seppuku*, is mentioned several times, more attention is given to Osamu Dazai, arguably the more important Japanese novelist, who threw himself into a river after completing his masterpiece, *No Longer Human*. In Zoë's view, Dazai detested hypocrisy above all, and it was the world's hypocrisy that killed him. She says, "Dazai and I basically share the same nature."[48] Whatever particular significance the references to foreign works in *Notes* and *Last Words* may individually have, they all imply the determination of the narrators in both works to defy through suicide the pain and oppression they experience. As Zoë asserts, she has no fear of death, for "the extinction of [her] physical body would set [her] free."[49]

Chiu also alludes to several foreign films to convey her queer identity and frustration. The unofficial introduction of foreign independent films into Taiwanese culture in the 1980s succeeded in smuggling what would otherwise have been seen as subversive gender and left-wing political attitudes issues into the country. One effect was to help incite the emerging Taiwanese gay movement over the next decade. From the 1950s through the 1970s, KMT censorship ensured that cinemas could

---

[44] Chiu, *Notes*, 70.
[45] Chiu, *Notes*, 104. In the story, the gender of the Crocodile is unstated. I will use "it" to refer to this character. See, Chiu, *Notes*, 57.
[46] Chiu, *Last Words*, 55–56. Perhaps Chiu also admires Marguerite Yourcenar for her lesbian relationship.
[47] Qtd. in Chiu, *Notes*, 118.
[48] Chiu, *Last Words*, 60.
[49] Chiu, *Last Words*, 61.

only show government propaganda, formulaic romance and martial arts films, and escapist Hollywood fare. To escape these shoddy potboilers, Taiwanese intellectuals and film buffs found underground sources for alternatives to the officially approved media. The chance of the general public seeing such films, including any that depicted homosexuality as other than a dirty perversion, was still minimal. This changed in 1980 when the KMT finally recognized the need to address the poor quality of Taiwanese films and agreed to cooperate with intellectuals to establish the Golden Horse Film Festival (金馬國際觀摩影展). Granted special juridical immunity, the festival became the only sanctuary where sensitive issues such as leftism and eroticism could be aired without being censored.

Erotic content—mainly homosexual in nature—was introduced into Taiwan by the festival under the rubric of "special themes." This not only elicited a great deal of interest among ordinary filmgoers but also challenged them to rethink numerous issues such as emerging youth subcultures, AIDS, drug use, ethnic discrimination, and of course sexuality. In 1992, the festival used the theme "Love in a Time of AIDS" (愛在愛滋蔓延時) to introduce twenty-four gay-themed films broadly representatives of New Queer Cinema—a description coined by B. Ruby Rich to describe the new wave of queer independent filmmaking in the early 1990s. The term *tongzhi* (同志), invented by Edward Lam (林奕華) to translate the new Western idea of queerness and provide a Chinese name for the first Hong Kong Lesbian and Gay Film Festival in 1989, was imported into Taiwan, replacing the pejorative *tongxinglian*. *Tongzhi* originally referred to comrades with revolutionary sentiments and aspirations in a political party. The appropriation of the term to capture a new sense of queer identity in Taiwan satisfied the need for a word that could express the emerging collective homosexual identity that, behind this appellation, gathered together all kinds of political entanglements from identity politics to differential politics and from human rights appeals to simple lust.

Although Chiu Miao-chin left Taipei for Paris when the term *tongzhi* was being popularized, her queer identity had already been formed by films featured in the festival or accessed through underground sources in the 1980s. Her passion for the kinds of films that raise questions about gender, sexuality, and identity continued in Paris, but here she was able to view with ease the latest releases, such as the most recent sensations and prizewinners from the Cannes Film Festival. Films mentioned in *Notes* and *Last Words* include the controversial Hollywood melodrama *Valley of the Dolls* (1967) and the avant-garde French directors, Leos Carax's *The Night Is Young* (1986), Jean-Jacques Beineix's *Betty Blue* (1986), and François Truffaut's *The 400 Blows* (1959). Chiu also alludes to the experimental British gay director Derek Jarman's *The Garden* (1990) and the renowned Greek director Theo Angelopoulos's *Reconstruction* (1970), *The Travelling Players* (1975), *Alexander the Great* (1980), *Landscape in the Mist* (1988), *The Suspended Step of the Stork* (1991), and *Ulysses' Gaze* (1995).

In *Notes*, Lazi explicitly cites some of these films as examples of how a stigmatized identity can be demonstrated. Carax's *The Night Is Young* can be read from a queer perspective if the sexually transmitted disease that sweeps the country in it and infects those who make love without emotional involvement is taken as a metaphor for the casual homosexual encounters thought at the time to be the underlying cause of the AIDS pandemic. References to Jarman—who was diagnosed as HIV positive in 1986—are particularly striking in *Notes*. The Crocodile adopts the name "Jarman" as a pseudonym at a crocodile Christmas party, where, using that name, it encounters another crocodile using the name "Genet," inspired by the French gay writer Jean Genet.[50] *Notes* ends with a shot of the Crocodile "Jarman" at the seacoast wearing a white gown and crouching in a bathtub surrounded by flowers, a scene conspicuously inspired by Jarman's *The Garden*. We see "Genet" filming "Jarman" in the tub as the Crocodile "Jarman" speaks its final words and kills itself. These words are "I have nothing more to say ... I wish all of you happiness" (我無話可說……祝你們幸福快樂).[51]

In the end, therefore, it is simply the importance of *xingfu* (幸福, literally "happiness") that Chiu wants to communicate to LGBTQ communities that have experienced discrimination and stigmatization. This message is also conveyed through epigraphs from Clarice Lispector's short story "Amor" and Angelopoulos's *The Suspended Step of the Stork*, inscribed at the beginning and the ending of *Last Words* respectively. Angelopoulos's statement in particular, after being read in a queer way again, shows her aspiration for a community where LGBTQ individuals will not be outed or spitefully asked about their identities:

> I wish you happiness and health
> but I cannot complete your journey
> I am a visitor.
> Everything I touch
> causes me real suffering
> and does not belong to me.
> There is someone who says:
> This is mine.
> But I did once say proudly,
> I have nothing of my own
> for now I know that nothing means
> nothing.
> That one does not even have a name.
> And that sometimes one must borrow one.[52]

Chiu quotes Angelopoulos's words to excuse herself for leaving the "journey" so early. Her life, as well as her queer identity, had been shaped by various forms of stigmatization—of promiscuity, of LGBTQ group as potential HIV carriers, of lesbian desire as deviant and perverse, of mental illness—and all caused her to suffer. At the end of this novel, she realizes that none of these stigmas can represent her because

---

[50] Chiu, *Notes*, 138–40.
[51] Chiu, *Notes*, 241–42. I translated this text by myself and do not follow the translation offered by Bonnie Huie.
[52] Theo Angelopoulos, dir., *The Suspended Step of the Stork*. Qtd. in Chiu, *Last Words*, 146.

she has no "name." She is, in Agamben's words, of "whatever singularity." Agamben's term refers not to a being in relation to a specific predicate or property (Asian, female, homosexual, etc.) but to a being *such as it is*.[53] Whatever singularity cannot be defined and categorized; it exists in an ambivalent position between image and thing, animal and human, proper and improper. In *Notes*, the Crocodile embodies a whatever singularity. It has no gender and is simultaneously human-like and animal-like. Chiu's point is that if the society can learn to accept this queer status of the Crocodile, that is, to acknowledge its whatever singularity, then a community of bliss and happiness comes.

Exporting Chiu Miao-chin

Chiu Miao-chin did not survive to witness the community of bliss and happiness, nor even to see the gay prides that Taiwan has held annually since 2003, nor the legalization of same-sex marriage in 2019, making Taiwan the most LGBTQ-friendly country in East Asia now. Perhaps she could not have imagined how her works would be translated into multiple languages and arouse a similar aspiration for a blissful, loving community in other parts of the world. Two of her translators have reflected on the power of the queer experience depicted in Chiu's works to attract global attention. Ari Larissa Heinrich, the English translator of *Last Words*, states that

> I (and many of her readers) can identify with the youthful earnestness of the twentysomething [Chiu]: not only in our shared coming-of-age within the queer literary confessional zeitgeist of the mid-1990s [...] but in her expatriatism, her solemn attachment to the ideas of the higher art and love, and her paradoxical ability to inhabit a spectrum of genders and identities across multiple platforms, cultural, linguistic, and otherwise.[54]

Bonnie Huie, the translator of *Notes*, calls that book a "survival manual for teenagers, for a certain age when reading the right book can save your life."[55]

The many positive reviews of Chiu's translated texts on Amazon and Goodreads certainly seem to confirm Heinrich's and Huie's accounts of the inspirational power of Chiu's writing. On Goodreads (Figures 11.1 and 11.2), only 9 percent of the reviewers of *Notes* and 7 percent of those commenting on *Last Words* give the books one or two stars. *Notes* gets four or five stars from 62 percent and *Last Words* the same high ratings from 64 percent for the rating details on Goodreads, accessed on September 3, 2021:[56]

---

[53] Giorgio Agamben, *The Coming Community*, trans. Michael Hardt (Minneapolis: University of Minnesota Press, 2007), 1.
[54] Ari Larissa Heinrich, "Formal Experiments in Qiu Miaojin's 'Lesbian *I Ching*,'" in *A New Literary History of Modern China*, ed. David Der-wei Wang (London: The Belknap Press of Harvard University Press, 2017), 842.
[55] Bonnie Huie, "The Kids Are Too Straight: Translating Qiu Miaojin's *Notes of a Crocodile*," *Kyoto Journal*, April 8, 2013.
[56] Both figures are used with permission of Goodreads LLC.

Figure 11.1 Ratings of *Notes* on Goodreads, September 3, 2021.

Figure 11.2 Ratings of *Last Words* on Goodreads, September 3, 2021.

Most of the readers making positive comments maintain how the works are reminiscent of their queer life in the closet. For example, a Goodreads user named Emily Davies, commenting on *Notes* on August 1, 2020, writes: "I saw a lot of myself in Lazi, her relationships with others, and her feelings and thoughts. I relate to her more than I care to admit." Another, with the alias "tatterpunk," wrote on July 17, 2018:

> I've been Lazi. I've dated Lazis. I still see and meet them. […] Despite the years passing and the laws changing and the cultural differences, queerness is still packaged with a certain measure of self-loathing and self-rejection. The drama of Lazi's push-pull relationships bore me to tears—now—but was I any different in college? Despite getting my degree more than two decades later, in a different country? No. And so I can't hate Lazi; I even love her a little, because she's so familiar.

The comments on *Last Words* on November 14, 2014, from a reviewer named Paul, drew my attention because they show how Chiu's queerness arouses strong empathy in people who have had similar experiences:

> I read this book with the mountainous burden of [Miao-chin's] heart which intertwined with mine so resolute [*sic*]. For I too had suffered a great loss, a love

disintegrated, a soul betrayed, perhaps karma redeeming. I too felt the cold hands of suicide trembling around my vital organs, bleeding from my eyes, lips, ears. I felt the searing stab. I read her as I read my own heart to itself. As a reflection of immense loss, in the huddling darkness. [...] I feel I share many of the same traits. The same qualities [and] flaws. We share the same qualms with society. Perhaps we share the same erratic romantic tendencies. [...] I take small solace in the fact that I am not alone [in being] cursed by this involuntary wretchedness. Small because she took her own life. She is gone. It brought me to tears. This [was truly] a traumatic reading experience because it held up this painful mirror of self [and] this particular moment in my life.

These comments attest to Venuti's notion that translation can be a force that helps constitute an identity in the target country. In addition to their perceived relevance to foreign reader's personal lives in their own countries, Chiu's works seem to remind them of many other texts, both domestic and foreign, including translated works, that evoke similar emotions and ideas for them such as James Baldwin's *Giovanni's Room*, Mieko Kawakami's *Breasts and Eggs*, Sylvia Plath's *The Bell Jar*, Elif Batuman's *The Idiot*, and the poems (and early death) of Theresa Hak Kyung Cha. A reader named Tony positions Chiu's *Last Words* with other stories by young women expatriates in Paris such as Elaine Dundy's *The Dud Avocado* and Carole Maso's *The American Woman in the Chinese Hat*. These associations, so disparate in relation to the sources or original languages of texts, correspond to Franco Moretti's concept of distant reading in which a reader focuses on specific devices, themes, tropes, genres, and systems.[57] As Moretti observes, when selecting books, readers do not follow a *tree*-like preference that prioritizes European, Chinese, Japanese, or any national tradition. Instead, their predilections are more analogous to *waves* that engulf diversity and disregard the grain of culture and history.[58]

The theory of distant reading also explains why foreign LGBTQ-themed works, compared with other translated works dealing with other issues, are more popular and attractive. This can also be perceived in how the commenters label their reviews as "LGBTQ" or "queer." However, as Moretti observes, distant reading in general refuses to follow any list of must-read books or a national canon but always goes against the "grain of national historiography."[59] While some readers point out that *Notes* is set in late 1980s Taipei, they still label it as "Chinese literature," or with the term "location China," or, in a more general and homogenizing sense, as "East Asian" or "Asian literature." The label "Taiwanese literature," to my knowledge, does not occur. Chiu's queerness and cosmopolitism, embodied by her Paris experience and the abundant allusions to foreign films and literature, enable her to enter the international book market but,

---

[57] Franco Moretti, "Conjectures on World Literature," in *Debating World Literature*, ed. Christopher Prendergast (London: Verso, 2004), 151.
[58] Moretti, "Conjectures on World Literature," 160–61.
[59] Moretti, "Conjectures on World Literature," 155.

paradoxically, may outshine how multiple factors have constituted the distinctiveness of Taiwanese queer history.

Conclusion

Taiwanese queer identity is not *purely* made in Taiwan but has been influenced by multiple foreign factors having to do with terminology, sexology, psychology, literature, and film. This can be seen in the way Chiu investigates her broken psyche, demonstrates how the Crocodile is depicted in a pseudo-scientific way, and alludes to so many films and literary works to express her secret, troubled queerness. Her works, after being translated, have become a powerful force in shaping queer identity in other countries. Readers adopt a strategy of distant reading to select LGBTQ books and find that Chiu's stories resonate strongly with their own youthful memories and experiences. This relatability has enabled Chiu's works to circulate globally while simultaneously, as predicted by Moretti's theory, avoiding any deep exploration of her own Taiwanese culture and traditions.[60] As a result, readers of the translations, especially in the West, can equate the LGBTQ situation in Taiwan with that of their own countries, unaware that premodern Taiwanese (and Chinese) societies were relatively tolerant of homosexuality or that modern Taiwanese queer identity—and the homophobic discourse that stigmatizes it—has been deeply shaped by foreign, especially Western, discourses. Thus, multiple, often heterogeneous, layers of meanings—domestic and foreign, past and present, friendly and hostile—are homogenized into one simplistic way of reading Chiu's translated texts. This is typified by the fact that, although most readers are well aware that Chiu is a Taiwanese author, they nevertheless label her works simply as "Chinese" or "Asian" literature. Analogous to Venuti's argument about how translation can form a person's identity, "Taiwanese literature" may sound unfamiliar to foreign readers' ears in this moment, but as the number of translations increases, it will slowly be accepted and perhaps ultimately form a new, richer understanding of Taiwan's distinctive queer culture for foreign readers.

---

[60] See Pei-yin Lin's chapter in this volume. She questions whether global circulation really means that a text "gains" currency or merely means a text has become homogenized.

12

Translation Matters: The Case of *The Butcher's Wife* in English

Sheng-chi Hsu

There has been increased academic attention to the study of world literature, which David Damrosch describes as encompassing "all literary works that circulate beyond their culture of origin, either in translation or in their original language."[1] However, this circulation by no means indicates these literary works roam aimlessly out of their places of origin. Instead, there must be a clear point of departure and a destination. He thus highlights the importance of readership and, taking after Claudio Guillén's questioning, adds that any literary work "only has an *effective* life as world literature whenever, and wherever, it is actively present within a literary system beyond that of its original culture."[2] In other words, as well as traveling between two points within the global space, a literary work as world literature is comprised of the work's global circulation and the readership it garners in new cultural contexts. It is the readership that helps to sustain the work's second life and ensure its effective existence and participation in a new context. With these in mind, Damrosch further adds a word of caution about the "variability of a work of world literature [as] one of its constitutive features,"[3] asserting that how world literature is handled and presented should demand equal attention.

Damrosch's elaborate language about his conception of world literature appears similar to that observed in a typical discussion about literary translation. It should naturally remind readers of several common terminologies, such as source and target, and the metaphors found in Walter Benjamin's essay, "The Task of the Translator": life and afterlife.[4] However, despite the terminological similarities and the multilingual and multicultural nature of these studies, there is a noticeable disconnection, or "an abyss between the study of world literature and the study of translation," as described

---

[1] David Damrosch, *What Is World Literature?* (Princeton: Princeton University Press, 2013), 4.
[2] Damrosch, *What Is World Literature?*, 4. Italics in the original.
[3] Damrosch, *What Is World Literature?*, 5.
[4] Walter Benjamin, "The Task of the Translator," trans. Steven Rendall, in *Translation Studies Reader*, ed. Lawrence Venuti (London: Routledge, 2021), 89–97. For discussions on the translation of "afterlife," see Antoine Berman, *The Age of Translation: A Commentary on Walter Benjamin's "The Task of the Translator,"* trans. Chantal Wright (London: Routledge, 2018), 75–6.

by Susan Bassnett.[5] She contends that translation studies are marginalized from literary studies because of long-term doubt and misconception about translation's reliability, institutions' reluctance to promote translation as an academic subject, and the Cultural Turn in the 1980s. Collectively, these factors resulted in a shift of attention away from engaging in linguistic aspects of translation studies. In light of this, she hopes "a fusion between translation studies and literary studies" can be achieved and that the important role translation plays in cultural and literary studies can receive its overdue acknowledgment.[6]

Bearing in mind the aforementioned context, this article sets out to respond to Bassnett's call to address the marginalized status of translation studies within the discourse of world literature. It will investigate the textual and paratextual material of two English translations of Li Ang's (李昂) novella *The Butcher's Wife* (殺夫, hereafter *Wife*) to comprehend how gender and sexuality are rendered and presented through translation. It will demonstrate how variable presentations of translated literature may influence readers' reading experience and the work's reception in new literary and cultural contexts.

Li Ang and *The Butcher's Wife* in Taiwan

Li Ang can be said to be one of Taiwan's most prominent feminist writers. Throughout her career, she has produced a huge repertoire of fictional writing that challenges Taiwan's normative concepts of gender and sexuality. Living in the period of martial law, Li astonished Taiwan's literary world with a series of "sexually-charged short stories" that bordered on the edge of causing controversy through her audacious exploration of women's sexual desire, a taboo subject matter that received little attention at the time.[7] It was at this point her reputation as a writer of contentious issues began to emerge. However, despite some harsh criticism, she never succumbed to pressure from Taiwan's relatively conservative social norms. She continued to produce more substantial prose writings, some of which directly engage with and allude to incidents and people in Taiwan's sociopolitical history.

Wife begins with two news reports about the murder of the pig butcher, Chen Jiangshui, committed by his wife, Chen Lin Shi. The narrative proper begins in her childhood when her mother was mistreated by their family clan as a result of her sexual act with an anonymous soldier in exchange for food. Having reached the marriageable age, Lin Shi is then married off to the ill-reputed and ill-tempered Chen Jiangshui. After the wedding night, Chen continues to abuse her verbally, physically, and sexually. The ceaseless domestic violence gradually leaves her on edge, causing her physical

---

[5] Susan Bassnett, "Introduction: The Rocky Relationship between Translation Studies and World Literature," in *Translation and World Literature*, ed. Susan Bassnett (London: Routledge, 2018), 1.
[6] Bassnett, "Introduction," 7.
[7] Michael Berry, "Taiwan Literature in the Post-Martial Law Era," in *The Columbia Companion to Modern Chinese Literature*, ed. Kirk Denton (New York: Columbia University Press, 2016), 425.

suffering and psychological instability. The story culminates in Lin's frantic attack on her husband. She dismembers his body with his butcher knife in a semiconscious state, and the story ends with their neighbors' speculation about possible motives behind her criminal act.

The novella received mixed reviews, ranging from accolades for its literary merits to fierce criticisms about its graphic descriptions of sexual violence and brutal killing. The harshest criticism came from an anonymous writer in the *Independence Evening Post*. The writer took a self-righteous position on the husband-killing plot, condemning the case's intolerable nature and its violation of law and civility. The editorial reads, "if literature sides with any criminal activities, it may as a result incite more vengeful killings. This will seriously damage society's civility, disrupt social order, and challenge the nation's legal system. The consequences are unimaginable."[8] Despite deep-rooted ambivalence about who or what this article really concerns, by relating the husband-killing plot to the legal and societal systems, it clearly conveys a high level of anxiety about challenges to the patriarchy. In other words, the review's writer reads the husband-killing plot as a symbolic catalyst that may motivate real-life challenges to existing male-dominant social systems.

The Butcher's Wife in English

Wife has been twice translated into English since its publication in Taiwan. The first of the two translations, completed by Howard Goldblatt and Ellen Yeung, is more commonly known. It was first published in 1986 by North Point Press, an independent publisher based in San Francisco. It was then republished by Cheng & Tsui Company in 1995 as part of a collection of Li Ang's work, entitled *The Butcher's Wife and Other Stories*. This collection signaled the recognition and visibility of Li Ang as an international writer. In the UK, Peter Owen Publishers launched the same translation of *Wife* as a monograph in their Modern Classics series in 1989; this was subsequently followed by Penguin's publication in the "Penguin International Writers Series" in 1991. In Asia, Goldblatt and Yeung's translation (hereafter referred to as "GY") was also reprinted and republished by Joint Publishing in Hong Kong and by Asiapac Books in Singapore in 1990. The other version, also a co-translation project, was completed by John Minford and Fan Wen-mei. This is less known and is often overlooked by general and academic readers, which may be due to it being only an excerpt of the novella: only the news reports at the beginning and the first two chapters. This translation, entitled "Butcher: Excerpts," was included in a special issue of *Renditions* dedicated to woman writers in 1987.

These two translations' publishing media suggest differing use of paratextual materials. Publishers would usually convey certain attributes and values they wish to

---

[8] "文學不可助長戾氣" [Literature Should Not Abet Brutality], 自立晚報 [*Independence Evening Post*], October 7, 1983. My translation.

emphasize through paratext, which by definition can include book titles, book cover design, and blurbs such as excerpts and quotes from book reviews. They facilitate a "threshold [...] that offers the world at large the possibility of either stepping inside or turning back."[9] GY, for instance, is published in the book form, either as a standalone volume or in a collection of Li Ang's stories. This medium provides space for the inclusion of various paratextual materials specific to Li Ang's novella. This means that readers, whether they are familiar with the Chinese language and culture, could gain access to the story from reading the paratext. The Cheng & Tsui and the Peter Owen editions have both taken advantage of the book form. As well as having blurbs on the back cover, both editions consist of Li Ang's preface, the author's profile, and the book's publishing history. In addition to these, the Peter Owens edition also includes "Translators' Note,"[10] which helps the translators to "indicate that the language of the translation originates with the translator in a decisive way."[11] In other words, Goldblatt and Yeung are afforded the space to present, explain, and justify their translation strategies, thus raising their visibility as translators and authenticating their involvement in the process of circulation. The comprehensive range of paratextual materials can likely enhance the marketability of *Wife* in the Anglophone world and as a result increase readership.

Fan and Minford's translation (hereafter referred to as FM), however, does not have similar paratextual materials. It is excerpted and published in *Renditions*, a Chinese-English literary translation journal. According to Charles Laughlin, *Renditions* provided a "rare venue for translations, most scholarly" and had the "narrower circles of academic circulation and distribution."[12] Although its official web page states that "[t]he general reader will be entertained and informed, finding in *Renditions* a unique and fascinating gateway to Chinese culture,"[13] the university affiliation could present the journal as highbrow and scholarly, thus restricting its readership. Meanwhile, as a subscription-based journal, it can be surmised that subscribers are likely those with a particular interest in translation and Chinese culture. Therefore, FM may reach a less general readership.

Included in a journal with works from multiple writers and translators, Fan and Minford are not afforded any space to justify and comment on their own translation work. Instead, the two scholars from the editorial board speak on behalf of the translators in the foreword section of the journal. They justify their textual selections by situating these Chinese women writers' stories about patriarchy in the sociohistorical context, conveying a clear ideological message in line with the West's dominant

---

[9] Gerard Genette, *Paratexts: Thresholds of Interpretation*, trans. Jane Lewin (Cambridge: Cambridge University Press, 1997), 2.
[10] Li Ang, *The Butcher's Wife*, trans. Howard Goldblatt and Ellen Yeung (London: Peter Owen Publishers, 2002).
[11] Lawrence Venuti, *Translator's Invisibility: A History of Translation* (London: Routledge, 2004), 331.
[12] Charles Laughlin, "The New Translators and Contemporary Chinese Literature in English: A Review of Journals *Chinese Literature Today*, *Pathlight*, and *Chutzpah! / Peregrine*," *Chinese Literature: Essays, Articles, Reviews* 35 (2013): 209.
[13] "Renditions," The Chinese University of Hong Kong, https://www.cuhk.edu.hk/rct/renditions/.

feminist ideas in the 1980s. The timing of the publication of this collection reflects the significance of contexts for translation production and publication. As von Flotow explains, "Contexts are of paramount importance when we produce translations [...]; they shape, influence, permit, or prohibit certain versions of certain texts at certain times."[14] Moreover, the editors' commentaries reflect a similar selection strategy, like that seen in many Chinese-English literary anthologies, where the "texts and authors [are] selected for predominantly ideological or social reasons,"[15] showing many voices and styles. However, there exists "a unified picture [... that offers] a way of judging and appreciating literature through a purposeful, collective presentation."[16] Therefore, the editors' words could exert an illocutionary force "to explain, elaborate, and justify the core text[s] [... and thus] guide and help the reader to read with understanding."[17] To put it differently, the editors' foreword and all the translation decisions can be considered paratextual materials of FM, as collectively they communicate the same feminist thematic concept.

Book Cover Design and Use of Illustration

Book covers and titles can help the audience comprehend how translated literature is positioned in the target language's culture to engage potential readership. Keith Harvey, examining the transformation and otherness of translated American gay fiction in the French context, terms these materials "binding" and explains that they work together to "support, legitimate and make readable what each individually represents and advances."[18] He further suggests that binding functions to reflect the content of a translated text and how its readership and the receiving culture are perceived.[19] However, despite the fact that translator's input to these paratextual materials can be minimized and that "commercial consideration might be the cause of many mutations [of titles],"[20] these materials can still enable an understanding of translations when they travel to a new cultural context.

Both English translations of *Wife* have illustrations. FM, for example, has a simple sketch of a serene-looking Chinese woman with the subheading "Special

---

[14] Luise von Flotow, "Tracing the Context of Translation: The Example of Gender," in *Gender, Sex, and Translation: The Manipulation of Identities*, ed. José Santaemilia (Manchester: St. Jerome, 2005), 39.
[15] Red Chan, "Intellectual Intervention and English Anthologies of Chinese Literature of the 1980s," *Asia Pacific Translation and Intercultural Studies* 2, no. 1 (2016): 54.
[16] Chan, "Intellectual Intervention and English anthologies of Chinese Literature of the 1980s," 48.
[17] Valerie Pellatt, "Translation of Chinese Paratext and Paratext of Chinese Translation," in *The Routledge Handbook of Chinese Translation*, ed. Chris Shei and Zhao-ming Gao (London: Routledge, 2017), 167.
[18] Keith Harvey, *Intercultural Movements: American Gay in French Translation* (Manchester: St. Jerome, 2003), 177.
[19] Harvey, *Intercultural Movements*, 180–82.
[20] Benjamin Schaper, "The Importance of the Literary Title and Its Implications for Translation Theory," *Focus on German Studies* 20 (2013): 111.

Issue Contemporary Women Writers" on the cover. This cover design brings the theme of feminism into focus, which frames and contextualizes *Wife*. In addition, the cover illustration of *Wife*'s Chinese original published in Taipei is placed within the translation.[21] It features the rear view of a woman, dressed in a loose blouse with her hair tied into a bun. Carrying a basket of eggs, she looks in the direction of some traditional Taiwanese-style houses behind a fence. The image in this picture elicits a sense of exoticism. Furthermore, the fence can be seen as a symbolic divide between two worlds. The woman, although appearing calm on this side of the fence, looks beyond the fence into an unknown world. In this sense, the illustration seems to emphasize Lin Shi as a newlywed venturing into a new life.

On the other hand, GY has had several cover designs since its first publication, among them the North Point Press's cover, which has been used for *Wife*'s translations into other languages.[22] It presents a haunting image of a typical female ghost. With her face covered in long, unkempt hair, the female figure, dressed in a loose white robe, is shown to hold a cleaver in one hand and a scimitar in the other. Her body language exhibits her engagement in an act of violence. The background's scattered random red lines further add to the overall visual effect of this ghostly figure as, seen together with the knives, they are suggestive of cuts, wounds, and blood. Meanwhile, the randomness of these lines gives a sense of motion, resembling splashing blood to represent chaos and violence at the murder scene. Therefore, this cover achieves its paratextual function by providing potential readers with access to the story. Kung claims that this cover functions "as a marketing device to aid in selling the book"[23] by projecting a sense of cultural otherness and exoticism through the ghostly image. However, this cultural otherness can also be observed in the cover's gender representation. The violent woman can be said to subvert the common stereotype of the 1980s portraying women "as weak, passive objects of a male gaze"[24] by aligning the image with the second-wave feminist notion of fighting for women's liberation and equality. Therefore, the gender representation in this illustration, while embedded in cultural otherness, in fact communicates a feminist message that can be easily assimilated into the Anglophone context.[25]

---

[21] *Wife*'s Taipei edition currently features a sketch of a frightened girl entangled in ropes. In contrast to the cover of the 1987 edition, which emphasizes more on the setting of the story, this current book cover seems to suggest the psychological aspect of the novella more explicitly.

[22] For more detail, see *The Li Ang Archive*, maintained by the National Chung Hsing University Research Center for Humanities and Social Sciences, http://li-ang-english.blogspot.com/.

[23] Szu-wen Kung, "How Translation Players Make Their Marks in the Case of Translated Chinese Literature from Taiwan," in *Perspectives on Translation*, ed. Anna Baszkowska (Newcastle: Cambridge Scholars Publishing, 2015), 229.

[24] Rosalind Gill, "Surveillance Is a Feminist Issue," in *The Routledge Handbook of Contemporary Feminism*, ed. Tasha Oren and Andrea Press (London: Routledge, 2019), 151.

[25] It is worth noting that the cultural otherness discussed in Szu-wen Kung's article can also be observed in the other translations' covers of *Wife*. However, these cover graphics all appear to reduce the feminist concept inherent to the North Point Press cover. Hong Kong's Joint Publishing edition (1990) removes references to femaleness on the cover. Instead, it shows a knife next to a pillow with a red blanket with traditional Chinese embroidery for newlyweds. This graphic implicates violence and a murder in a couple's bedroom. The Penguin edition (1991) features an oil painting of a woman with two chicks. This cover, like the Taipei edition (1986), highlights the village setting of the story. The Peter Owen Modern Classics edition (2002) uses a picture of young Li Ang, in line with the rest of the covers in the series. For more detail and illustrations, see the website *The Li Ang Archive*.

A comparison of the two translations' illustrations clearly shows how both publishers use them to convey *Wife*'s feminist theme. Encompassed within a collection of female writers' works, FM is accompanied by the same image as that on the cover of the Chinese original. The adoption of the original illustration conveys a degree of authenticity to readers, thus enhancing the authority and reliability of this translation. Furthermore, as this image gives very little away about the story of *Wife*, it can also become "a source of mystery that succeeds in triggering the curiosity of the reader."[26] Contrastingly, the cover illustration of GY demonstrates a higher degree of control and manipulation of readers' perceptions of the book. By presenting the murder scene on the cover, not only can the reader gain access to the story but they can also discern the illustration's inherent feminist message.

Translating the Title

Shafu, the Chinese title of *The Butcher's Wife*, can be literally translated into English as "kill husband." As demonstrated in the literal translation, the agent that performs the action of killing is absent from the phrase. Moreover, as the Chinese verbs do not incur inflectional changes to identify a subject, suggest plurality, or indicate the tense, the title leaves a certain level of ambiguity. Translating this title would then require the translator to interpret who the killer is and when the killing occurs. Following the verb *sha*, *fu* as the object may provide clues for the missing subject as it implicitly suggests a marital relationship through the allusion to a common Chinese compound, *fuqi* (夫妻), meaning husband and wife. It is therefore possible to infer that the missing subject could be "wife." With this in mind, it would then be necessary to consider the presentation of this title to readers.

There have been different translations of this title. In the academic context, Sheung-Yeun Daisy Ng translates the title as "husband killing"[27] by nominalizing the phrase in English, which reflects what Nord terms "documentary translation" that functions as "a text about a text."[28] In other words, Ng seeks to illuminate the original text by keeping her translated title fairly literal, with only some reversal of word order. This nominalization indicates Ng's intention to see the novel as the documentary record of an event; meanwhile, it simultaneously erases the directness expressed in the Chinese title's verb phrase.

In contrast to Ng's more literal approach, the two translations under discussion have both been given a less literal title. Goldblatt and Yeung render the title as "The

---

[26] Valerie Pellatt, "Translation of Chinese Paratext and Paratext of Chinese Translation," in *The Routledge Handbook of Chinese Translation*, ed. Chris She and Zhao-Ming Gao (London: Routledge, 2017), 170.

[27] Shueng-Yuen Daisy Ng, "Feminism in the Chinese Context: Li Ang's The Butcher's Wife," in *Gender Politics in Modern China*, ed. Tani Barlow (Durham: Duke University Press, 1993), 266.

[28] Christiane Nord, *Translating as a Purposeful Activity: Functionalist Approaches Explained* (London: Routledge, 2018), 46–48.

Butcher's Wife," while Fan and Minford, "Butcher." It is apparent that the translators exploit the meanings of the word "butcher" in their rendering. As a noun, "butcher" means "a person whose trade is the preparation and selling of meat [...] and a person who deals with both the slaughter of livestock and the preparation of animal flesh for food."[29] Goldblatt and Yeung's title "The Butcher's Wife" is said to have been "slightly altered" from the Chinese title and has "concealed the novel's theme to a certain extent [and] brought forward the overall conceptual perception of the whole novel."[30] To put it simply, rather than conjuring an explicit image of abuse and violence, this title appears to present the novella's feminist theme indirectly. This is succinctly achieved by using the possessive, "butcher's," to modify the noun "wife." The two-word noun phrase headed by "wife" signposts readers to the protagonist of the story. However, the possessive adjective, "butcher's," deserves equal attention as it raises the question of why the husband's profession should matter. On the one hand, the profession evokes an image of flesh, blood, and killing through its association with butchering. On the other hand, the possessive suffix tagged to "butcher" directly communicates the meaning of ownership, objectifying the wife as a possession of the butcher. It also implicitly belittles and degrades the wife, therefore signaling male dominance. Through this owner-possession juxtaposition, this English rendering reverses the hierarchy of power in the Chinese title. While the focus remains on the wife, which is the head noun of the phrase, the phrase presents the husband as superior and having control over the wife. As a result, "The Butcher's Wife" succinctly highlights the core issue of male dominance and patriarchy that second-wave feminists contested.

Fan and Minford's title, by comparison, appears more ambiguous. Ambiguity, according to Katie Wales, is "one of the special or defining features" of literary language as "the reader is expected [...] to hold the different interpretations in mind, and to give them equal serious meaningful value."[31] The word "butcher" stands alone without any formal changes or modifications, conveying a degree of lexical ambiguity that allows space for interpretation. As already shown in the foregoing discussion, "butcher" can be a noun. However, it can also be a verb that simultaneously conjures up the image of "slaughter[ing] in a brutal or bloody manner [and] indiscriminately."[32] If Fan and Minford's title is seen as a zero-article noun, there would be no specificity ascribed to it. This title therefore suggests a symbolic prevalence, which seeks to underscore the issue of violence that is prevalent in Taiwanese society. What is equally noteworthy is how this English title retains and transforms the sense of ambiguity also detected in the Chinese title. However, dissimilar to the Chinese title and Goldblatt and Yeung's title, this title renders gender undetectable in the gender-neutral noun "butcher." This gender-neutrality is highly significant in the way it suggests both males and females can assume the role to carry out the act of butchering, both literally as in dealing with animal flesh for food trading and metaphorically as in abusing or murdering a

---

[29] See the entry "butcher, n." in *Oxford English Dictionary Online*, www.oed.com/view/Entry/25324.
[30] Kung, "How Translation Players Make Their Marks in the Case of Translated Chinese Literature from Taiwan," 221.
[31] Katie Wales, *A Dictionary of Stylistics* (London: Routledge, 2011), 16.
[32] See the entry "butcher, v." in *Oxford English Dictionary Online*, www.oed.com/view/Entry/25325.

partner. This leads to a successful blending of semantic references and related images into one word, thus purposefully encouraging readers to work through the ambiguity. Meanwhile, it also brings to prominence the sociomoral question of who the victim is in the murder case depicted in the novella.

Contrasting these two English titles to the Chinese one, it becomes apparent that both of them follow a nonliteral strategy by exploiting the meanings of the word "butcher." By linking a word in the title to a key character in the story, both titles become what David Lodge describes as "a part of the text [… that] has considerable power to attract and condition the reader's attention."[33] Furthermore, this also ensures both titles are "internally oriented content titles" that "describe subject, theme, form, character, and symbols" and can "be directed toward an aspect that is part of the novel."[34]

How a lexical choice can effectively elicit images of relevance is significant in the two translated titles. For a story that is saturated with vivid descriptions of cruel animal killing, varied forms of abuse, and murder, the word "butcher" fittingly encapsulates these violent images. The lexical choice intensifies the level of descriptiveness that augments and sensationalizes the effect of the word *sha* in the Chinese title. However, these two English titles frame the story differently. "The Butcher's Wife" evidently underscores the gender politics and power structure between the two protagonists. On the other hand, "Butcher" is an ambiguous title that demands readers' engagement to critically reflect on the novella's sociomoral issues.

Book Reviews

Book reviews, a type of paratext also known as "epitext," also act as a gateway into the world of a book.[35] However, in the reviews of translated literary works, it appears that a translator's work is often overlooked and superseded by discussions about the book's author, contents, and thematic messages. As Esther Allen laments, reviewers only mention "the name [of the translator whose work is being reviewed] and a single adverb [to evaluate the quality of translations]" as their way of evaluating works in translation.[36] She recommends that reviewers value literary translators' vital role, evaluate their work with care, and give them their due credit. The reviewers' comments on GY could sufficiently demonstrate Allen's concern. The reviews revolve around Li Ang's feminist concerns and daring descriptions of sexual violence; only an adjective, such as "masterful"[37] in Leung's review and "seamless"[38] in Burgin's review, is given to

---

[33] David Lodge, *The Art of Fiction* (London: Vintage, 2011), 193.
[34] Charles Briffa and Roseline Caruan, "Stylistic Creativity when Translating Titles" (presentation, PALA 2009 Conference, the Netherlands, 2009).
[35] Gerard Genette, *Paratexts: Thresholds of Interpretation*, trans. Jane Lewin (Cambridge: Cambridge University Press, 1997), 5.
[36] Esther Allen, "Lost in the Book Review," *In Other Words*, no. 44 (2014): 26.
[37] K. C. Leung, review of *The Butcher's Wife and Other Stories*, by Li Ang, trans. Howard Goldblatt and Ellen Yeung, *World Literature Today* 70, no. 4 (1996): 1028.
[38] Richard Burgin, review of *The Butcher's Wife*, by Li Ang, trans. Howard Goldblatt and Ellen Yeung, *New York Times*, December 28, 1986.

evaluate the translator's work. Moreover, Joseph Allen's review discusses the novella's grotesque nature without mentioning the translators nor commenting on their translation.[39] A similar tendency of translator's under-acknowledgment can also be identified in reader reviews. In the study of Taiwanese literature in the global context, Chiu asserts the importance of translation in the global circulation of literary works. She proposes what she terms "international recognition indicators," which surveys reader reviews from Amazon and Goodreads to evidence "the effective life of literary works as world literature."[40] In the word cloud based on the frequency of words in the reviews,[41] the words appear to be mostly about the content of the story, and neither the word "translation" nor the word "translator" is mentioned. This survey highlights the issue of translators' continued invisibility and under-recognition.

Textual Comparison

Language, after all, is central to translation. Without translator's efforts in selecting words in the translating language to add "an entirely new set of resonances and allusions designed to imitate the source text,"[42] literary works would not be able to cross borders and circulate into other cultural and linguistic contexts. With this in mind, Venuti argues for the importance of paying attention to the form and meaning of translator's language choices. In a different context, Damrosch also underscores the significance of language in reading world literature in translation. He contends that, without access to the source language, readers can better understand the original by comparing different translations of the same text. Using different English translations of Voltaire's *Candide* as examples, he incisively demonstrates how language is manipulated in accordance with varied sociohistorical contexts by different translators. He asserts that such textual comparison "can reveal a host of choices that different translators have made."[43]

In light of the calls for attention on translators' language, what follows will be a textual comparison of Goldblatt and Yeung's "The Butcher's Wife," Fan and Minford's "Butcher," and Li Ang's Chinese original. The comparison will examine how the translators use stylistic features to present *Wife*'s gender issues in English for Anglophone readers. It will consequently show how the translators "create something new with [their] subtly distinct voice"[44] and how this voice can "bear the fingerprint of the translator's idiolect or preferred translation strategies."[45]

---

[39] Joseph Allen, review of *The Butcher's Wife*, by Li Ang, trans. Howard Goldblatt and Ellen Yeung, *World Literature Today* 61, no. 2 (1987): 347.
[40] Kuei-fen Chiu, "'Worlding' World Literature from the Literary Periphery: Four Taiwanese Models," *Modern Chinese Literature and Culture* 30, no. 1 (2018): 15.
[41] Chiu, "'Worlding' World Literature from the Literary Periphery," 20.
[42] Lawrence Venuti, "How to Read a Translation," in *Translation Changes Everything: Theory and Practice* (London: Routledge, 2013), 110.
[43] David Damrosch, *How to Read World Literature* (Chichester: Wiley-Blackwell, 2009), 68.
[44] Jeremy Munday, *Style and Ideology in Translation* (London: Routledge, 2008), 14.
[45] Munday, *Style and Ideology in Translation*, 17.

The novella begins with two news articles reporting on the murder of Lin Shi's husband and her subsequent sentencing, as well as the reporter's commentaries at length. However, the reports are written in first person and focalized through the reporter. In other words, Lin Shi's account is reported rather than quoted, suggesting that her voice is replaced by the reporter's. The reporter further speaks on behalf of the public in condemning and calling for attention to the woman-murderer's violation of the sociomoral codes. It is in this way that the reporter's dominating voice foregrounds the overall tone of the narrative in the novella. Kuei-fen Chiu argues that this "voice of public moral censorship" is in fact what renders Lin Shi "the victim of the language of other people" and therefore commits "symbolic rape."[46] The reporter's voice can thus be understood as a source of violence and oppressive practice, and it is worth investigating how this voice is constructed stylistically in the Chinese original and the corresponding translations. What follows are three excerpts from the opening paragraph of *Wife* and its two English translations:

The Chinese original:

XX年X月X日訊。

一對住鹿城北角陳厝的夫婦,男陳江水,四十多歲,以殺豬為業,妻陳林市,年二十餘。X日陳林市突然以丈夫殺豬用的屠刀,謀害親夫,支解屍體,將屍體斬為八塊,裝置藤箱中企圖滅屍,幸賴隔鄰警覺,及時發現報警。[47]

Goldblatt and Yeung's translation:

> Date: _____, 19___
>
> On the morning of _____, Chen Lin Shi, a woman in her twenties, murdered her husband, Chen Jiangshui, a pig butcher in his forties, in the couple's home in the Chencuo district of northern Lucheng. Using the victim's own butcher knife, she dismembered his body, chopping it up into eight pieces, which she placed in a rattan basket for later disposal. Fortunately, a watchful neighbor discovered the crime and reported it to the police before she could carry out her plan.[48]

Fan and Minford's translation:

> XX News Agency, ___. ___, 19___, Chen Jiangshui, a forty-year-old butcher from Chen Village, North Point, Deer Town, has been murdered by his wife, Chen Linshi, a woman in her twenties. On __. __., she suddenly attacked him with his

---

[46] Kuei-fen Chiu, "Taking Off: A Feminist Approach to Two Contemporary Women's Novels in Taiwan," *Tamkang Review* 23, no. 1–4 (1992): 724.
[47] Li Ang, 殺夫 [*The Butcher's Wife*] (Taipei: Linking Books, 2011), 73.
[48] Li Ang, "The Butcher's Wife," in *The Butcher's Wife and Other Stories*, trans. Howard Goldblatt and Ellen Yeung (Boston: Cheng & Tsui Company, 1986), 3.

butcher's knife and killed him. She then hacked the body into eight pieces, and was attempting to dispose of it in a rattan case, when fortunately her neighbor became suspicious and contacted the police.[49]

Analysis of the Chinese Original and the Translation

The passage is reported from the reporter's point of view, and it begins with a sentence about the two characters involved in the crime and their matrimonial relationship. Following this is a long sentence led by the wife's name, Lin Shi, as the subject of the sentence to outline the process of her crime, from killing to attempting to dispose of the body. There is a noticeable directness in the descriptions, especially in the way that the wife's name is repeated twice in this brief passage. The repetition reiterates the female gender of the murderer and can be considered an intentional arrangement to amplify the unusual nature of this murder case. In addition, despite its brevity, the passage's lexical items can reveal the reporter's biased subject position that creates the sensationalizing effect in the narrative.

Several lexical items can be seen to suggest bias in the passage. For example, the Chinese compound verb *mouhai* (謀害, literally "plot harm") suggests Lin Shi's husband-killing is a premeditated operation, not unsolicited, and the concept of planning is then reinforced by another compound *qitu* (企圖, literally "attempt" or "plan"). These verbs evidently reflect the reporter's belief that the crime had been plotted. In addition, a range of adverbs are deployed to aid the dynamic descriptions of the crime report; meanwhile, these adverbs also generate a commentary effect to reflect the reporter's viewpoints. The adverb *turan* (突然, literally "suddenly"), for instance, is an adverb of time and manner. It describes the instantaneity and unexpectedness of the murder, which can suggest the reporter's astonishment about the crime. Meanwhile, *turan* can also indicate the reporter speaking on behalf of the husband, as it implies the husband's vulnerability at the time of the attack. Adding to these are two adverbs, *xing* (幸, literally "luckily" or "fortunately") and *jishi* (及時, literally "in time"), which create a dramatic transition in the mood and tone of the narrative in the passage. By referring to the neighbor's discovery and reporting of the killing to the police as fortunate, these two adverbs communicate a sense of relief, thus strengthening the commentary nature in the latter two segments of this sentence. Collectively, these adverbs demonstrate how the reporter conveys personal bias and moral judgments, projecting a sense of injustice and unfairness toward Lin Shi.

From the outset, it is clear that both translations' opening sentences amalgamate the character introduction with partial crime descriptions, leading to the syntactic deformation of the sentence in the Chinese original. This corresponds to what Antoine Berman terms rationalization, which is a negative analytic denoting a deforming

---

[49] Li Ang, "Butcher: Excerpts," *Renditions*, no. 27/28 (1987): 61.

tendency that inevitably occurs in the act of translation.⁵⁰ Doing this may be seen as necessary to rationalize the information in a certain order to meet Anglophone readers' expectations of journalistic writing.

However, there appears to be some effort to mitigate these deforming tendencies in both translations. They achieve this mitigation similarly by using appositives and parallel verb phrases to stylistically imitate how commas divide the Chinese sentence into parallel verb phrases.

There is, however, a noticeable difference in how active or passive voice is used in the translations' respective opening sentences. GY, for example, follows the Chinese syntax and uses active voice, namely "murdered her husband," to create a direct statement of fact in the simple past tense. This statement attributes the responsibility of the crime to Lin Shi by nominating her as the agent of this sentence. Doing this, however, is stylistically defamiliarizing as it goes against the common practice in English, where news articles would tend to report similar criminal activities in a passive voice.⁵¹ Moreover, in addition to the date and location outlined in the Chinese original, the translators have added two adjuncts—"on the morning" and "in the couple's own home"—to supplement the setting of the incident in the news report. However, shifting this information from a latter part of the novella to the opening sentence suggests that the translators are contextualizing the crime as domestic violence.

Immediately after the sentence about the characters is a participle clause led by the present participle "using." Rather than submerging this piece of information into the description of the murder process, the translators shift it to the start of the sentence to highlight that the killing weapon is the exact tool the victim used to make a living. The possessive, "victim's," is reinforced by the word "own" to create an emphatic effect. Collectively, they arouse sympathy and commiseration for the victim, and at the same time, they characterize Lin Shi as a merciless and ungrateful killer. To describe how she deals with her husband's remains, the sentence ends with a nondefining relative clause that places a comma before the relative pronoun "which." This syntactic construction suggests the information communicated through the relative clause is supplementary and nonessential. Combining this with the fact that the neighbor could not have known what Lin Shi would do with her husband's remains and when, details such as "for later disposal" are assumptions made by the reporter. This exhibits the reporter's interference and portrays the killing as a murder, which can be perceived as an attempt to incite. Meanwhile, the nondefining relative clause renders this piece of information less significant, which in turn offers a contrasting effect to increase the significance of the killing descriptions in the main clause. In this vein, it can be argued that, instead of relying on the use of "suddenly," the literal translation of *turan*, the translators have effectively exploited the use of English syntactic and grammatical features to generate dramatic effects in the reporter's biased voice.

---

⁵⁰ Antoine Berman, "Translation and the Trials of the Foreign," trans. Lawrence Venuti, in *The Translation Studies Reader*, ed. Lawrence Venuti (London: Routledge, 2012), 240–53.
⁵¹ See Nancy Henley, Michelle Miller, and Jo Beazley, "Syntax, Semantics, and Sexual Violence: Agency and the Passive Voice," *Journal of Language and Social Psychology* 14 (1995): 60–84.

The last sentence of this passage commences with an adverb of attitude, "fortunately," to signal a shift in the tone of the narrative. This adverb, separated from the rest of the sentence with a comma, modifies the entire sentence. With an emphatic tone in the first word of the sentence, it brings about a sense of relief from the horror and tension in the preceding descriptions of killing. It is obvious that this adverb imparts the reporter's opinion, therefore functioning as a commentary on the neighbor's "lucky" discovery of the criminal act. By revealing an attitude, "fortunately" can be conceived of as a way to invite readers to offer their sympathy for the victim and simultaneously incite hatred for the perpetrator. Another noteworthy lexical item is the modifier *jingjue* (警覺, literally "vigilant and aware") used to describe the neighbor in this sentence. Rather than translating it literally, the translators have opted for "watchful" in English instead. By definition, there is no doubt that the English word can be said to be equivalent to its Chinese counterpart. However, "watchful" adds a vivid graphic that illustrates the neighbor's constant surveillance, patrolling, and guarding of the neighborhood. Moreover, the time adverbial—*jishi* (及時, literally "in time") in the Chinese original—has not been translated into English literally but has been expanded into a subordinate clause headed by "before." This expansion of a single adverb into a subordinate clause retains the time reference in the original and allows the translators to reiterate the nature of the crime as intended, which justifies the sense of relief expressed through "fortunately." As a temporal reference, this subordinate clause offers another opportunity to restate the crime as premeditated, further demonizing Lin Shi.

In Fan and Minford's version, the translators begin the paragraph in passive voice using present perfect tense, namely "has been murdered." This can be interpreted as a way to naturalize the syntax into a writing style familiar to English-language readers. However, rather than keeping the sentence agentless like common passive configurations, this sentence specifies the *doer* of the action that is usually removed entirely from the sentence. Retaining the feature implies an intention to highlight the agency of the doer. In other words, despite the fact that this sentence does name the victim in a prominent part of the sentence, the naming of the doer is unusual and therefore comparatively more significant. It can be argued that the translators have intentionally done this to draw attention to Lin Shi as a female murderer and her status as the spouse of the victim.

The sentence that follows presents some distinctions in its linguistic patterning from those in GY, which consequently evidences Fan and Minford's different reading and approach to create dramatic effects. As opposed to the indirectness inherent to the passive voice used in the opening sentence, the translators adopt a compound sentence to give a concise and direct description of the crime. The adverb "suddenly" in the Chinese original is retained for dramatic effect, but to enhance this, it is obvious that the translators have made use of internal rhyme by repeating the short vowel sound [*i*] to strengthen the prominence of this sentence. This phonological feature, as a result, adds force and punchiness to this direct statement and simultaneously draws attention to the repetitive masculine object pronoun "him" and possessive pronouns "his." Following this, the rest of the passage appears shorter in length in comparison to that in GY, and there is an apparent difference in the way Fan and Minford indicate tone and mood shift in their translation. Unlike GY, which uses the adverb "fortunately" in the head position to modify the entire sentence about the neighbor's discovery, FM situates the adverb in the middle of a complex sentence after the subordinate conjunction "when." This means the description of the lucky discovery of the killing is subordinated as a dependent clause within the complex sentence structure. Although it still brings about a tonal shift within the sentence, it appears to have a reduced level of dramatic force by comparison.

There is also a distinct difference between the two translations in what the neighbor sees. GY details the descriptions of Lin Shi's physical actions, which, as a result, appears to suggest that these actions are focalized through the neighbor. In other words, this translation sets out to present the neighbor as a witness who has observed every step of the murder process. This is very much in line with the style in the Chinese original. Contrastingly, in FM, the last sentence appears to not only emphasize what the neighbor sees but also underscore what the neighbor feels. In this complex sentence, the past progressive in "was attempting" and the past simple in "became suspicious" work in conjunction to establish that the two actions take place simultaneously. Unlike in GY, where "watchful" is employed to render *jingjue* in the Chinese original to describe the neighbor's character trait, "became suspicious" in FM signals a shift of the neighbor's mind and illustrates the cause-and-effect relationship of the actions. As a result, the reporter in FM appears to speak more logically and less emotionally than the reporter in GY.

This textual comparison demonstrates how translators can render the same text differently. Using linguistic and stylistic resources available in the same translating language, the translators of *Wife* have created two diverse and domesticated translations of the same text. Even though both translations can be said to adequately present the feminist theme in the novella, there is an apparent level of difference in how their literary effects have been achieved stylistically. Based on the foregoing analysis, GY can be said to be direct and action-oriented, showing more freedom and creativity in its occasional deviation from the Chinese original. This can be seen clearly in the additions, lexical transformations, and syntactic reconstructions, which collectively shape the reporter's condescending voice that spares no mercy for Lin Shi. The voice appears purposefully manipulative and inflammatory to augment and sensationalize the report, adequately recreating similar effects observed in the Chinese original. However, this is by no means to say that it is inappropriate for the translators to do so; instead, this type of shock tactic may be necessary to enhance the power of the hook of this novella. On the other hand, Fan and Minford's rendering seems more indirect and reserved in its phrasing and lexical choices; it also appears stylistically closer to the Chinese original. The indirectness is established by the passive voice used at the start of the first report. Rather than persistently villainizing the female protagonist as it does in GY, more emphasis appears to be placed on the husband's victimhood, which contributes to the reporter's gentler and less forceful voice.

Conclusion

Kuo-ch'ing Tu proposes four key points that can help lead more Taiwanese literary works to the world stage: the texts that can adequately represent Taiwan, the importance of translation, the discovery of potential translators, and the focus on studies in translation theory and practice.[52] It is noteworthy that three out of the four points in Tu's proposition concern the quality and presentation of translated literature, whose impact on the circulation and reception of translated literature is certainly not too difficult to imagine. As demonstrated in this preliminary study of two translations of *Wife*, different textual and paratextual presentations of the same text in translation generate varying effects that can impact readers' perception of the novella. Ultimately, these effects will also contribute to readers' perception of the cultural and linguistic context where *Wife* originates. It is in this way that there remains a continual need to critically reflect on how a literary text should be translated to be positioned "in the hierarchy of values, beliefs, and social representations in the receiving situation."[53]

---

[52] Kuo-ch'ing Tu, "台灣文學走向世界路有多遠" [How Long Is Taiwan Literature's Journey to the World?], 台灣文學與世華文學 [*Taiwanese Literature and World Literatures in Chinese*] (Taipei: Taiwan University Press, 2015), 459–65.

[53] Lawrence Venuti, *Contra Instrumentalism: A Translation Polemic* (Lincoln: University of Nebraska Press, 2019), 18.

Notes on Contributors

John Balcom is Professor Emeritus at the Middlebury Institute of International Studies. An award-winning translator of Chinese literature, he is also a former president of the American Literary Translators Association.

Blake Brownrigg graduated with a bachelor's degree in philosophy from Iowa State University, a master's degree in translation from Fu Jen Catholic University, and is currently in the PhD program for translation at National Taiwan Normal University. He has twelve years of experience in translation, with a focus on the humanities and sciences. His research includes study of the works of James Joyce in Chinese translation.

Kuei-fen Chiu is Chair Professor of Taiwan Literature at National Chung Hsing University, Taiwan. She is the coeditor of *The Making of Chinese-Sinophone Literatures as World Literature* (2022) and coauthor of *New Chinese-Language Documentaries: Ethics, Subject, and Place* (2014).

Gwennaël Gaffric is Assistant Professor of Chinese Language and Literature at the Jean Moulin University Lyon 3. His PhD thesis was about ecological issues in Taiwan literature. He is also translator of contemporary Chinese, Hong Kong, and Taiwanese novels. His research interests include literary studies (especially science fiction), ecocriticism, postcolonialism, and translation studies. He has published the book *La Littérature à l'ère de l'Anthropocène: une étude écocritique autour des œuvres de l'écrivain taïwanais Wu Ming-yi* (2019).

Sheng-chi Hsu is a PhD candidate in translation studies at the University of Warwick. His thesis investigated gender and sexuality in Howard Goldblatt's translations of Taiwanese novels. His translation of Lin Yu-hsuan's "A Daughter" and co-translation (with Howard Chiang) of Hsu Yu-cheng's "Violet" have appeared in *Queer Taiwanese Literature: A Reader*. He was a tutor and lecturer in English and teacher education in the UK and is currently teaching English in Taiwan.

Ying-che Huang (alias Eitetsu Ko) is Professor of Modern Chinese Studies at Aichi University. He was a visiting professor at Columbia University from 2001 to 2002. He is the author of *Uprooting Japan, Implanting China: Cultural Reconstruction in Postwar Taiwan, 1945–1947* (2017) and *Diaspora and Border-Crossing: Intellectuals Moving across the Strait* (2016), as well as the coeditor of *What Is "Postwar": Asia after 1945* (2015) and *Challenge to Taiwan's Democratization: The Competition and Coexistence of Taiwanese, Japanese, and Chinese Cultures* (2021).

Sherlon Chi-yin Ip holds a BA and an M.Phil. in translation from the University of Hong Kong. Having served as Managing Editor of *Renditions*, an international journal for English translations of Chinese literature, and as Project Editor at the Hong Kong University Press, she is now dividing her time teaching at universities in Hong Kong and taking on new, challenging translation and editing projects that pique her interest.

Nicholas A. Kaldis is Director of Chinese Studies at Binghamton University (SUNY). He sits on the editorial boards of *Modern Chinese Literature and Culture* and the *Journal of Chinese Cinemas*. He is also Literature Studies Book Review Editor for *Modern Chinese Literature and Culture*. His publications include *The Chinese Prose Poem: A Study of Lu Xun's "Wild Grass" (Yecao)* and numerous essays on contemporary Chinese cinemas, world literature, modern Chinese fiction and poetry, Taiwan nature writing, and many translations.

Wen-chi Li is Susan Manning Fellow at the University of Edinburgh after he acquired his PhD in sinology from the University of Zurich. A translator of Taiwanese literature, he won first prize in the 2018 John Dryden Translation Competition. In Taiwan, he has published a few poetry collections and coedited the book *Under the Same Roof: A Poetry Anthology for LGBT*.

Pei-yin Lin received her PhD in languages and cultures of East Asia from the School of Oriental and African Studies, University of London. She taught at the National University of Singapore and the University of Cambridge before joining the University of Hong Kong in January 2012, where she is currently Associate Professor at the School of Chinese. She is the author of *Colonial Taiwan: Negotiating Identities and Modernity through Literature* (2017) and was a Harvard Yenching visiting scholar in 2015/16 and Chair of Taiwan Studies at Leiden University in fall 2020.

Yi-chen Liu is a PhD candidate at Meiji University. She received her master's degree in Japanese language and literature from National Taiwan University. For her PhD dissertation, she explores how Western and Japanese literary movements influenced Taiwanese writers under Japanese rule. She is the co-translator of Sankichi Tōge's *Poems of the Atomic Bomb* (2022). Her research articles can be seen in some Japanese books and magazines such as *Gendaishi Techo*.

Federica Passi is Associate Professor of Chinese Language and Literature at the Department of Asian and North African Studies, Ca' Foscari University of Venice, where she teaches Chinese language and translation. She earned her PhD from University of Naples "L'Orientale" in 1998 and became a researcher at Ca' Foscari University of Venice in 2004. Her research mainly focuses on Taiwanese literature, particularly on fiction, narratology, historiography, and translation. In addition to the translation of two books by Chinese writer Hong Ying, she has published *Letteratura taiwanese. Un profilo storico* (2007) and articles on different issues concerning Taiwanese literature.

Carlos Rojas is Professor of Chinese Cultural Studies, Gender, Sexuality & Feminist Studies, and Cinematic Arts at Duke University. He is the author of *The Naked Gaze: Reflections on Chinese Modernity* (2008), *The Great Wall: A Cultural History* (2010), and *Homesickness: Culture, Contagion, and National Transformation in Modern China* (2015). He is also the coeditor of eight volumes, including *Writing Taiwan: A New Literary History*, with David Der-wei Wang (2007), and *The Oxford Handbook of Modern Chinese Literatures*, with Andrea Bachner (2016), and the translator of sixteen volumes of literary fiction and critique.

Darryl Sterk holds a PhD from the University of Toronto (2009) in East Asian studies. He wrote his dissertation on the significance of Indigenous-Han romance in cultural production, mainly film and fiction, from Taiwan. Since graduation, he has reoriented his research toward translation between the Indigenous language Seediq and colonial languages, mainly Mandarin but also Japanese and English, particularly in a monograph about the translation of the screenplay of the biggest film in Taiwan box office history, *Indigenous Cultural Translation: A Thick Description of Seediq Bale* (2020). He is currently studying the translation of TEK (traditional environmental knowledge) in terms of "autoethnobotany."

Karen Thornber is Harry Tuchman Levin Professor in Literature and Professor of East Asian Languages and Civilizations at Harvard University. She is the award-winning author of four single-author scholarly monographs (*Empire of Texts in Motion: Chinese, Korean, and Taiwanese Transculturations of Japanese Literature*; *Ecoambiguity: Environmental Crises and East Asian Literatures*; *Global Healing: Literature, Advocacy, Care*; and *Gender Justice and Contemporary Asian Literatures*), four (co)edited volumes, and more than eighty articles/chapters on comparative literature, world literature, Asian literatures and cultures, environmental humanities, medical and health humanities, gender justice and other forms of justice, diaspora/migration, indigeneity, and trauma, among other fields. Thornber is also a prize-winning translator of Japanese literature.

Acknowledgments

This book has been a long time coming. The initial idea of editing this volume sprang from an informal email exchange among a small group of people who are dedicated scholars of Taiwanese literature both in and outside of Taiwan. Among them, Professor Kuei-fen Chiu, Professor Shu-mei Shih, and Professor Karen Thornber have given us a lot of warm encouragement. We all believe that a new conceptualization of studying the rich literary heritage from Taiwan as part of world literature is timely and meaningful, and we are glad that this project can be included in Bloomsbury's Literatures as World Literature series. We would like to thank the series editor Professor Thomas Beebee for expressing an interest in this project to start with.

Along the process of preparing the manuscript, there are many individuals we would like to thank. In addition to our contributors, we would like to thank Amy Martin, Bloomsbury's acquisitions editor in literary studies, for her professional help and patience in responding to our various inquiries. Our two translators, Blake Brownrigg and Sherlon Chi-yin Ip, as well as our copyeditors, Valerie Gwynn and John McAllister, also deserve our special mention. Blake and Sherlon have rendered the Chinese essays into English faithfully and fluently. John helped polish a few chapters to ensure that they were coherently written before we sent them to Valerie. Valerie's enormous skill and meticulous precision in her copyediting service substantially helped improve the clarity and stylistic consistency of this book.

Finally, we would like to express our gratitude for the generous financial support from the Hsu Long-sing Research Fund at the University of Hong Kong. And upon compiling the manuscript, we were also awarded a publication subsidy from the European Association of Taiwan Studies. This project would not have been possible without these grants.

Index

Aboriginal. *See* Indigenous
AIDS 97, 101–9, 172, 179–83
Akutagawa, Ryūnosuke 78
alienation 81, 86, 95, 101–6, 118, 134
alternative 11, 15, 24, 64, 76, 79–80, 87, 91, 105, 108, 113, 124, 126–7, 133, 145, 147, 155, 182
American dream 55
Angelopoulos, Theo 182–3
Anglophone 118, 122, 127, 146, 168, 175, 192, 194, 198, 201
animism 60
anthologize 113–14, 126
anticommunist 1, 10, 12, 123, 125, 132
Apter, Emily 5, 82
archipelagic thinking 146
Austronesian 84, 87–8, 91–2, 160
autobiographical 14, 53, 58–9, 61, 65, 97, 173
automatic writing 72, 74
automatism 14, 79
avant-garde 10, 71, 123, 133, 182

Bacon, Francis 72
Bamboo Hat Society, The 121, 125–6
Bassnett, Susan 190
Baudelaire, Charles 72–3
Benjamin, Walter 189
biculturalism 30
bildungsroman 14, 53, 62–6, 97
Blue Stars Poetry Society, The 120
Books from Taiwan 13, 127, 154
border 20, 37, 40, 42–3, 45–6, 53, 198
Borges, Jorge Luis 32
Breton, André: *Surrealist Manifesto* 74
butterfly effect 35, 44–6

Cambria Press 13, 20, 122, 127
canonization 2, 5, 113, 130, 136, 138
capitalism 8, 11, 87, 92, 94–5, 168

Casanova, Pascale 5, 19, 24, 27, 30, 33, 45–7, 82, 129–30, 134–5, 144–6, 150, 153–5
CCA (Council for Cultural Affairs) 12, 38, 157, 161, 166–8
CCP (Chinese Communist Party) 2, 127, 132–3
Chang, Iris 57
Chang, Jung 56–7
Chang Hsi-kuo 116, 118, 150, 162
Chang Ing, Nancy: *The Chinese PEN* 118; *Winter Plum* 115, 118
Chang Kuei-hsing 26, 167
Chang Ta-chun 117, 162
Chen Fang-ming 11, 40, 57
Chen Jo-hsi 116, 131–2, 148
Chen Li 29
Chi, Pang-yuan: *An Anthology of Contemporary Chinese Literature* 12, 114–15, 132, 135; *The Great Flowing River* 115
Chi Hsien 10, 119, 121, 133
Chi Ta-wei 136, 166–7
China-centrism 3, 22, 32
Chinese: culture 15, 62–4, 115, 133, 149, 152, 157, 160, 192; Filipino 64; heritage 133, 138; language 3, 6, 8, 21, 25–6, 31–2, 61, 117, 124, 133–4, 144–6, 155, 159, 167, 192; letters 45; literature 2–7, 20–2, 28, 30–3, 51, 116, 135, 145, 148–55, 157, 159–63, 167–8, 176, 186; poetry 30–2, 119–20, 123
Chineseness 4, 20, 24, 26–7, 32–3, 62–4, 132, 141–2
Chiu Miao-chin: *Last Words from Montmartre* 151, 173, 180–6; *Notes of a Crocodile* 166–7, 173, 178, 180–6
Chu T'ien-hsin 154, 162
Chu T'ien-wen: *Notes of a Desolate Man* 14, 97–109, 165, 172; *The Old Capital* 162

Chung Li-he 117
circulation 5–8, 14, 23, 27, 29, 51–3, 58–9, 62, 65–6, 129, 132, 137, 144, 161, 166, 173–4, 189, 192, 198, 204
civilization 59, 63, 72
Cocteau, Jean 69, 73–9
colonial 1–12, 14, 20–3, 28, 39, 60, 62, 69, 71, 78, 113, 117–18, 120–2, 124–5, 143, 152, 158–9, 161,164–5, 176
colonizer 9, 60
commodification 92, 94, 107
Communist China 32, 115, 132, 157
continent-centric 60
cosmopolitanism 14, 30, 32–3, 98
creolization 31, 173
cross-cultural 21, 53, 64
cultural: alterity 65, 90; assimilation 61, 65; capital 4, 7, 15, 129, 137, 144; exchange 13, 27, 143, 147, 155; Cultural Revolution, The 123, 131–3

Dadaism 70, 72, 74
Damrosch, David 5, 19, 23, 27, 35–7, 47, 51–2, 82, 99, 151, 189, 198
Dante Alighieri 37
Darwinistic 46
Dazai, Osamu 181
dehistoricize 174
Deleuze, Gilles, and Félix Guattari: minor literature 15, 141, 143, 145, 155–6; nomad 9, 136, 137, 142
democracy 54, 84, 123, 141, 159
democratization 2, 133, 141, 157–8
Dickens, Charles 62
discrimination 8, 116–17, 177–8, 182–3
dissemination 113
domestication 174

ecocosmopolitanism 81–2
ecological 60, 87–8, 138, 153
economic miracle 115, 118
Eliot, T. S. 101
environmental world literature 21, 30, 81–2, 85–8, 91, 96
epic 56, 58
Epoch Poetry Society, The 120
Eroticism 176–7, 180, 182

Eurocentric 6, 144–5
eventualities 39
exile 25, 89, 98, 115, 121–2, 172
exoticism 155, 194

family saga 14, 51, 53, 56–7, 65
Fantasy and Science Fiction Award, The 136
February 28 Incident, The 2, 54, 56, 58, 124, 163
female-centric 57, 65
Fishing Luck 95
flâneur 100, 107
Foucault, Michel 61, 104, 172
Four-Way Voice 40
francophone 144, 168
Free China 1, 4, 115–16, 126–7, 172

Galápagos archipelago, The 46–7
Gao Xingjian 22, 47
gender 11, 13, 63–4, 166, 172–4, 181–4, 190, 193–8
Genet, Jean 183
Genette, Gérard paratext 131, 192
Gide, André 10, 180
Glissant, Édouard 8–9, 13
global indigenism 82
Global North, The 5–6, 80
Global South, The 5, 36, 113, 168
globalization 12, 79–80, 153, 179
Goethe, Johann Wolfgang von 5, 51, 62, 65
Golden Horse Film Festival, The 182
Goll, Yvan 73
Great Kantō earthquake, The 73

habitus 98
Hakka: cultural tradition 28; dialect 159; literature 121, 127; novelist 158
Han: cultural assimilation 61; culture 59, 61; ethnicity 28, 30; people 42, 59, 160; readers 60; settlers 20, 52; society 59; writers 20
Han-centric 59
Han-Indigenous relations 59, 61
Haruyama Yukio 70–5
Hauʻofa, Epeli 8, 13

Hegelian history 104
hegemony 2, 8, 11, 15, 20, 28, 59–60
heterogeneity 98, 130, 141, 175
heteronormativity 98, 106, 176
heterosexual 103, 107–8
historiography 58, 65, 113, 186
HIV. *See* AIDS
Homer 37
homogenize 4, 6, 65, 156, 186–7
homophobia 106, 178, 187
homosexuality 14, 107–8, 122, 165, 175–82, 187
Hong Kong 3, 12, 15, 21–2, 24, 36, 46, 63–4, 146, 150, 156–7, 179, 182, 191
Hori Tatsuo 73–80
Horiguchi Daigaku 78
Hou Hsiao-hsien 54, 138
Hsia, C. T. 1–2, 132, 134
Hsia Yu 46
Hualien 41
Huang, Juan 53
Huang Chun-ming 28, 115–16, 118, 131, 140, 158
humanism 104
hybrid 9, 27, 43, 63, 70, 164–5, 173
hybridization 152, 173
hyphenated 66

I-narrator 59, 98, 100
identity: queer 173, 176, 180–3, 187; cultural 12, 114, 133, 152
imagined community 82
indigeneity 81, 85–6, 89–91
Indigenous: Bunun 81, 88, 91–5; Husluman Vava 96; literature 20, 25–6, 28, 30, 52–3, 59, 122, 127, 168; Pangcah 91–2; Sakinu Ahronglong 96; Syaman Rapongan 26, 52, 58, 85, 89, 96; Tao, 59–61, 85, 89, 95; Walis Nokan 135, 139
intellectualism 14, 70–5
intertextuality 33, 88
intra-Asian 53, 59, 64

Japanese: Empire 1, 4, 39, 80, 164; occupation 69, 71, 118, 120–3, 126; rule 3, 12–13, 71, 79, 80, 117, 125, 161

Japanophone 1, 4
Jarman, Derek 183
juxtaposition 165, 196

Kan Yao-ming 28
Kingston, Maxine Hong 57
KMT (Chinese Nationalist Party, Kuomintang) 1–2, 11–12, 32, 54–5, 80, 83–4, 116–19, 123–4, 132, 157, 172, 181–2
Kwan-Terry, John 119

language: dominated 144, 146–7, 153; dominating 144, 146–7; national 164
Lau, Joseph S. M.: *Chinese Stories from Taiwan* 2, 115–16; *The Unbroken Chain* 115, 117–18
Le Guin, Ursula 85
Le Moulin 10, 14, 69–80
Lefevere, André 113, 126
left-wing 71, 76, 181
legitimacy: literary 135; of a minority group 106; of literatures 144; of the KMT rule 1, 117
Li, Kotomi 52
Li Ang: *The Butcher's Wife* 15, 149, 151, 161, 172, 190–204; *The Lost Garden* 162
Li Chang-jui 71, 73, 76, 79
Li Yung-ping 26, 62, 115
Lien Ming-wei 52, 61–6
Lin Heng-tai 125
Lin Hsui-erh 69, 73–4, 78
literary: capital 33, 121, 129–30, 137, 144, 155–6; consecration 129, 144; exchange 143–4; field 46, 129, 143–7, 153–6; magazine 131, 156; tradition 6, 31–3, 46, 87, 113,118, 120, 127, 132, 144, 159; value 132, 140, 145
Literary Journal 115
literature: comparative 5, 19, 35, 173; dialect 127; dominated 146, 156; dominating 155–6; East Asian 144–5, 186; European 156; French 9, 10, 55, 74, 156; marginal 164; modern 115–16, 159; national 21, 26, 31, 33, 65, 156,

162, 173; overseas Chinese 22; popular 165; queer 122, 173; of Southeast Asia 146; Western 6, 19–20, 30, 74
literature in Chinese (Chinese-language literature) 6, 13, 22, 26, 122, 145–6, 167
littérisation 24, 27
Lo Ching 11, 121
Lo Fu 4, 119, 121, 123, 133, 138
Lōa Hô 9, 28, 76, 117, 161
Localization 14, 71, 73, 86
Lung Ying-tai 169
Lung Ying-tsung 10, 12

mainland China 24, 46, 115–16, 119–21, 123–7, 132, 146, 152, 159–61
mainlander 11, 72, 116, 121, 124–5, 149
Malaysian Chinese 3, 21–2, 25–6, 28, 30, 45
Malinowski, Bronisław 60
Mallarmé, Stéphane 77
Man Booker International Prize, The 21, 29, 47–8
Mandarin 2, 63, 84, 138, 164
Mann, Thomas 180
marginality 155, 164, 168
marginalization 2–3, 98, 123–4
marginalized 1–2, 11, 60, 99, 106, 118, 123–4, 145, 155, 165
marketability 113, 126, 192
Marxism 104
Mau Mau Uprising, The 62
May Fourth, The: period 122–3; Movement 120, 124, 159, 161, 173, 176
migrants 12, 40
minor 7, 15, 30, 39, 53, 61, 65, 91, 141, 143, 145, 155–6
minority 3, 25, 84, 99, 106, 141, 166, 167
Mishima, Yukio 181
Mo Yan 149
MoC (Ministry of Culture) 12–13, 134, 154, 157, 166, 168–9
Modern Literature 115, 121, 132
modernism 10, 70–9, 115, 123–7, 133, 173
modernist 1, 11, 46, 70–1, 73, 76, 78, 116, 119–27, 138, 176
Modernist School, The 120

modernity 12, 59–60, 87–8, 93–4, 115, 133, 171, 180
monocultural 84
monolingual 84
Moretti, Franco 19, 27, 82, 144, 186–7
Mudan Incident, The 38–9
multilingualism 66, 150
Murakami, Haruki 165

National Central Library, The 148
National Institute of Compilation and Translation, The 116
native science 59
nativism 124–7
nativist 25, 28, 46, 119, 121, 124–5, 127, 138, 158
neoclassicism 125
neocolonial 6, 158
neoliberalism 168
Ng Kim Chew: "The World Republic of Southern Letters," 145–6
Nieh Hua-ling 180
Nishiwaki Junzaburō: *Supernaturalism* 72; *Surrealist Poetics* 72–3
NMTL (National Museum of Taiwanese Literature) 12–13, 134
Nobel Prize, The 6, 47, 145
nominalization 195
non-Chinese 23, 34
non-Western 6, 14–15, 32, 37, 51, 53, 66
novel for the masses 165

ocean-centric 59, 65
Oceania 60
Orchid Island 59, 60, 85, 95
otherness 26, 99, 106, 193–4

Pacific: Island, 81; Ocean 59
Pai Hsien-yung: *Crystal Boys* 149, 165, 172
Palandri, Angela C.Y. Jung: *Modern Verse from Taiwan* 115, 120
performativity 140–1
Picasso, Pablo 77
plurality 195
poésie 73
poetics 7–10, 31–4, 71–4, 77–80, 113, 120, 123, 139

postcolonial 4, 7, 11–12, 21, 57, 62, 162, 168
postmodern 11, 87, 97–109, 138
postwar Taiwan 4, 10, 80, 163
potentiality 53, 146, 155–6
PRC (People's Republic of China) 98, 117, 123, 133, 139, 141, 150
primitivism 86, 94–5
proletarian 79

Qing dynasty 63, 164
queer 6, 15, 122, 139, 149, 151, 166–7, 172–87

Radiguet, Raymond 78
readership 7, 13, 15, 23, 28–9, 51, 53–4, 56, 58–9, 64–5, 99, 107, 114, 137, 143, 145, 151, 173, 189, 192–3
realism 6, 10, 21, 30, 72, 76–7, 85–6, 88, 116, 118, 126, 161
resistance 6, 20, 26–7, 39, 61, 63, 71, 79, 134, 159, 161, 165–6, 172, 175
Retrocession 125
Reverdy, Pierre 74
Rilke, Rainer Maria 32
ROC (Republic of China) 4, 119, 120, 132–3, 164
romanticism 76, 87
Rushdie, Salman 49
Ryan, Shawna Yang 52–8, 65
Ryukyu 38–9

same-sex marriage 122, 184
SARS 35, 56
SARS-CoV-2 35
sentimentality 76–7, 79
sentiments 153, 165, 175, 182
settler colonialism 3, 20, 52, 64
sexuality 15, 104, 172, 174, 178, 182, 190
Shang Chin 119, 121, 123, 125, 133
Shih, Shu-mei 3, 6–9, 13, 19–22, 24, 30, 167
Sinicization 1, 31–2, 80
Sinitic 3, 20–3, 28, 52, 65
Sinocentric 4, 32
Sinophone: communities 140, 145, 176–7; literature 14, 19–22, 24–6, 30, 34, 46, 51, 122, 167–9; Malaysian 25–8, 61–2, 64, 167

slow violence 96
sociohistorical 65, 155, 192, 198
sociopolitical 55, 65, 115, 139, 190
South Seas 46–7, 146
Spender, Stephen 32
subconscious. *See* unconscious
sublime 74
Sung Tse-lai 28, 158
supernaturalism 72–3
surrealism 10, 14, 69–80, 120, 173
symbiosis 14, 60

Taishō period, The 73, 159
Taiwan-centric 2, 55
Taiwan Creative Content Agency, The 127
Taiwan Literature Award for Migrants, The 40
Taiwan Literature: English Translation Series 13, 121
Taiwanese New Literature during the Japanese Occupation Period 117
Takahashi Shinkichi: *Poetry and Poetics* 70, 73, 75–6
Tan, Amy 56–7
Tang Wen-piao 119
Tekken (Iron Dog) Heterotopia Literary Prize, The 52
Thiong'o, Ngũgĩ wa 6
trans-Indigenous 60, 65
transcultural 6–7, 9, 29–30, 32–3, 52, 60, 73, 136
transculturation 4, 6, 7, 9, 12–14, 29–30, 34, 88
translation: English 12–14, 37, 96, 114, 121–2, 127, 132, 137; French 130–1, 137, 141; Italian 146–7, 155; Japanese 158–61, 168–9
translingual generation 125, 169
transpacific 53, 58
Truffaut, François 182
Tsuji Jun 70
Tu, Kuo-ch'ing 13, 121, 167, 204
Twain, Mark 62–3

UN (United Nations) 55, 82–3, 117, 166
unconscious 74–5
urban 107

USSR (Union of Soviet Socialist Republics) 84
Utopiales Festival, The 136
utopian 6, 88, 108

Venuti, Lawrence 174–5, 198
vernacular 4, 9, 28, 125, 159, 164
Verne, Jules: *Around the World in Eighty Days* 35–8

Wallerstein, Immanuel 51
Wang Chen-ho 28, 116–17, 149–51
Wang, David Der-wei 3, 7, 13, 114, 118, 122, 147–8, 167
Wang Wen-hsing 11, 115–16, 132–3
Weltanschauung 145
Western-centric 51
westernized 64, 97, 109, 119, 121, 178
White Terror, The 4, 53, 58, 122, 139, 163, 172
Wittgenstein, Ludwig 40
world literatures in Chinese. *See* literature in Chinese
world-making 44
worlding 7, 14, 28, 53, 59, 64–5, 135, 143, 153–4

Wu Cho-liu 117, 158
Wu He 46
Wu Ming-yi: *The Magician on the Skywalk* 169; *The Man with the Compound Eyes* 37, 40–9, 81, 83–96, 127, 136, 152, 154; *The Stolen Bicycle* 48

Xi Xi 46, 150

Ya Hsien 4, 46, 119, 121
Yang Chih-chang 10, 69–79, 125
Yang Kuei 10, 76, 117
Yang Mu 4, 7, 29–34, 46, 119, 121, 151–2
Yeh Shih-tao: *The Complete Pre-retrocession Taiwanese Literature* 117; *A History of Taiwan Literature* 2, 127, 163
Yeh, Michelle: *Anthology of Modern Chinese Poetry* 122; *Frontier Taiwan* 122, 124
Yesi 46
Yip, Wai-lim: *Modern Chinese Poetry* 115, 119
Yourcenar, Marguerite 181
Yu Kuang-chung 119, 121, 138

Zheng, Egoyan 168

www.ingramcontent.com/pod-product-compliance
Lightning Source LLC
Chambersburg PA
CBHW062221300426
44115CB00012BA/2160